D1229312

RYAN **PARROTT** • MARCO **RENNA** • WALTER **BAIAMONTE**

VOLUME TWO

Published by

BOOM!
S T U D I O S

SERIES DESIGNERS
**SCOTT NEWMAN
& MADISON GOYETTE** (CHAPTER 8)

COLLECTION DESIGNER
CHELSEA ROBERTS

ASSISTANT EDITOR
GWEN WALLER

EDITOR
DAFNA PLEBAN

HASBRO SPECIAL THANKS
ED LANE, **BETH ARTALE**,
AND **MICHAEL KELLY**

Ross Richie CEO & Founder
Joy Huffman CFO
Matt Gagnon Editor-in-Chief
Filip Sablik President, Publishing & Marketing
Stephen Christy President, Development
Lance Kreiter Vice President, Licensing & Merchandising
Bryce Carlson Vice President, Editorial & Creative Strategy
Kate Henning Director, Operations
Spencer Simpson Director, Sales
Scott Newman Manager, Production Design
Elyse Strandberg Manager, Finance
Sierra Hahn Executive Editor
Dafna Pleban Senior Editor
Shannon Watters Senior Editor
Eric Harburn Senior Editor
Elizabeth Brei Editor
Sophie Philips-Roberts Associate Editor
Amanda LaFranco Associate Editor
Jonathan Manning Associate Editor
Gavin Gronenthal Assistant Editor
Gwen Waller Assistant Editor
Allyson Gronowitz Assistant Editor
Ramiro Portnoy Assistant Editor
Kenzie Rzonca Assistant Editor
Shelby Netschke Editorial Assistant
Michelle Ankley Design Lead
Marie Krupina Production Designer
Grace Park Production Designer
Chelsea Roberts Production Designer
Madison Goyette Production Designer
Crystal White Production Designer
Samantha Knapp Production Design Assistant
Esther Kim Marketing Lead
Breanna Sarpy Marketing Coordinator, Digital
Grecia Martinez Marketing Assistant
Amanda Lawson Marketing Assistant, Digital
José Meza Consumer Sales Lead
Morgan Perry Retail Sales Lead
Harley Salbacka Sales Coordinator
Megan Christopher Operations Coordinator
Rodrigo Hernandez Operations Coordinator
Zipporah Smith Operations Coordinator
Jason Lee Senior Accountant
Sabrina Lesin Accounting Assistant
Lauren Alexander Administrative Assistant

Licensed by:

MIGHTY MORPHIN Volume Two, August 2021. Published by
BOOM! Studios, a division of Boom Entertainment, Inc. ™ & ©
2021 SCG Power Rangers LLC and Hasbro. Power Rangers and
all related logos, characters, names, and distinctive likenesses
thereof are the exclusive property of SCG Power Rangers LLC.
All Rights Reserved.   Used Under Authorization. Originally
published in single magazine form as MIGHTY MORPHIN No.
5-8 © 2021 SCG Power Rangers LLC and Hasbro. All Rights
Reserved. BOOM! Studios™ and the BOOM! Studios logo are
trademarks of Boom Entertainment, Inc., registered in various
countries and categories. All characters, events, and institutions
depicted herein are fictional. Any similarity between any of the
names, characters, persons, events, and/or institutions in this
publication to actual names, characters, and persons, whether
living or dead, events, and/or institutions is unintended and
purely coincidental. BOOM! Studios does not read or accept
unsolicited submissions of ideas, stories, or artwork.

BOOM! Studios, 5670 Wilshire Boulevard, Suite 400, Los Angeles,
CA 90036-5679. Printed in Canada. First Printing.

ISBN: 978-1-68415-702-0, eISBN: 978-1-64668-246-1

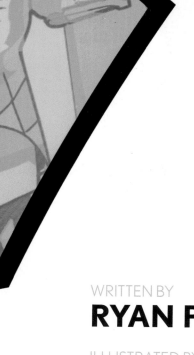

WITHDRAWN

WRITTEN BY
RYAN PARROTT

ILLUSTRATED BY
MARCO RENNA

COLORS BY
WALTER BAIAMONTE
WITH ASSISTANCE BY **KATIA RANALLI**
& SARA ANTONELLINI

LETTERS BY
ED DUKESHIRE

COVER BY
INHYUK LEE

ELTARIAN, GREEN RANGER, CHAOS PUTTIES,
PUTTY PRIME, AND BANDORIAN MONK
CHARACTER DESIGNS BY
DAN MORA

CHAPTER FIVE

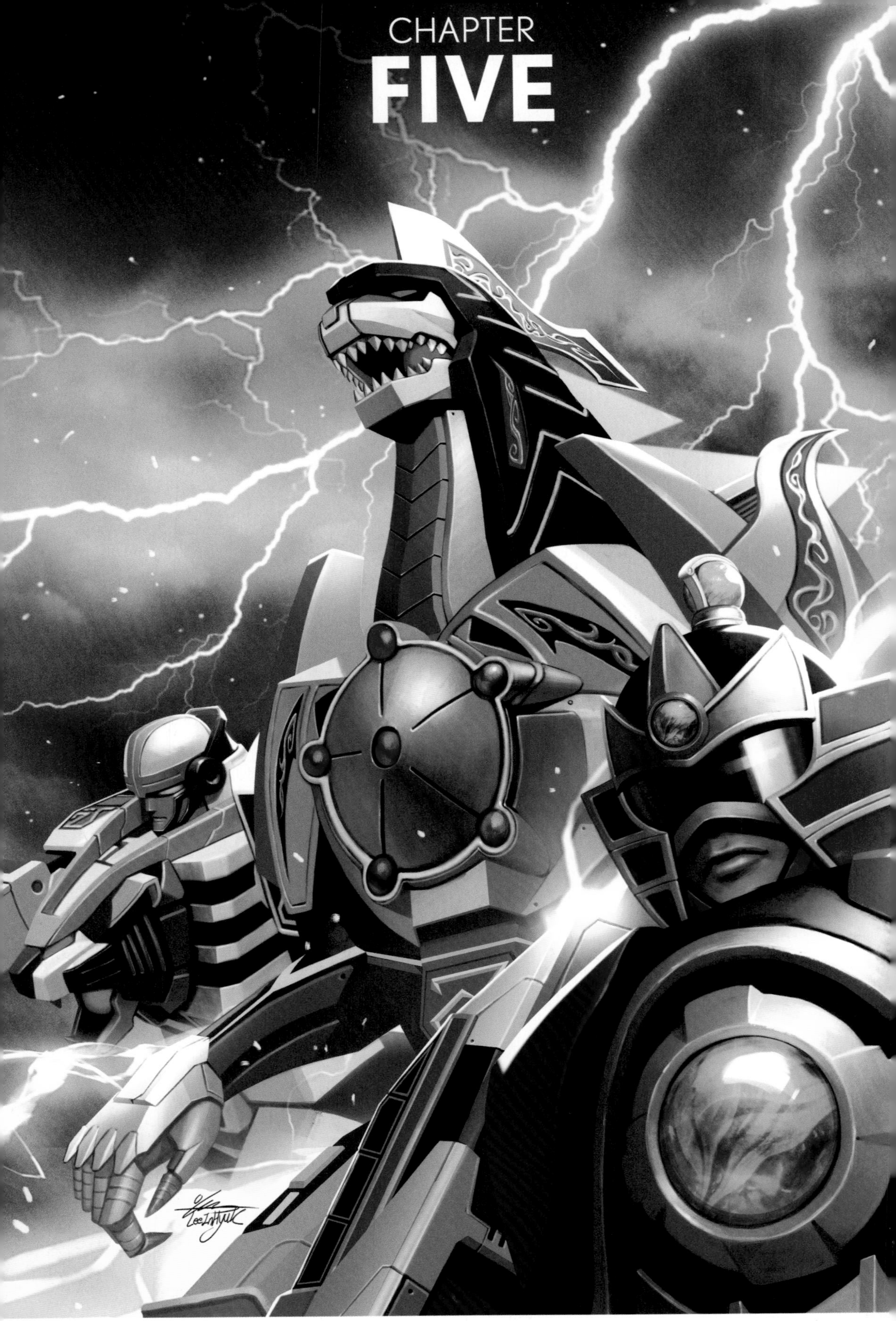

INHYUK LEE | ISSUE FIVE COVER

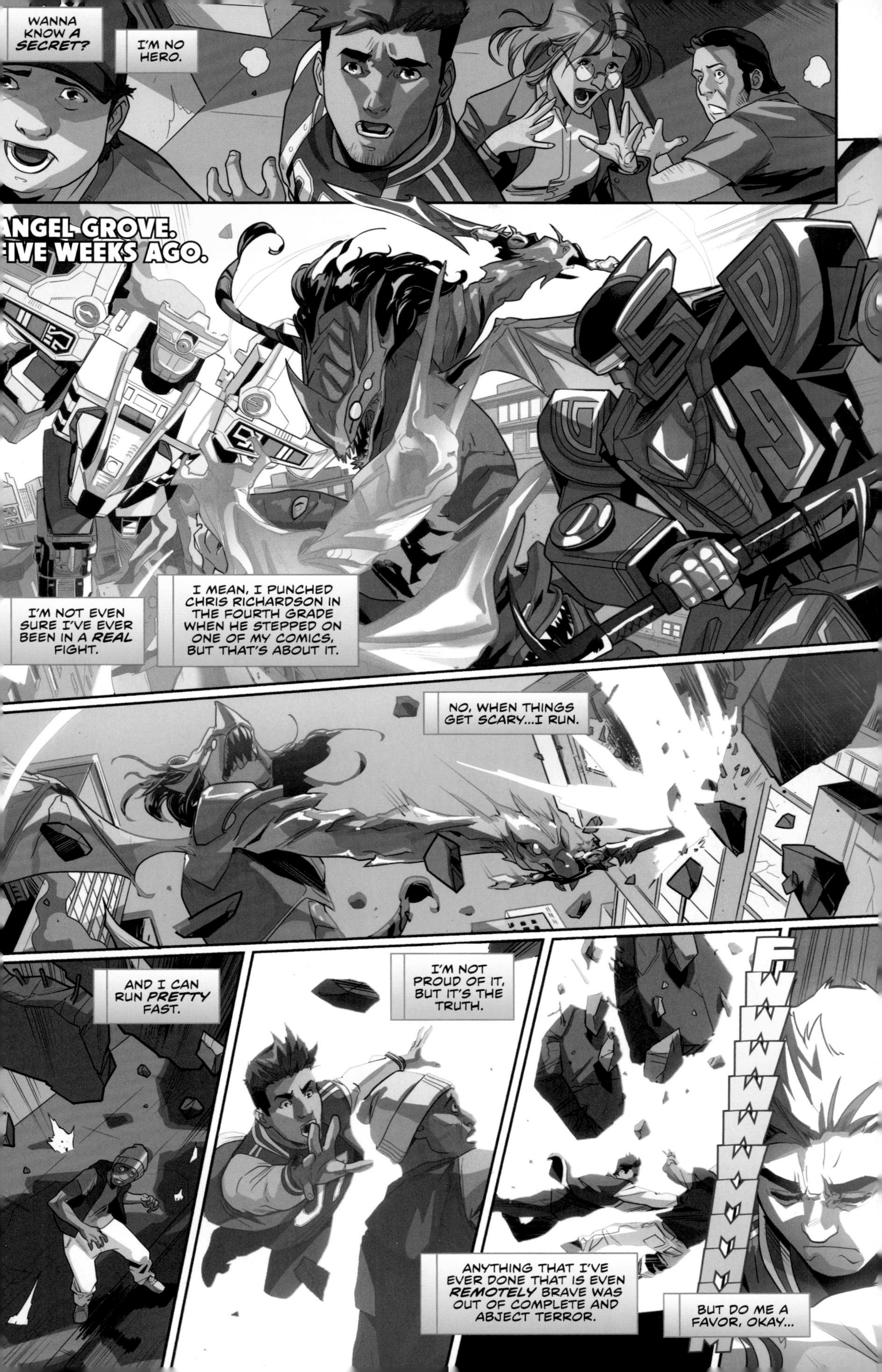
WANNA KNOW A SECRET?
I'M NO HERO.
ANGEL GROVE. FIVE WEEKS AGO.
I'M NOT EVEN SURE I'VE EVER BEEN IN A REAL FIGHT.
I MEAN, I PUNCHED CHRIS RICHARDSON IN THE FOURTH GRADE WHEN HE STEPPED ON ONE OF MY COMICS, BUT THAT'S ABOUT IT.
NO, WHEN THINGS GET SCARY...I RUN.
AND I CAN RUN PRETTY FAST.
I'M NOT PROUD OF IT, BUT IT'S THE TRUTH.
FWAAAAAAAAAM
ANYTHING THAT I'VE EVER DONE THAT IS EVEN REMOTELY BRAVE WAS OUT OF COMPLETE AND ABJECT TERROR.
BUT DO ME A FAVOR, OKAY...

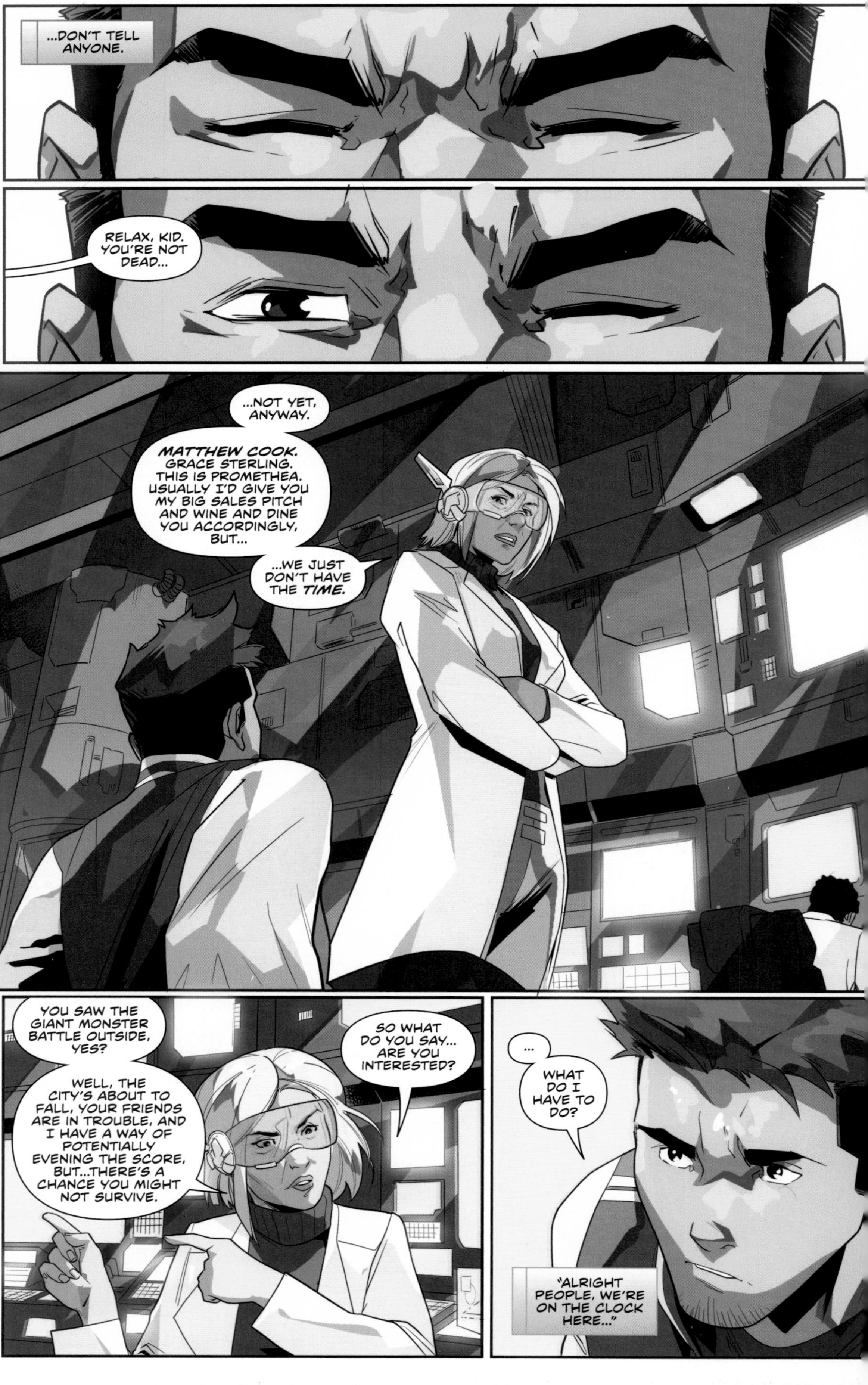
...DON'T TELL ANYONE.
RELAX, KID. YOU'RE NOT DEAD...
...NOT YET, ANYWAY.
MATTHEW COOK. GRACE STERLING. THIS IS PROMETHEA. USUALLY I'D GIVE YOU MY BIG SALES PITCH AND WINE AND DINE YOU ACCORDINGLY, BUT...
...WE JUST DON'T HAVE THE TIME.
YOU SAW THE GIANT MONSTER BATTLE OUTSIDE, YES?
WELL, THE CITY'S ABOUT TO FALL, YOUR FRIENDS ARE IN TROUBLE, AND I HAVE A WAY OF POTENTIALLY EVENING THE SCORE, BUT...THERE'S A CHANCE YOU MIGHT NOT SURVIVE.
SO WHAT DO YOU SAY... ARE YOU INTERESTED?
...
WHAT DO I HAVE TO DO?
"ALRIGHT PEOPLE, WE'RE ON THE CLOCK HERE..."

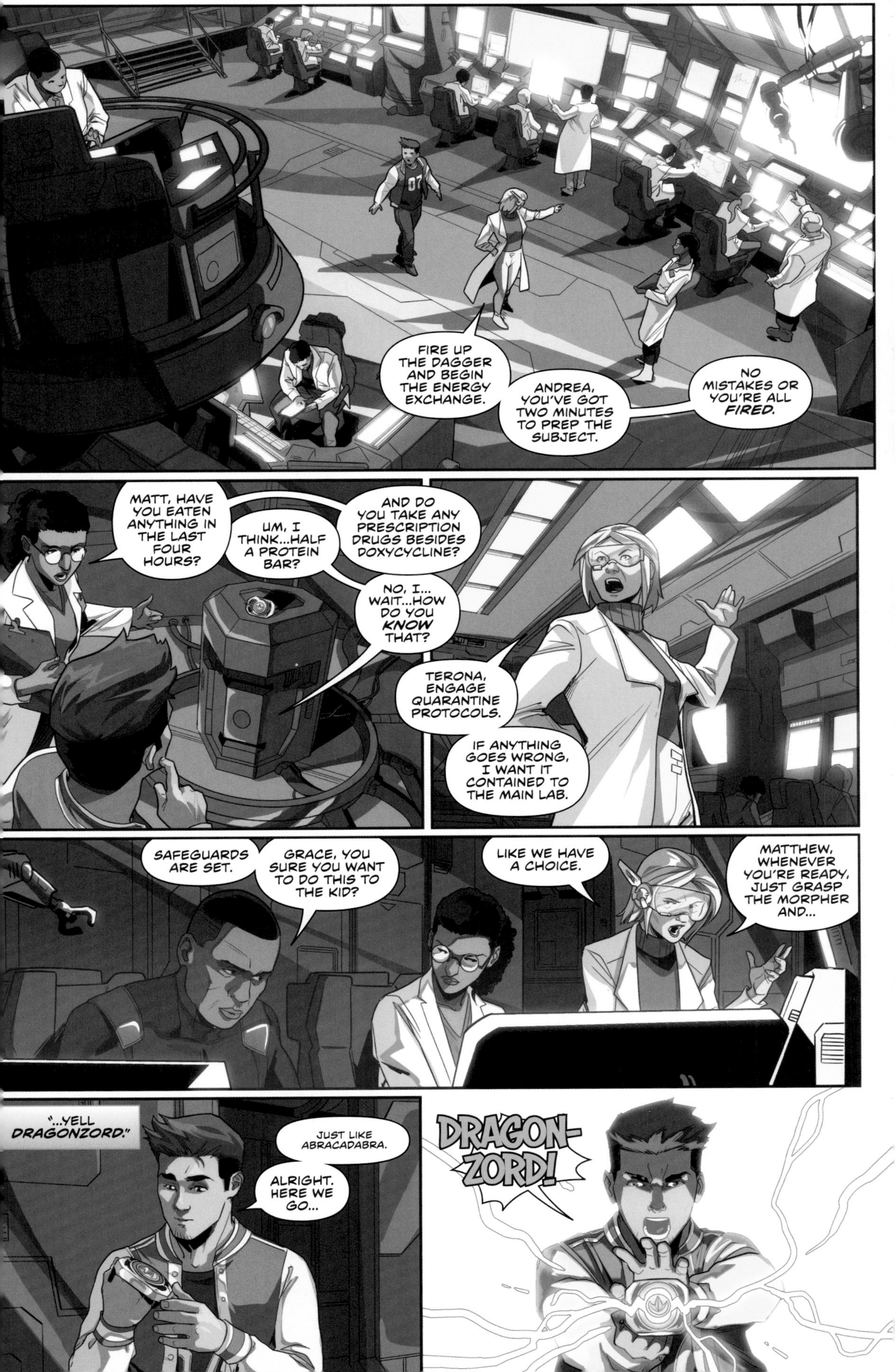
FIRE UP THE DAGGER AND BEGIN THE ENERGY EXCHANGE.
ANDREA, YOU'VE GOT TWO MINUTES TO PREP THE SUBJECT.
NO MISTAKES OR YOU'RE ALL *FIRED.*
MATT, HAVE YOU EATEN ANYTHING IN THE LAST FOUR HOURS?
UM, I THINK...HALF A PROTEIN BAR?
AND DO YOU TAKE ANY PRESCRIPTION DRUGS BESIDES DOXYCYCLINE?
NO, I... WAIT...HOW DO YOU *KNOW* THAT?
TERONA, ENGAGE QUARANTINE PROTOCOLS.
IF ANYTHING GOES WRONG, I WANT IT CONTAINED TO THE MAIN LAB.
SAFEGUARDS ARE SET.
GRACE, YOU SURE YOU WANT TO DO THIS TO THE KID?
LIKE WE HAVE A CHOICE.
MATTHEW, WHENEVER YOU'RE READY, JUST GRASP THE MORPHER AND...
"...YELL *DRAGONZORD.*"
JUST LIKE ABRACADABRA.
ALRIGHT. HERE WE GO...
DRAGON-ZORD!

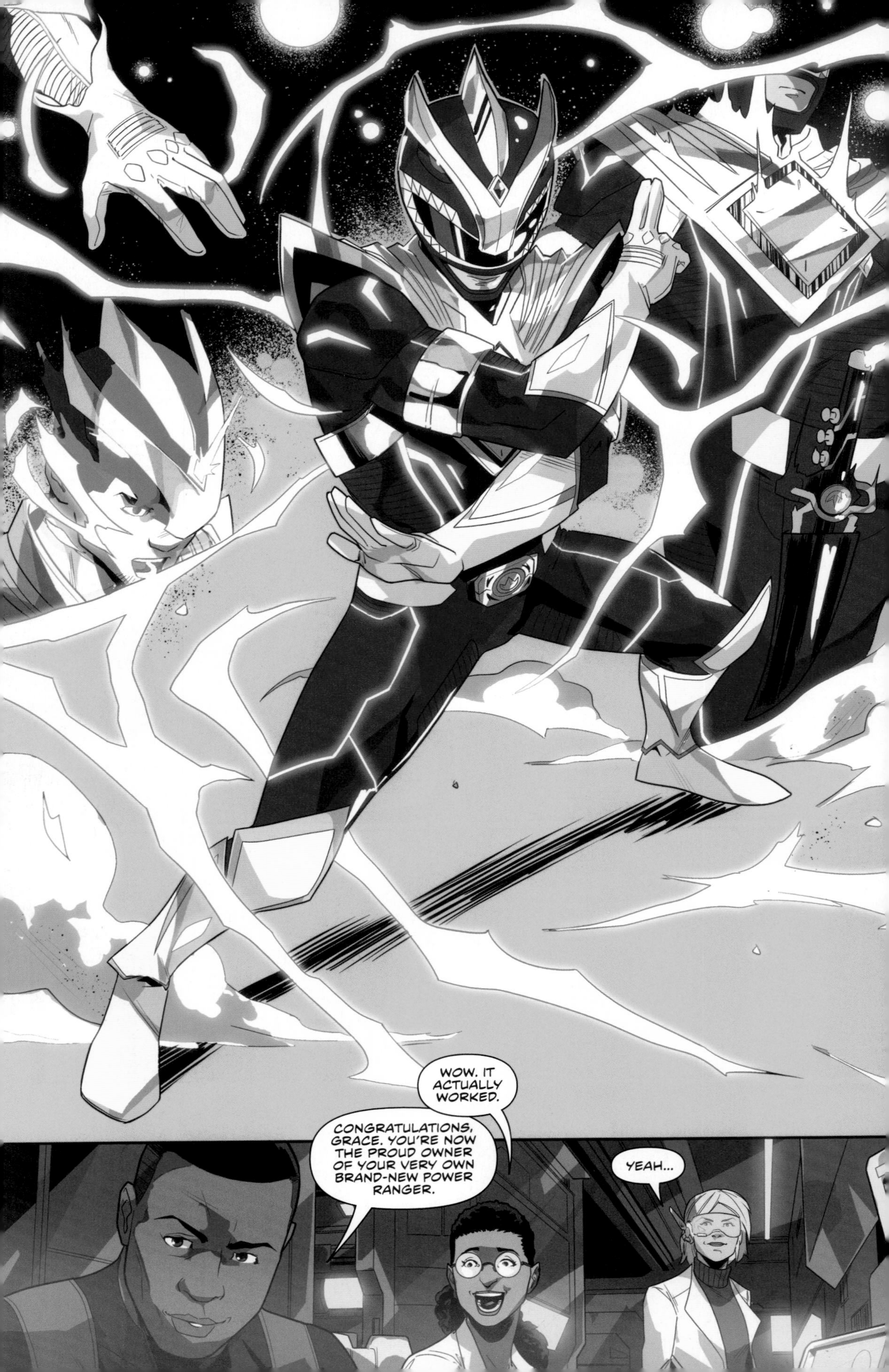
WOW. IT ACTUALLY WORKED.
CONGRATULATIONS, GRACE. YOU'RE NOW THE PROUD OWNER OF YOUR VERY OWN BRAND-NEW POWER RANGER.
YEAH...

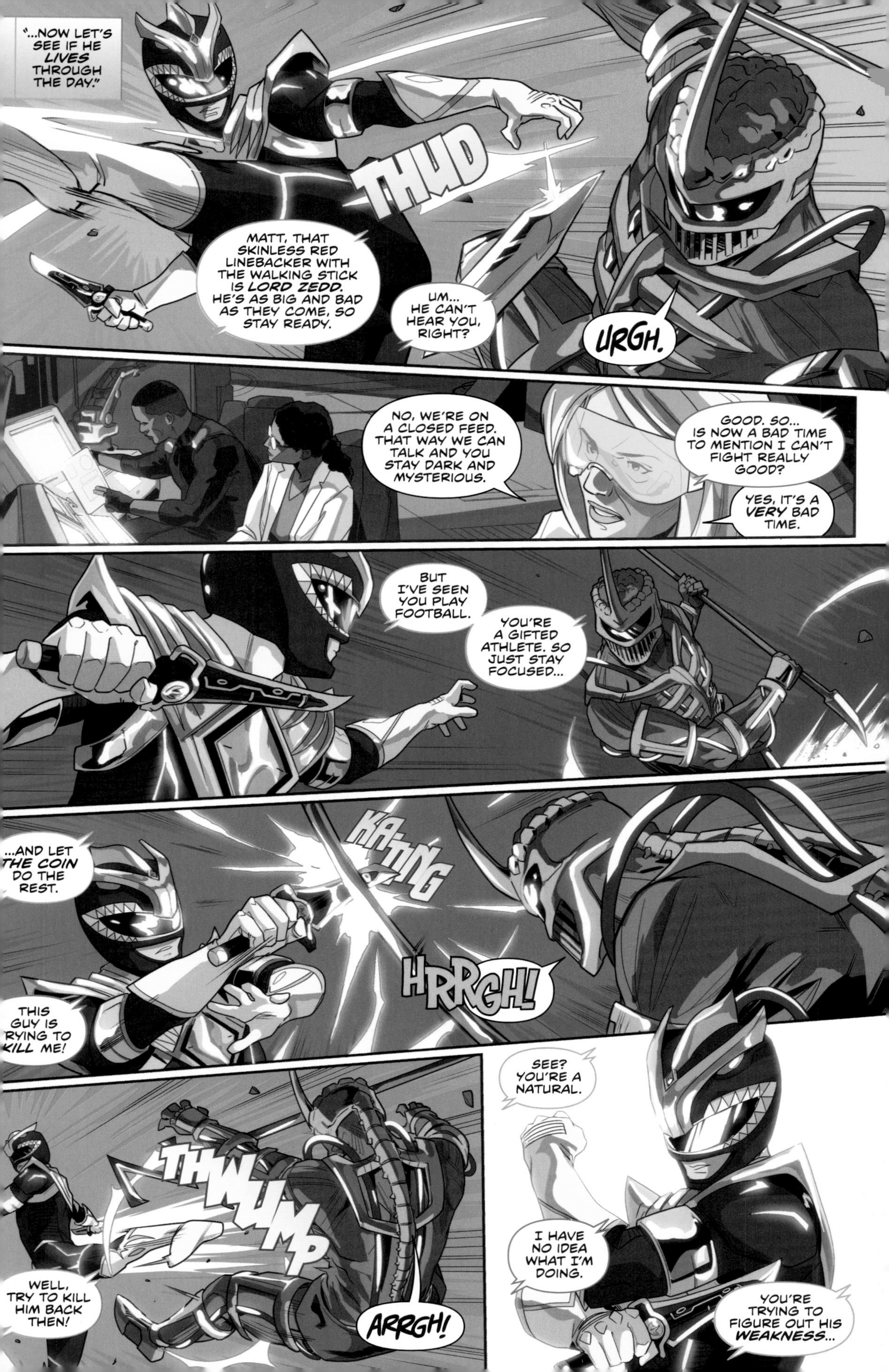
"...NOW LET'S SEE IF HE LIVES THROUGH THE DAY."
THUD
MATT, THAT SKINLESS RED LINEBACKER WITH THE WALKING STICK IS LORD ZEDD. HE'S AS BIG AND BAD AS THEY COME, SO STAY READY.
UM... HE CAN'T HEAR YOU, RIGHT?
URGH.
NO, WE'RE ON A CLOSED FEED. THAT WAY WE CAN TALK AND YOU STAY DARK AND MYSTERIOUS.
GOOD. SO... IS NOW A BAD TIME TO MENTION I CAN'T FIGHT REALLY GOOD?
YES, IT'S A VERY BAD TIME.
BUT I'VE SEEN YOU PLAY FOOTBALL.
YOU'RE A GIFTED ATHLETE. SO JUST STAY FOCUSED...
...AND LET THE COIN DO THE REST.
KA-TING
HRRRGH!
THIS GUY IS TRYING TO KILL ME!
THWUMP
WELL, TRY TO KILL HIM BACK THEN!
ARRGH!
SEE? YOU'RE A NATURAL.
I HAVE NO IDEA WHAT I'M DOING.
YOU'RE TRYING TO FIGURE OUT HIS WEAKNESS...

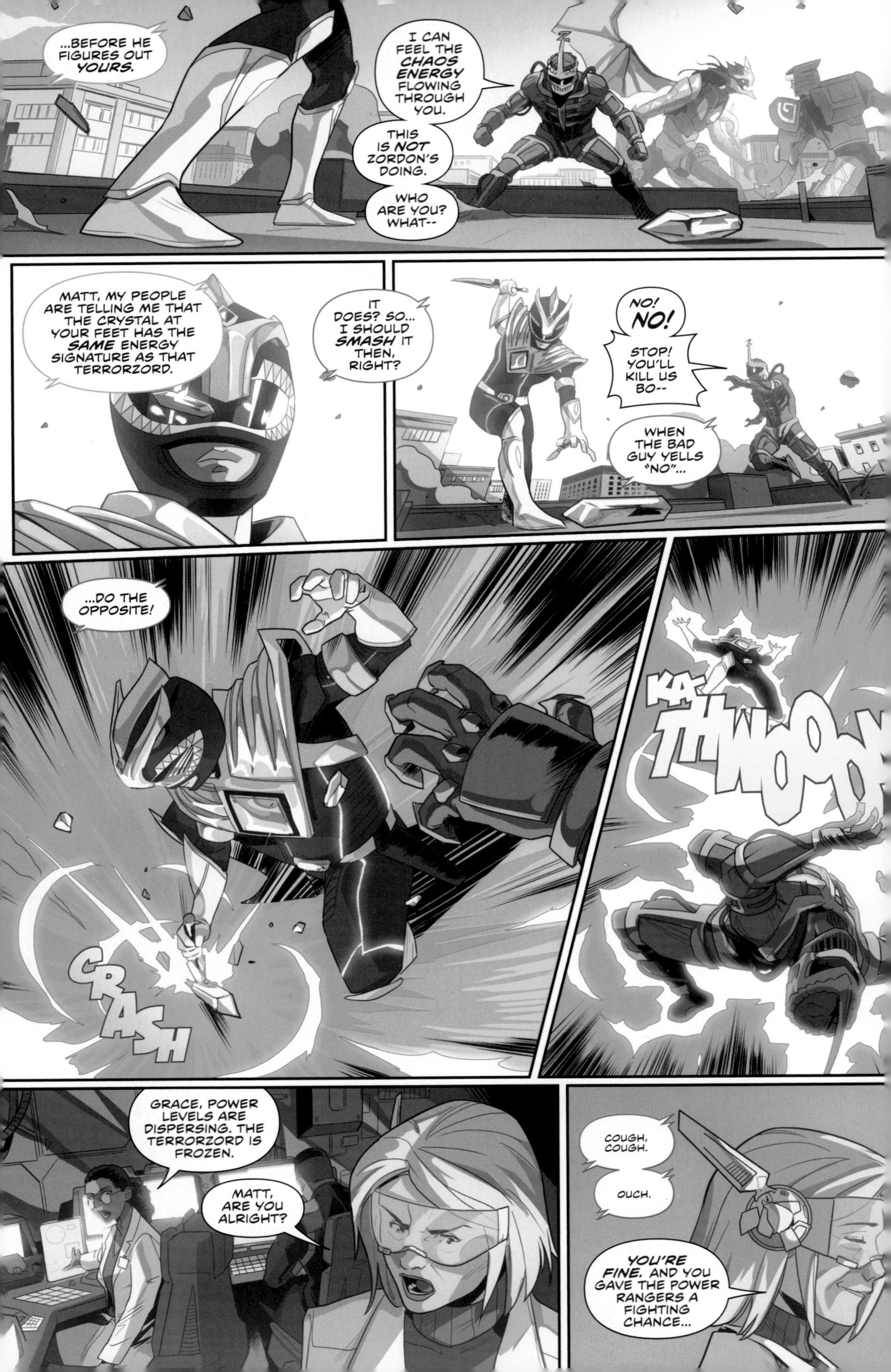
...BEFORE HE FIGURES OUT YOURS.
I CAN FEEL THE CHAOS ENERGY FLOWING THROUGH YOU.
THIS IS NOT ZORDON'S DOING.
WHO ARE YOU? WHAT--
MATT, MY PEOPLE ARE TELLING ME THAT THE CRYSTAL AT YOUR FEET HAS THE SAME ENERGY SIGNATURE AS THAT TERRORZORD.
IT DOES? SO... I SHOULD SMASH IT THEN, RIGHT?
NO! NO!
STOP! YOU'LL KILL US BO--
WHEN THE BAD GUY YELLS "NO"...
...DO THE OPPOSITE!
CRASH
KA-THWOOM
GRACE, POWER LEVELS ARE DISPERSING. THE TERRORZORD IS FROZEN.
MATT, ARE YOU ALRIGHT?
COUGH, COUGH.
OUCH.
YOU'RE FINE. AND YOU GAVE THE POWER RANGERS A FIGHTING CHANCE...

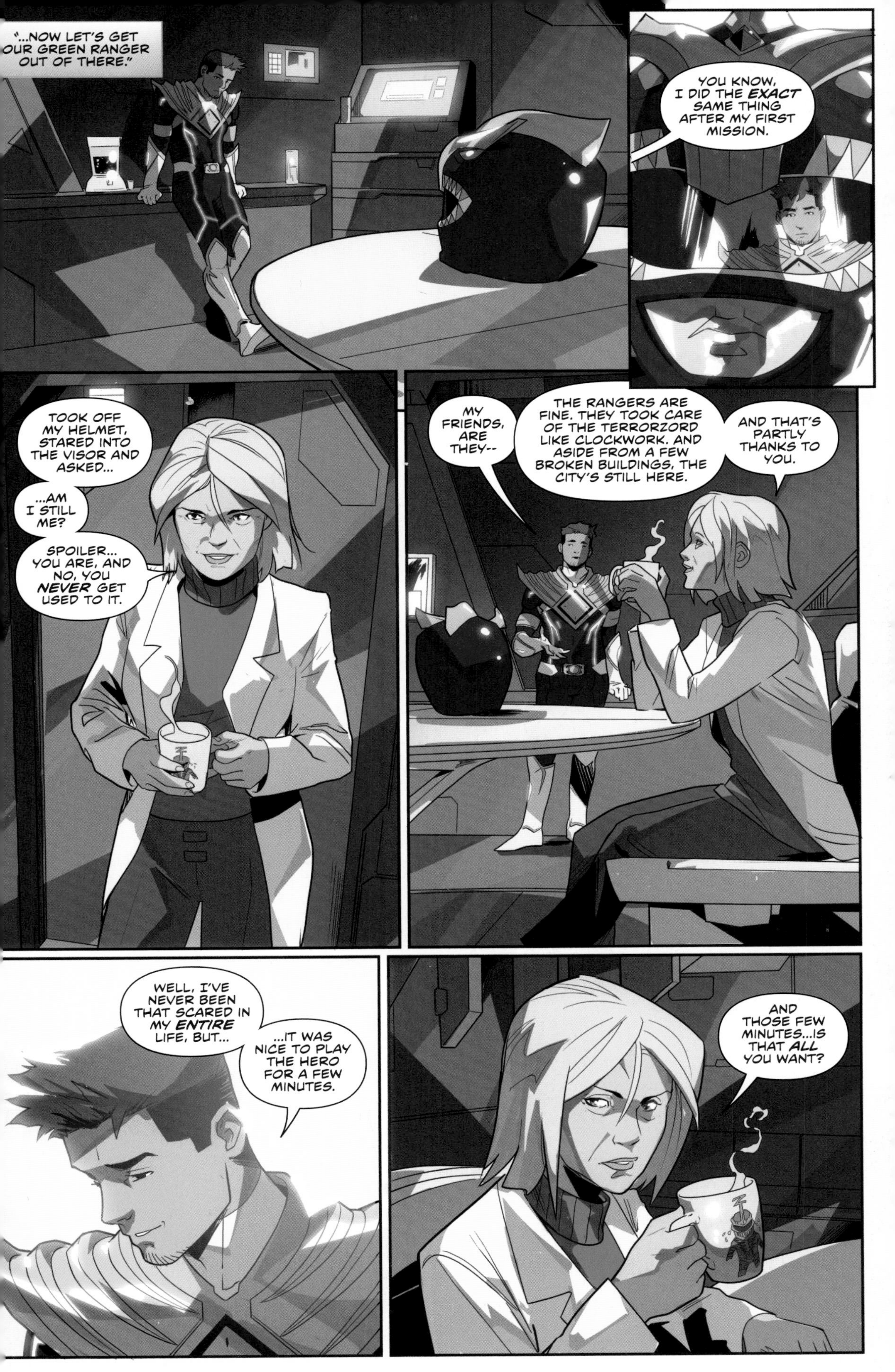
"...NOW LET'S GET OUR GREEN RANGER OUT OF THERE."
YOU KNOW, I DID THE EXACT SAME THING AFTER MY FIRST MISSION.
TOOK OFF MY HELMET, STARED INTO THE VISOR AND ASKED...
...AM I STILL ME?
SPOILER... YOU ARE, AND NO, YOU NEVER GET USED TO IT.
MY FRIENDS, ARE THEY--
THE RANGERS ARE FINE. THEY TOOK CARE OF THE TERRORZORD LIKE CLOCKWORK. AND ASIDE FROM A FEW BROKEN BUILDINGS, THE CITY'S STILL HERE.
AND THAT'S PARTLY THANKS TO YOU.
WELL, I'VE NEVER BEEN THAT SCARED IN MY ENTIRE LIFE, BUT...
...IT WAS NICE TO PLAY THE HERO FOR A FEW MINUTES.
AND THOSE FEW MINUTES...IS THAT ALL YOU WANT?

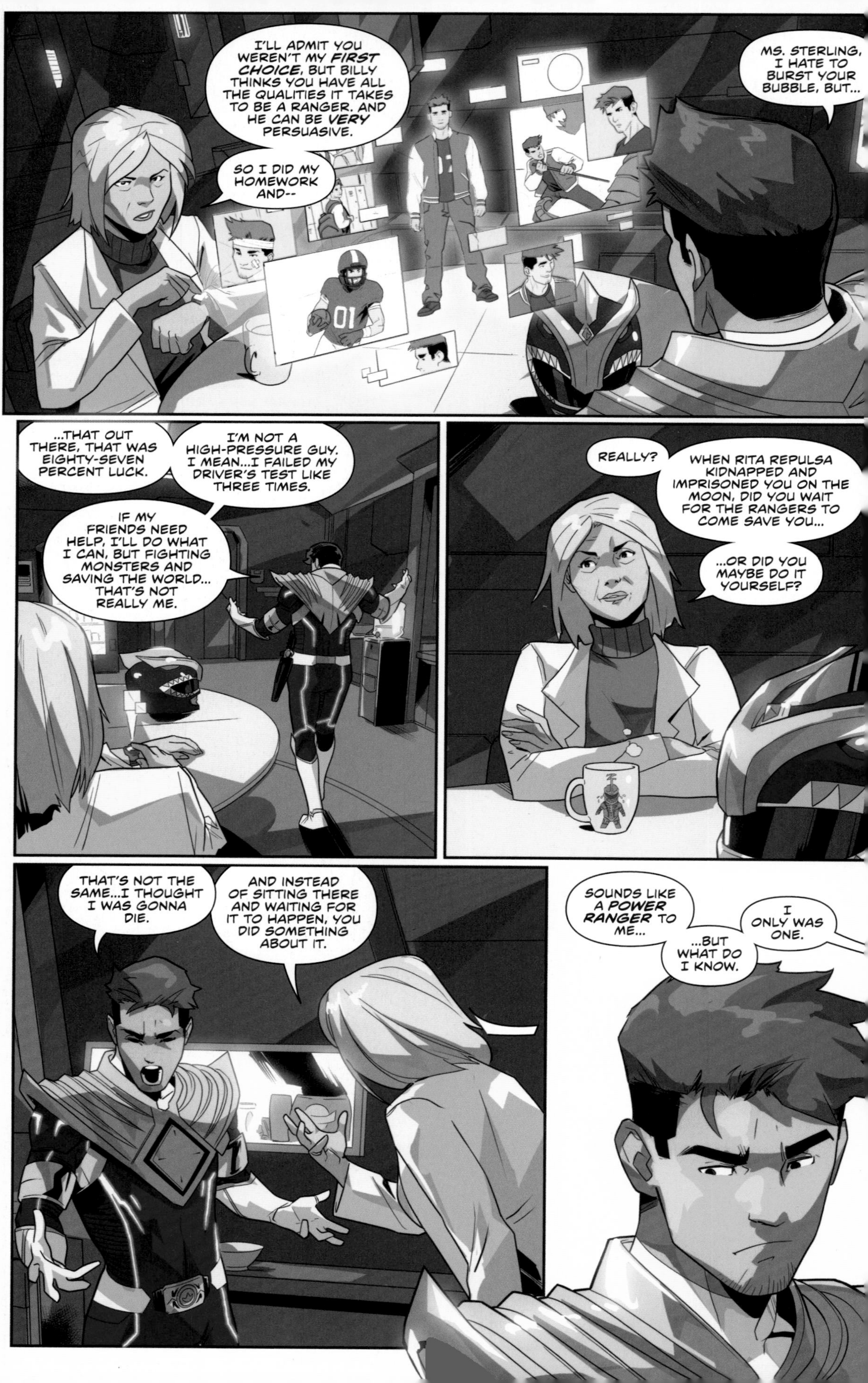
I'LL ADMIT YOU WEREN'T MY FIRST CHOICE, BUT BILLY THINKS YOU HAVE ALL THE QUALITIES IT TAKES TO BE A RANGER. AND HE CAN BE VERY PERSUASIVE.
SO I DID MY HOMEWORK AND--
MS. STERLING, I HATE TO BURST YOUR BUBBLE, BUT...
...THAT OUT THERE, THAT WAS EIGHTY-SEVEN PERCENT LUCK.
I'M NOT A HIGH-PRESSURE GUY. I MEAN...I FAILED MY DRIVER'S TEST LIKE THREE TIMES.
IF MY FRIENDS NEED HELP, I'LL DO WHAT I CAN, BUT FIGHTING MONSTERS AND SAVING THE WORLD... THAT'S NOT REALLY ME.
REALLY?
WHEN RITA REPULSA KIDNAPPED AND IMPRISONED YOU ON THE MOON, DID YOU WAIT FOR THE RANGERS TO COME SAVE YOU...
...OR DID YOU MAYBE DO IT YOURSELF?
THAT'S NOT THE SAME...I THOUGHT I WAS GONNA DIE.
AND INSTEAD OF SITTING THERE AND WAITING FOR IT TO HAPPEN, YOU DID SOMETHING ABOUT IT.
SOUNDS LIKE A POWER RANGER TO ME...
...BUT WHAT DO I KNOW.
I ONLY WAS ONE.

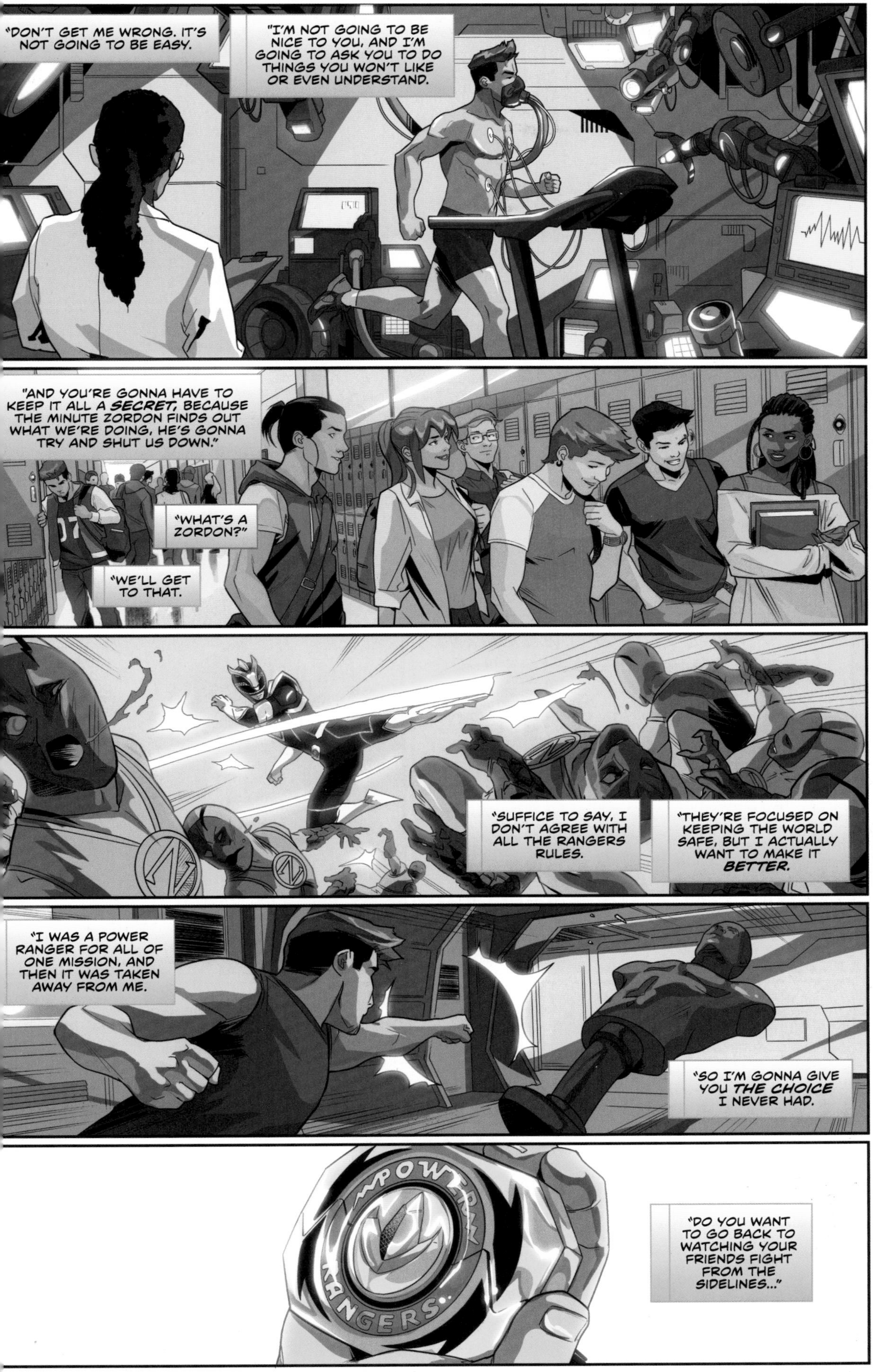
"DON'T GET ME WRONG. IT'S NOT GOING TO BE EASY.
"I'M NOT GOING TO BE NICE TO YOU, AND I'M GOING TO ASK YOU TO DO THINGS YOU WON'T LIKE OR EVEN UNDERSTAND.
"AND YOU'RE GONNA HAVE TO KEEP IT ALL A SECRET, BECAUSE THE MINUTE ZORDON FINDS OUT WHAT WE'RE DOING, HE'S GONNA TRY AND SHUT US DOWN."
"WHAT'S A ZORDON?"
"WE'LL GET TO THAT.
"SUFFICE TO SAY, I DON'T AGREE WITH ALL THE RANGERS RULES.
"THEY'RE FOCUSED ON KEEPING THE WORLD SAFE, BUT I ACTUALLY WANT TO MAKE IT BETTER.
"I WAS A POWER RANGER FOR ALL OF ONE MISSION, AND THEN IT WAS TAKEN AWAY FROM ME.
"SO I'M GONNA GIVE YOU THE CHOICE I NEVER HAD.
POWER RANGERS
"DO YOU WANT TO GO BACK TO WATCHING YOUR FRIENDS FIGHT FROM THE SIDELINES..."

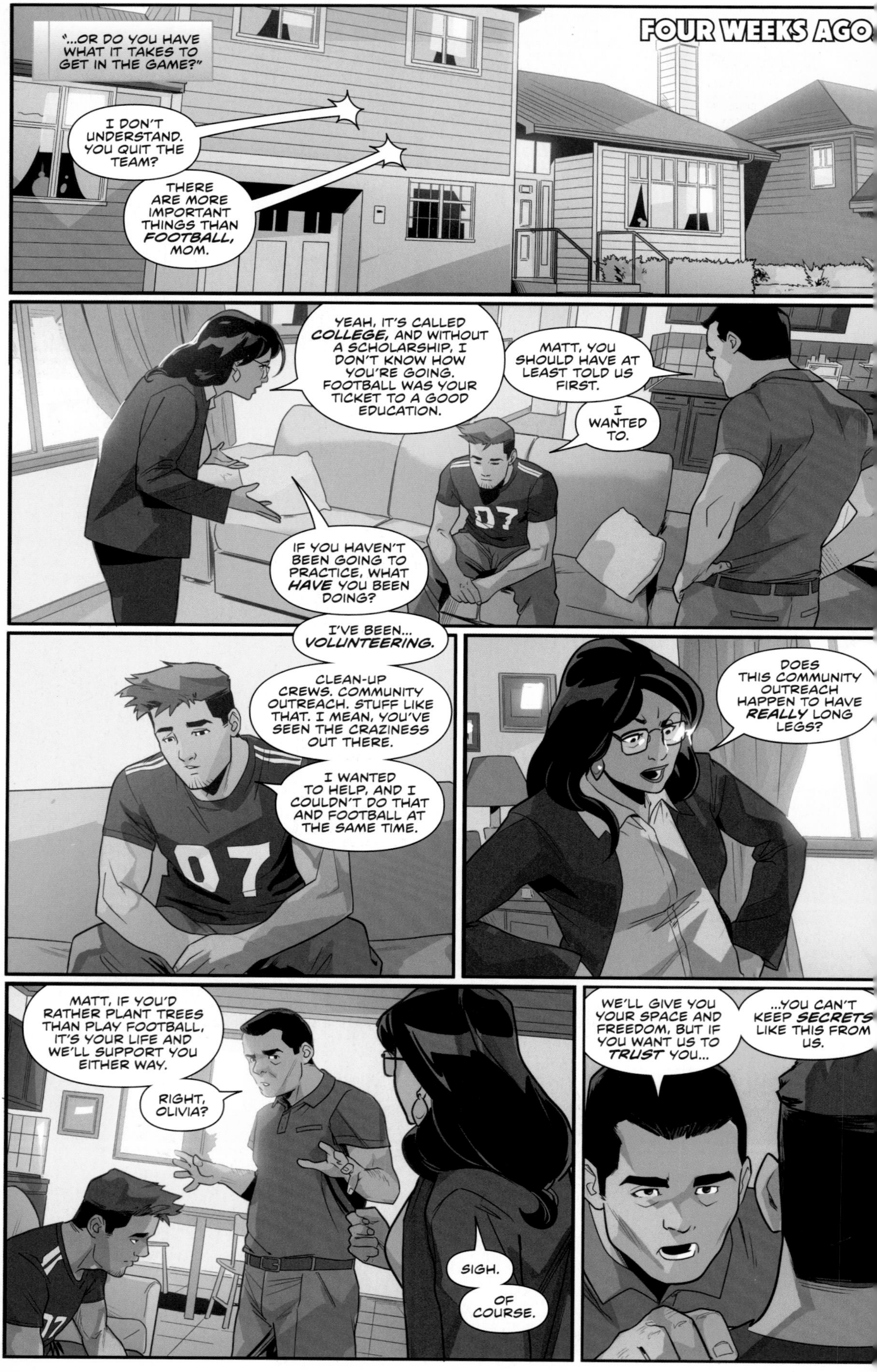
FOUR WEEKS AGO
"...OR DO YOU HAVE WHAT IT TAKES TO GET IN THE GAME?"
I DON'T UNDERSTAND. YOU QUIT THE TEAM?
THERE ARE MORE IMPORTANT THINGS THAN FOOTBALL, MOM.
YEAH, IT'S CALLED COLLEGE, AND WITHOUT A SCHOLARSHIP, I DON'T KNOW HOW YOU'RE GOING. FOOTBALL WAS YOUR TICKET TO A GOOD EDUCATION.
MATT, YOU SHOULD HAVE AT LEAST TOLD US FIRST.
I WANTED TO.
IF YOU HAVEN'T BEEN GOING TO PRACTICE, WHAT HAVE YOU BEEN DOING?
I'VE BEEN... VOLUNTEERING.
CLEAN-UP CREWS. COMMUNITY OUTREACH. STUFF LIKE THAT. I MEAN, YOU'VE SEEN THE CRAZINESS OUT THERE.
I WANTED TO HELP, AND I COULDN'T DO THAT AND FOOTBALL AT THE SAME TIME.
DOES THIS COMMUNITY OUTREACH HAPPEN TO HAVE REALLY LONG LEGS?
MATT, IF YOU'D RATHER PLANT TREES THAN PLAY FOOTBALL, IT'S YOUR LIFE AND WE'LL SUPPORT YOU EITHER WAY.
RIGHT, OLIVIA?
SIGH.
OF COURSE.
WE'LL GIVE YOU YOUR SPACE AND FREEDOM, BUT IF YOU WANT US TO TRUST YOU...
...YOU CAN'T KEEP SECRETS LIKE THIS FROM US.

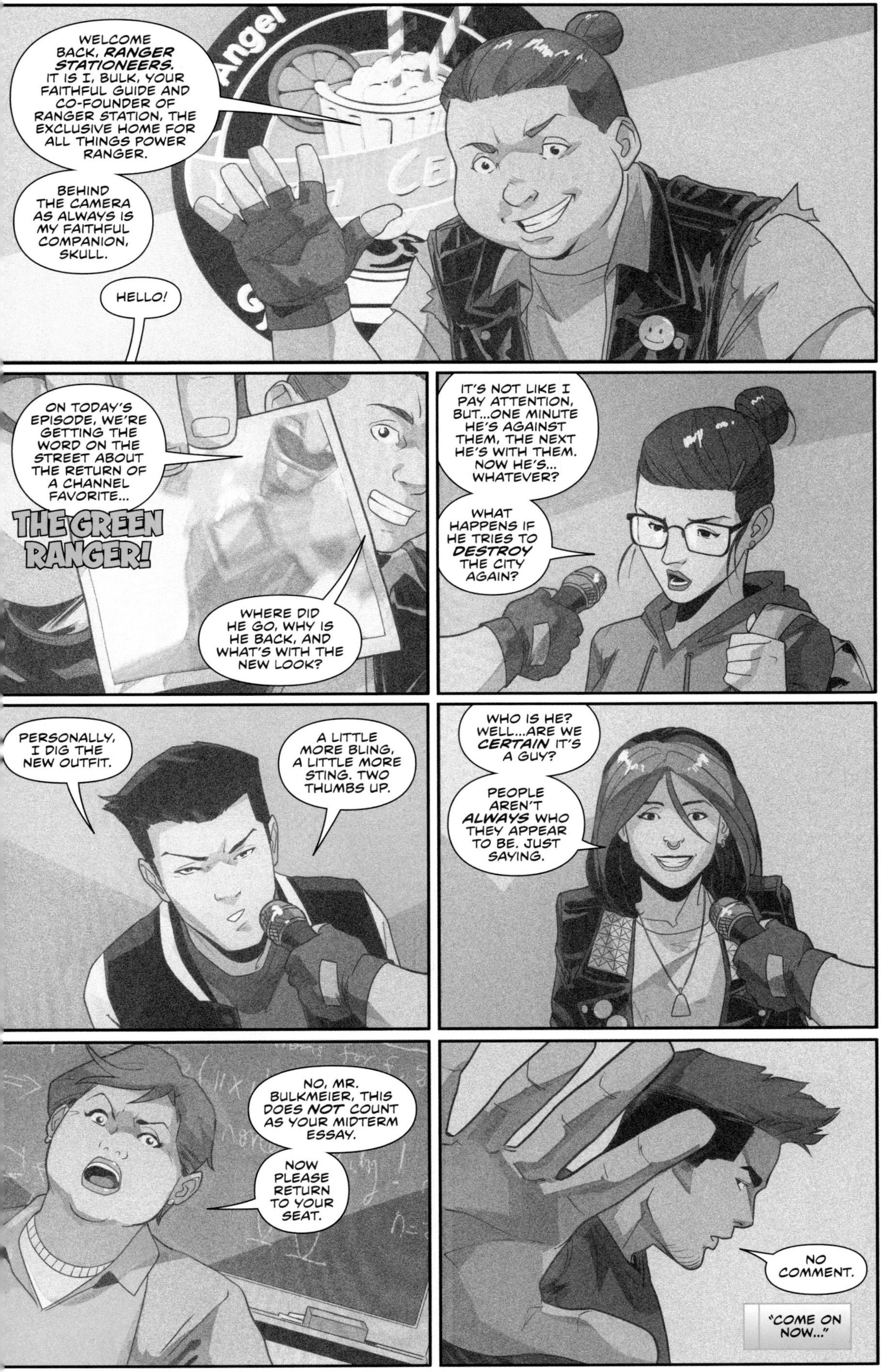

WELCOME BACK, RANGER STATIONEERS. IT IS I, BULK, YOUR FAITHFUL GUIDE AND CO-FOUNDER OF RANGER STATION, THE EXCLUSIVE HOME FOR ALL THINGS POWER RANGER.
BEHIND THE CAMERA AS ALWAYS IS MY FAITHFUL COMPANION, SKULL.
HELLO!
ON TODAY'S EPISODE, WE'RE GETTING THE WORD ON THE STREET ABOUT THE RETURN OF A CHANNEL FAVORITE...
THE GREEN RANGER!
WHERE DID HE GO, WHY IS HE BACK, AND WHAT'S WITH THE NEW LOOK?
IT'S NOT LIKE I PAY ATTENTION, BUT...ONE MINUTE HE'S AGAINST THEM, THE NEXT HE'S WITH THEM. NOW HE'S... WHATEVER?
WHAT HAPPENS IF HE TRIES TO DESTROY THE CITY AGAIN?
PERSONALLY, I DIG THE NEW OUTFIT.
A LITTLE MORE BLING, A LITTLE MORE STING. TWO THUMBS UP.
WHO IS HE? WELL...ARE WE CERTAIN IT'S A GUY?
PEOPLE AREN'T ALWAYS WHO THEY APPEAR TO BE. JUST SAYING.
NO, MR. BULKMEIER, THIS DOES NOT COUNT AS YOUR MIDTERM ESSAY.
NOW PLEASE RETURN TO YOUR SEAT.
NO COMMENT.
"COME ON NOW..."

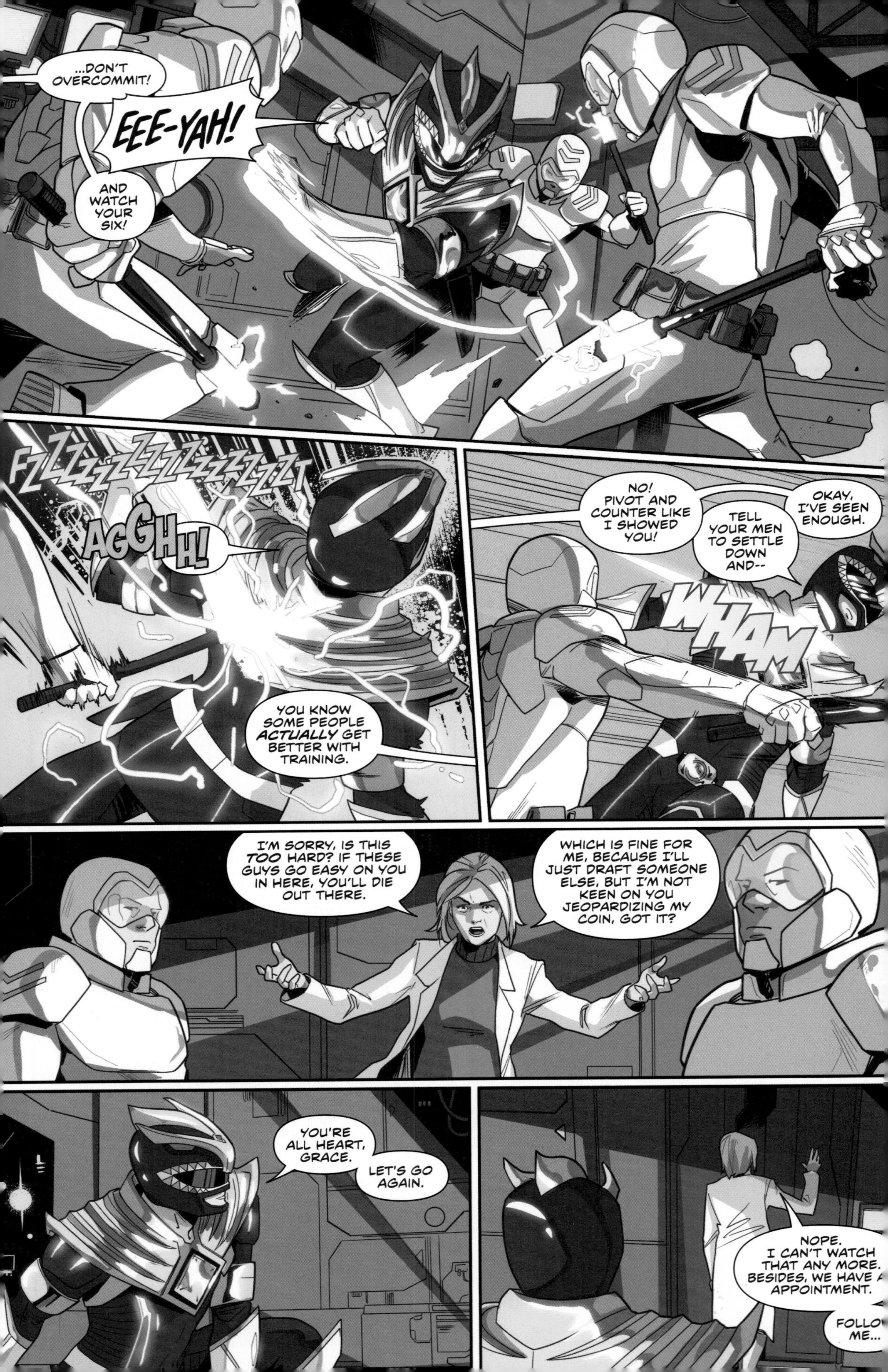
...DON'T OVERCOMMIT!
EEE-YAH!
AND WATCH YOUR SIX!
FZZZZZZZZZZZZZZZZZT
AGGHH!
YOU KNOW SOME PEOPLE ACTUALLY GET BETTER WITH TRAINING.
NO! PIVOT AND COUNTER LIKE I SHOWED YOU!
OKAY, I'VE SEEN ENOUGH.
TELL YOUR MEN TO SETTLE DOWN AND--
WHAM
I'M SORRY, IS THIS TOO HARD? IF THESE GUYS GO EASY ON YOU IN HERE, YOU'LL DIE OUT THERE.
WHICH IS FINE FOR ME, BECAUSE I'LL JUST DRAFT SOMEONE ELSE, BUT I'M NOT KEEN ON YOU JEOPARDIZING MY COIN, GOT IT?
YOU'RE ALL HEART, GRACE.
LET'S GO AGAIN.
NOPE. I CAN'T WATCH THAT ANY MORE. BESIDES, WE HAVE AN APPOINTMENT.

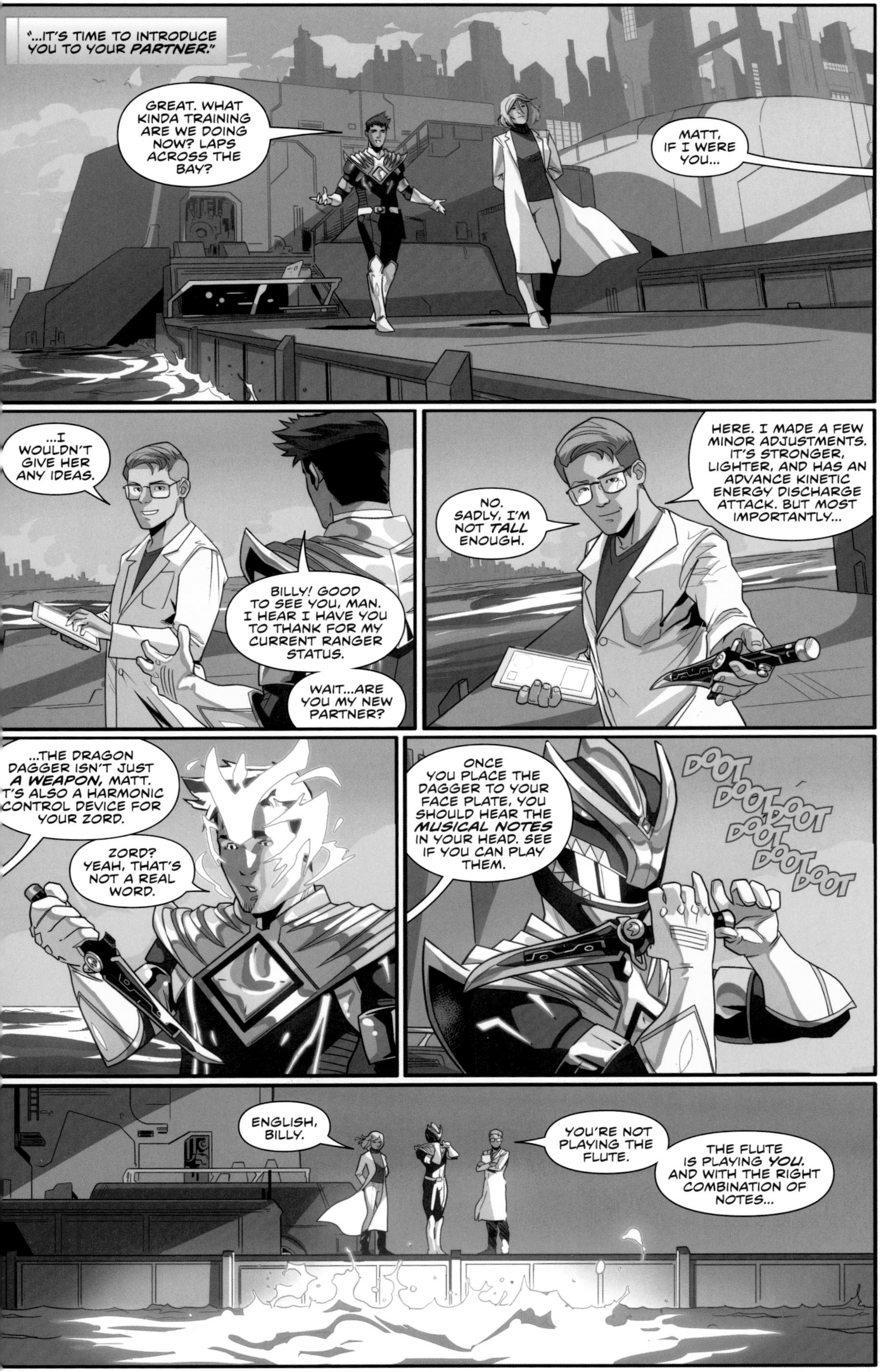
"...IT'S TIME TO INTRODUCE YOU TO YOUR PARTNER."
GREAT. WHAT KINDA TRAINING ARE WE DOING NOW? LAPS ACROSS THE BAY?
MATT, IF I WERE YOU...
...I WOULDN'T GIVE HER ANY IDEAS.
BILLY! GOOD TO SEE YOU, MAN. I HEAR I HAVE YOU TO THANK FOR MY CURRENT RANGER STATUS.
WAIT...ARE YOU MY NEW PARTNER?
NO. SADLY, I'M NOT TALL ENOUGH.
HERE. I MADE A FEW MINOR ADJUSTMENTS. IT'S STRONGER, LIGHTER, AND HAS AN ADVANCE KINETIC ENERGY DISCHARGE ATTACK. BUT MOST IMPORTANTLY...
...THE DRAGON DAGGER ISN'T JUST A WEAPON, MATT. IT'S ALSO A HARMONIC CONTROL DEVICE FOR YOUR ZORD.
ZORD? YEAH, THAT'S NOT A REAL WORD.
ONCE YOU PLACE THE DAGGER TO YOUR FACE PLATE, YOU SHOULD HEAR THE MUSICAL NOTES IN YOUR HEAD. SEE IF YOU CAN PLAY THEM.
DOOT DOOT DOOT DOOT DOOT DOOT
ENGLISH, BILLY.
YOU'RE NOT PLAYING THE FLUTE.
THE FLUTE IS PLAYING YOU. AND WITH THE RIGHT COMBINATION OF NOTES...

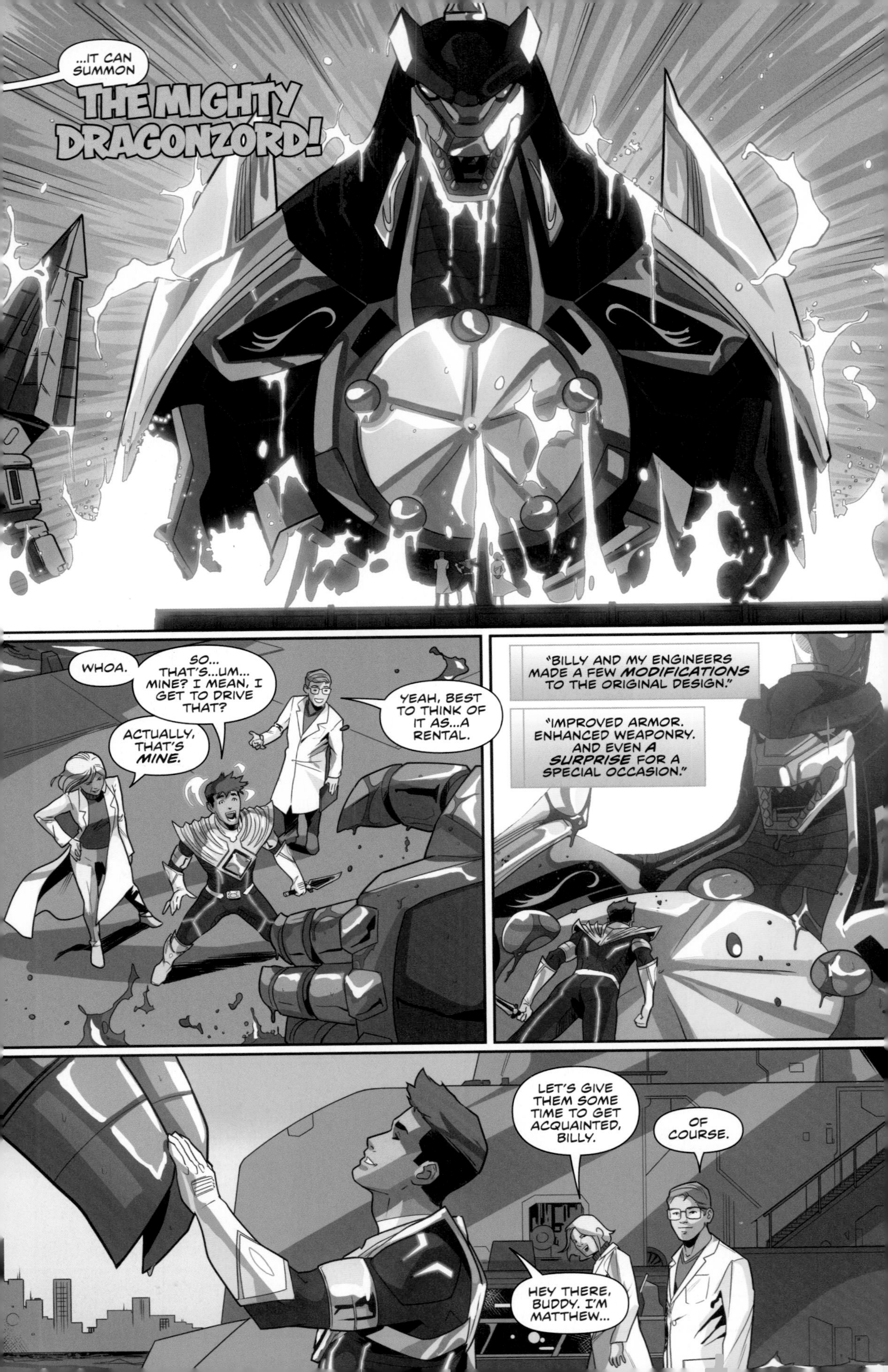
...IT CAN SUMMON
THE MIGHTY DRAGONZORD!
WHOA.
SO... THAT'S...UM... MINE? I MEAN, I GET TO DRIVE THAT?
ACTUALLY, THAT'S *MINE.*
YEAH, BEST TO THINK OF IT AS...A RENTAL.
"BILLY AND MY ENGINEERS MADE A FEW *MODIFICATIONS* TO THE ORIGINAL DESIGN."
"IMPROVED ARMOR. ENHANCED WEAPONRY. AND EVEN *A SURPRISE* FOR A SPECIAL OCCASION."
LET'S GIVE THEM SOME TIME TO GET ACQUAINTED, BILLY.
OF COURSE.
HEY THERE, BUDDY. I'M MATTHEW...

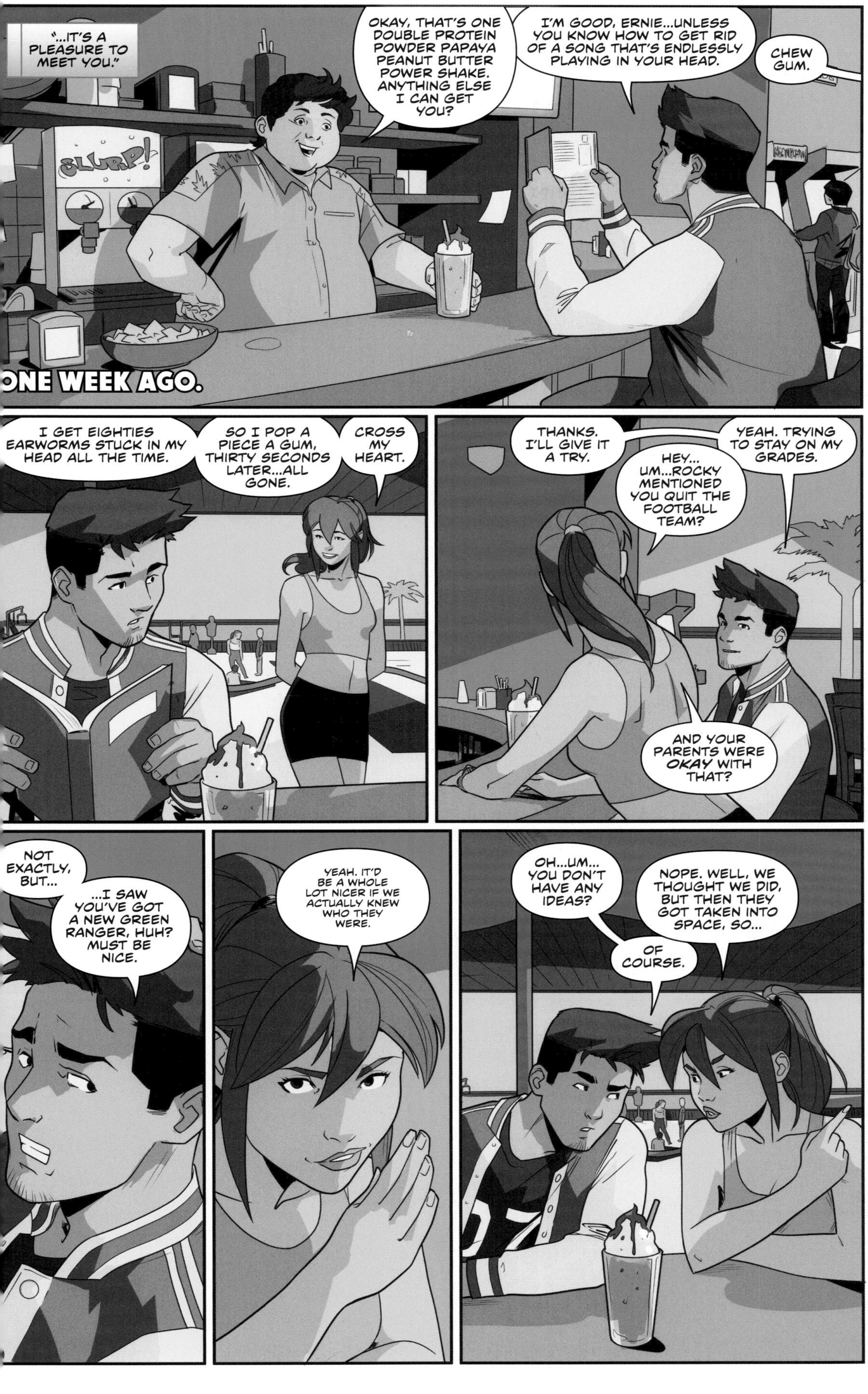
"...IT'S A PLEASURE TO MEET YOU."
SLURP!
OKAY, THAT'S ONE DOUBLE PROTEIN POWDER PAPAYA PEANUT BUTTER POWER SHAKE. ANYTHING ELSE I CAN GET YOU?
I'M GOOD, ERNIE...UNLESS YOU KNOW HOW TO GET RID OF A SONG THAT'S ENDLESSLY PLAYING IN YOUR HEAD.
CHEW GUM.
ONE WEEK AGO.
I GET EIGHTIES EARWORMS STUCK IN MY HEAD ALL THE TIME.
SO I POP A PIECE A GUM, THIRTY SECONDS LATER...ALL GONE.
CROSS MY HEART.
THANKS. I'LL GIVE IT A TRY.
HEY... UM...ROCKY MENTIONED YOU QUIT THE FOOTBALL TEAM?
YEAH. TRYING TO STAY ON MY GRADES.
AND YOUR PARENTS WERE OKAY WITH THAT?
NOT EXACTLY, BUT...
...I SAW YOU'VE GOT A NEW GREEN RANGER, HUH? MUST BE NICE.
YEAH. IT'D BE A WHOLE LOT NICER IF WE ACTUALLY KNEW WHO THEY WERE.
OH...UM... YOU DON'T HAVE ANY IDEAS?
NOPE. WELL, WE THOUGHT WE DID, BUT THEN THEY GOT TAKEN INTO SPACE, SO...
OF COURSE.

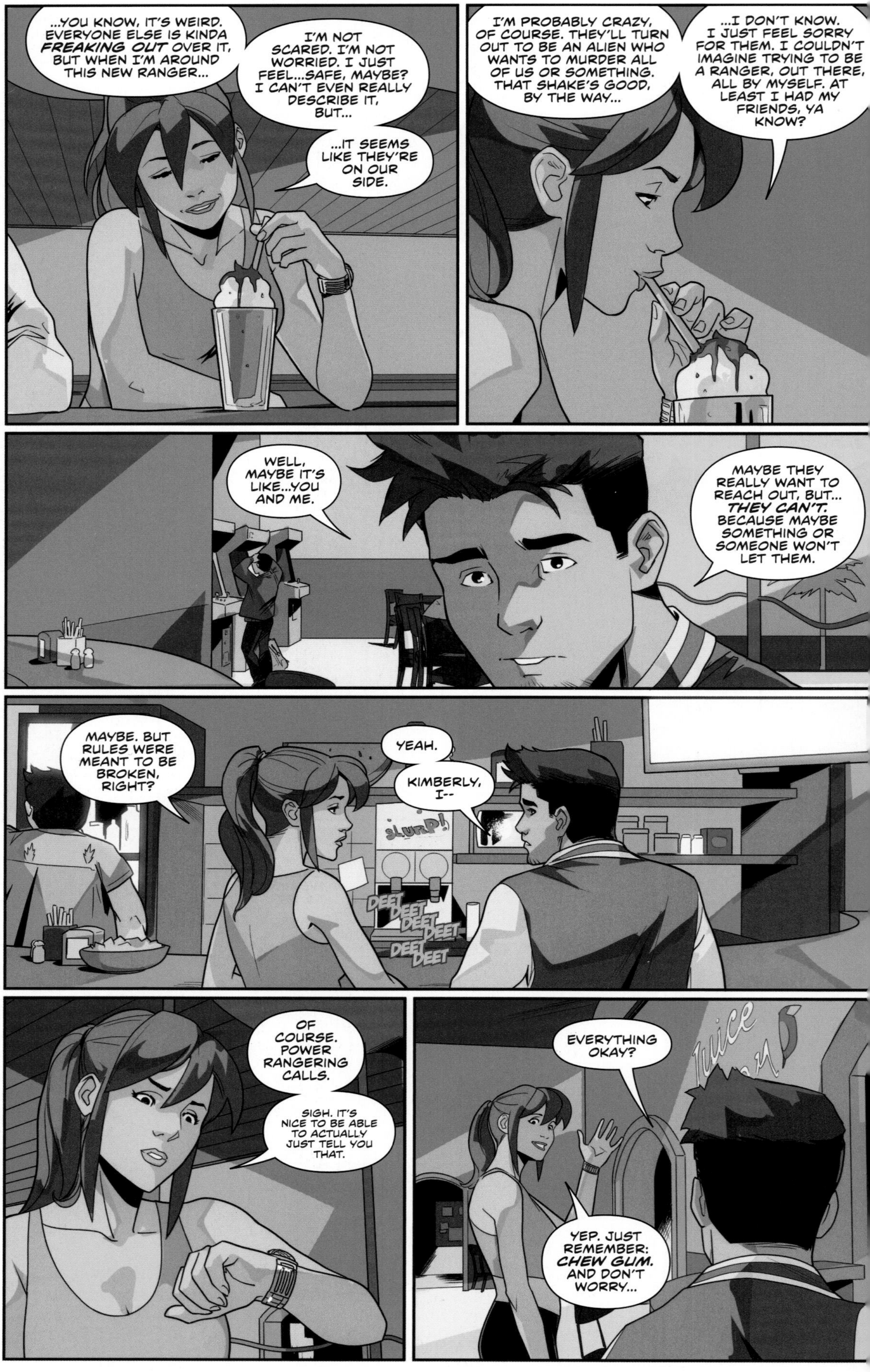
...YOU KNOW, IT'S WEIRD. EVERYONE ELSE IS KINDA *FREAKING OUT* OVER IT, BUT WHEN I'M AROUND THIS NEW RANGER...
I'M NOT SCARED. I'M NOT WORRIED. I JUST FEEL...SAFE, MAYBE? I CAN'T EVEN REALLY DESCRIBE IT, BUT...
...IT SEEMS LIKE THEY'RE ON OUR SIDE.
I'M PROBABLY CRAZY, OF COURSE. THEY'LL TURN OUT TO BE AN ALIEN WHO WANTS TO MURDER ALL OF US OR SOMETHING. THAT SHAKE'S GOOD, BY THE WAY...
...I DON'T KNOW. I JUST FEEL SORRY FOR THEM. I COULDN'T IMAGINE TRYING TO BE A RANGER, OUT THERE, ALL BY MYSELF. AT LEAST I HAD MY FRIENDS, YA KNOW?
WELL, MAYBE IT'S LIKE...YOU AND ME.
MAYBE THEY REALLY WANT TO REACH OUT, BUT... *THEY CAN'T.* BECAUSE MAYBE SOMETHING OR SOMEONE WON'T LET THEM.
MAYBE. BUT RULES WERE MEANT TO BE BROKEN, RIGHT?
YEAH.
KIMBERLY, I--
SLURP!
DEET DEET DEET DEET DEET DEET
OF COURSE. POWER RANGERING CALLS.
SIGH. IT'S NICE TO BE ABLE TO ACTUALLY JUST TELL YOU THAT.
EVERYTHING OKAY?
YEP. JUST REMEMBER: *CHEW GUM.* AND DON'T WORRY...

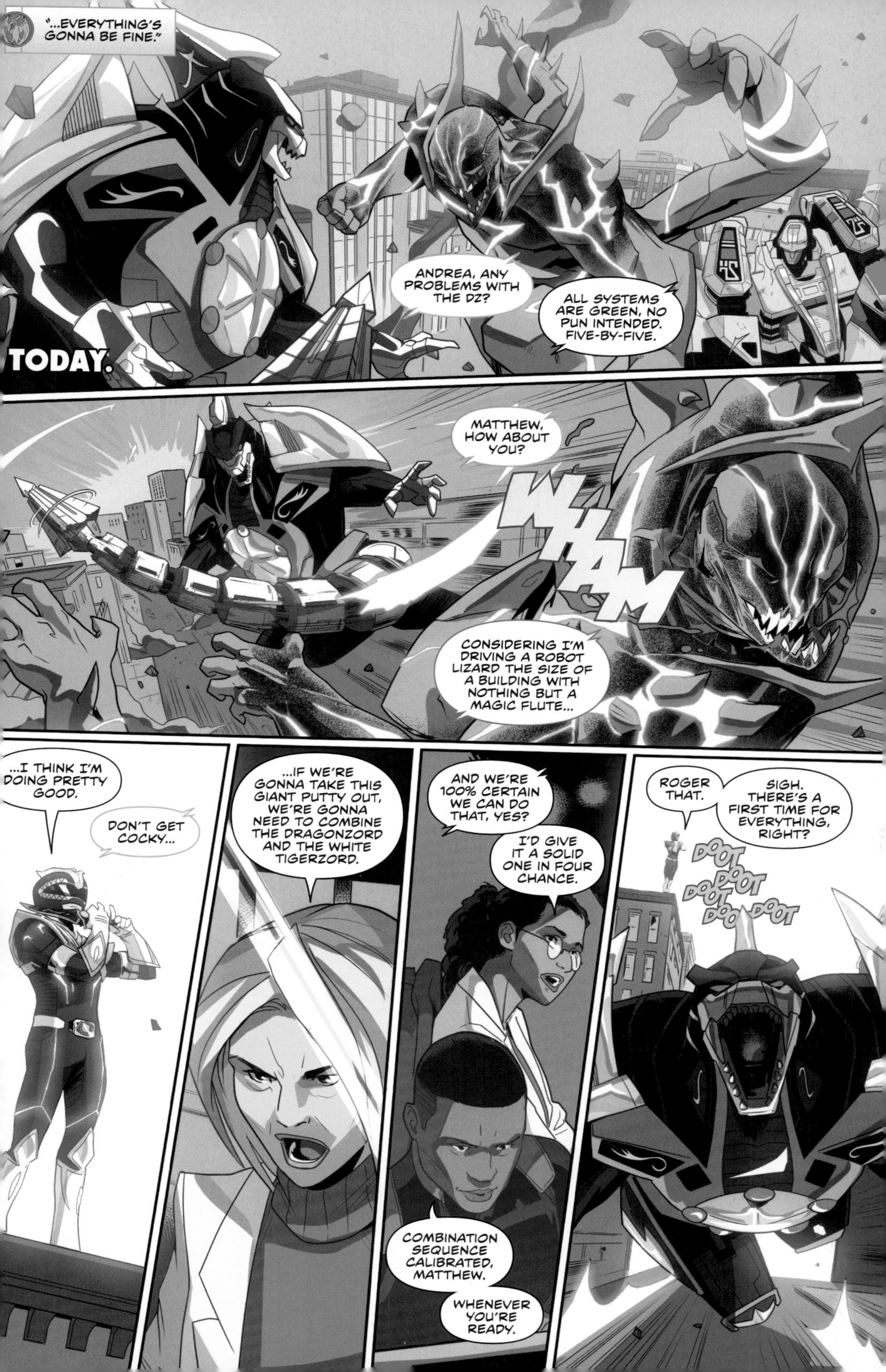
"...EVERYTHING'S GONNA BE FINE."
TODAY.
ANDREA, ANY PROBLEMS WITH THE DZ?
ALL SYSTEMS ARE GREEN, NO PUN INTENDED. FIVE-BY-FIVE.
MATTHEW, HOW ABOUT YOU?
WHAM
CONSIDERING I'M DRIVING A ROBOT LIZARD THE SIZE OF A BUILDING WITH NOTHING BUT A MAGIC FLUTE...
...I THINK I'M DOING PRETTY GOOD.
DON'T GET COCKY...
...IF WE'RE GONNA TAKE THIS GIANT PUTTY OUT, WE'RE GONNA NEED TO COMBINE THE DRAGONZORD AND THE WHITE TIGERZORD.
AND WE'RE 100% CERTAIN WE CAN DO THAT, YES?
I'D GIVE IT A SOLID ONE IN FOUR CHANCE.
COMBINATION SEQUENCE CALIBRATED, MATTHEW.
WHENEVER YOU'RE READY.
ROGER THAT.
SIGH. THERE'S A FIRST TIME FOR EVERYTHING, RIGHT?
DOOT DOOT DOOT DOO DOOT

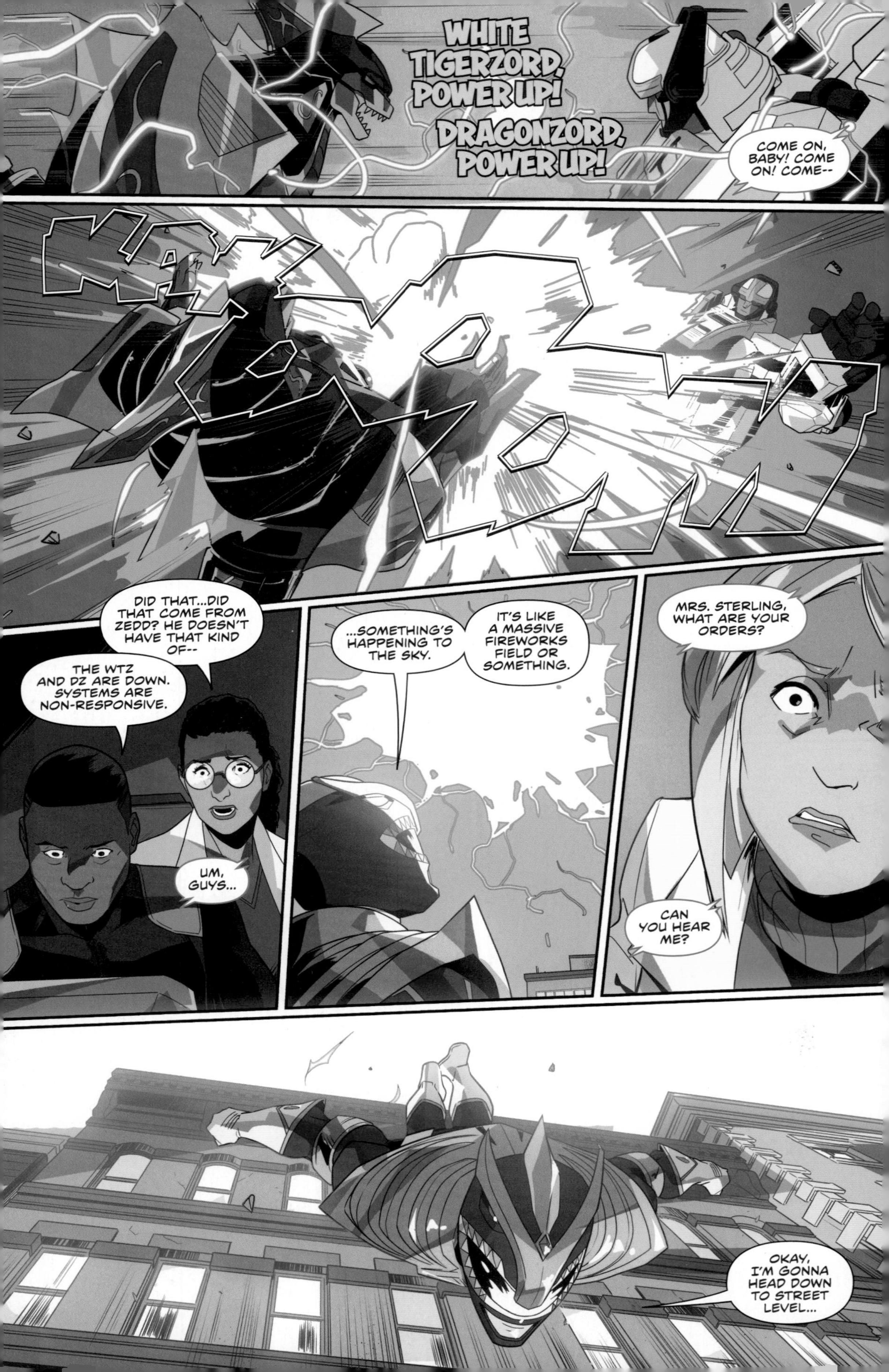
WHITE TIGERZORD, POWER UP!
DRAGONZORD, POWER UP!
COME ON, BABY! COME ON! COME--
DID THAT...DID THAT COME FROM ZEDD? HE DOESN'T HAVE THAT KIND OF--
THE WTZ AND DZ ARE DOWN. SYSTEMS ARE NON-RESPONSIVE.
UM, GUYS...
...SOMETHING'S HAPPENING TO THE SKY.
IT'S LIKE A MASSIVE FIREWORKS FIELD OR SOMETHING.
MRS. STERLING, WHAT ARE YOUR ORDERS?
CAN YOU HEAR ME?
OKAY, I'M GONNA HEAD DOWN TO STREET LEVEL...

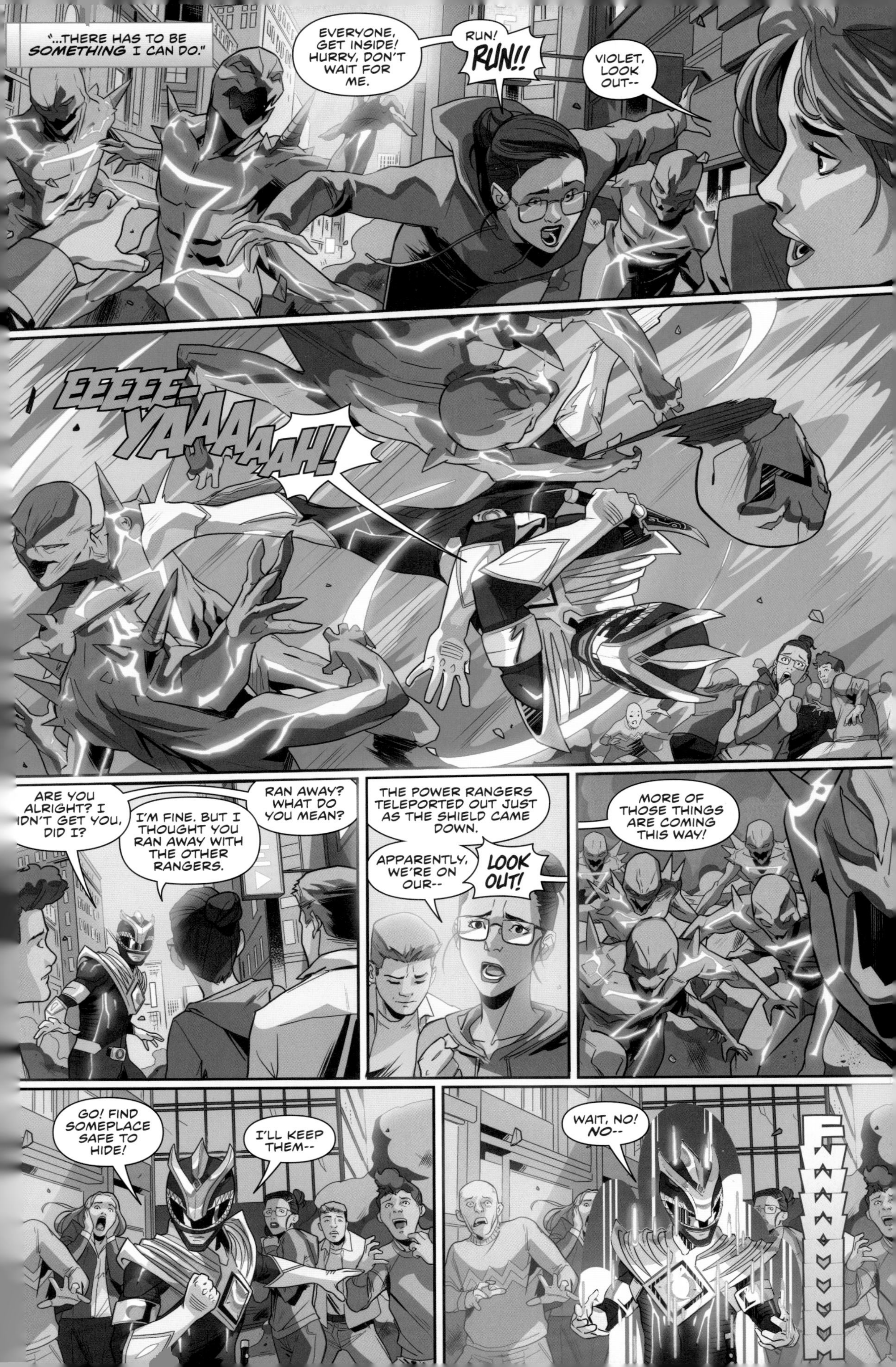
"...THERE HAS TO BE SOMETHING I CAN DO."
EVERYONE, GET INSIDE! HURRY, DON'T WAIT FOR ME.
RUN! RUN!!
VIOLET, LOOK OUT--
EEEEE-YAAAAAAH!
ARE YOU ALRIGHT? I DIDN'T GET YOU, DID I?
I'M FINE. BUT I THOUGHT YOU RAN AWAY WITH THE OTHER RANGERS.
RAN AWAY? WHAT DO YOU MEAN?
THE POWER RANGERS TELEPORTED OUT JUST AS THE SHIELD CAME DOWN.
APPARENTLY, WE'RE ON OUR--
LOOK OUT!
MORE OF THOSE THINGS ARE COMING THIS WAY!
GO! FIND SOMEPLACE SAFE TO HIDE!
I'LL KEEP THEM--
WAIT, NO! NO--
FWAAAAAAAAMM

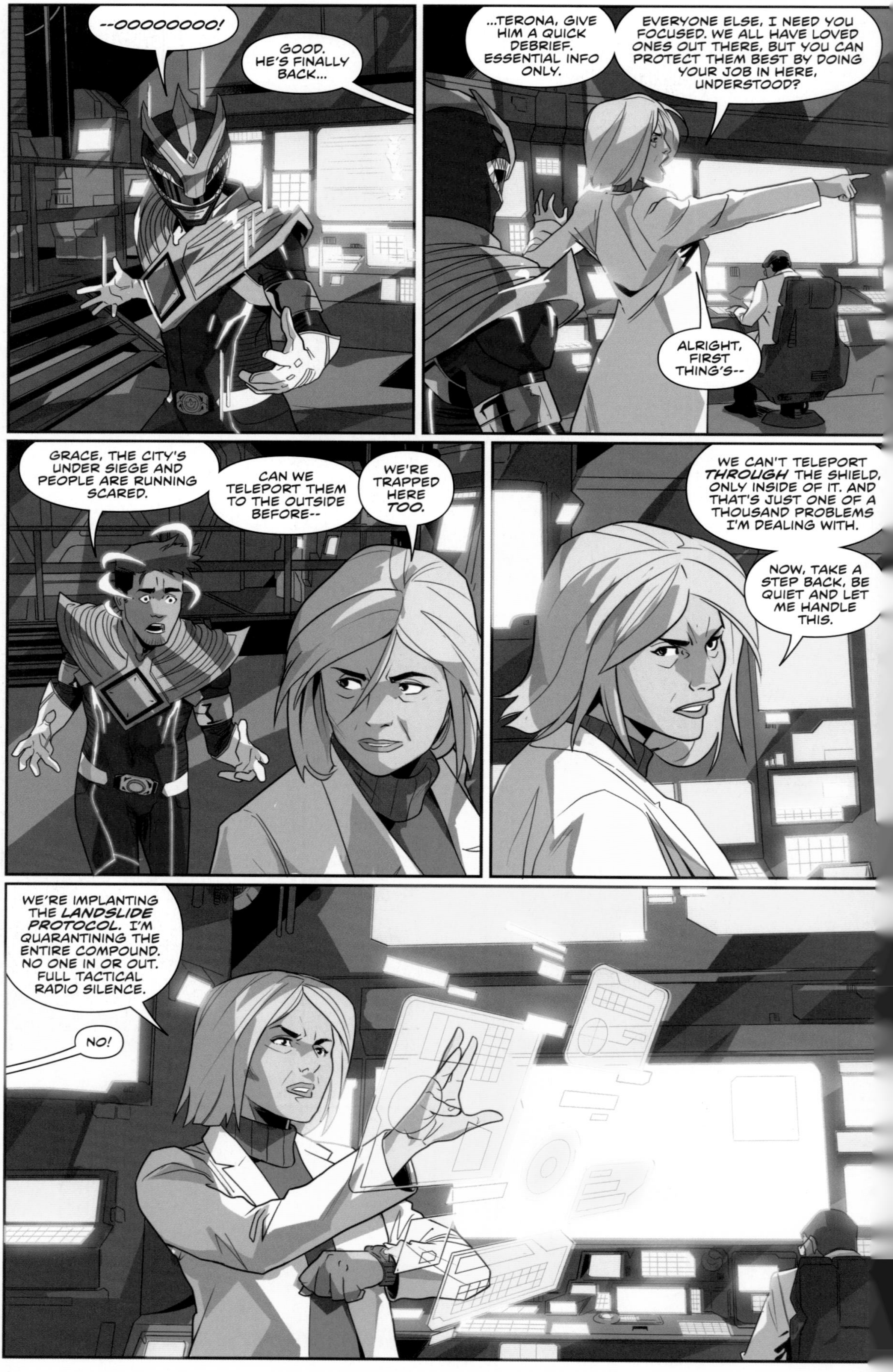
--OOOOOOOO!
GOOD. HE'S FINALLY BACK...
...TERONA, GIVE HIM A QUICK DEBRIEF. ESSENTIAL INFO ONLY.
EVERYONE ELSE, I NEED YOU FOCUSED. WE ALL HAVE LOVED ONES OUT THERE, BUT YOU CAN PROTECT THEM BEST BY DOING YOUR JOB IN HERE, UNDERSTOOD?
ALRIGHT, FIRST THING'S--
GRACE, THE CITY'S UNDER SIEGE AND PEOPLE ARE RUNNING SCARED.
CAN WE TELEPORT THEM TO THE OUTSIDE BEFORE--
WE'RE TRAPPED HERE *TOO*.
WE CAN'T TELEPORT ***THROUGH*** THE SHIELD, ONLY INSIDE OF IT. AND THAT'S JUST ONE OF A THOUSAND PROBLEMS I'M DEALING WITH.
NOW, TAKE A STEP BACK, BE QUIET AND LET ME HANDLE THIS.
WE'RE IMPLANTING THE ***LANDSLIDE PROTOCOL***. I'M QUARANTINING THE ENTIRE COMPOUND. NO ONE IN OR OUT. FULL TACTICAL RADIO SILENCE.
NO!

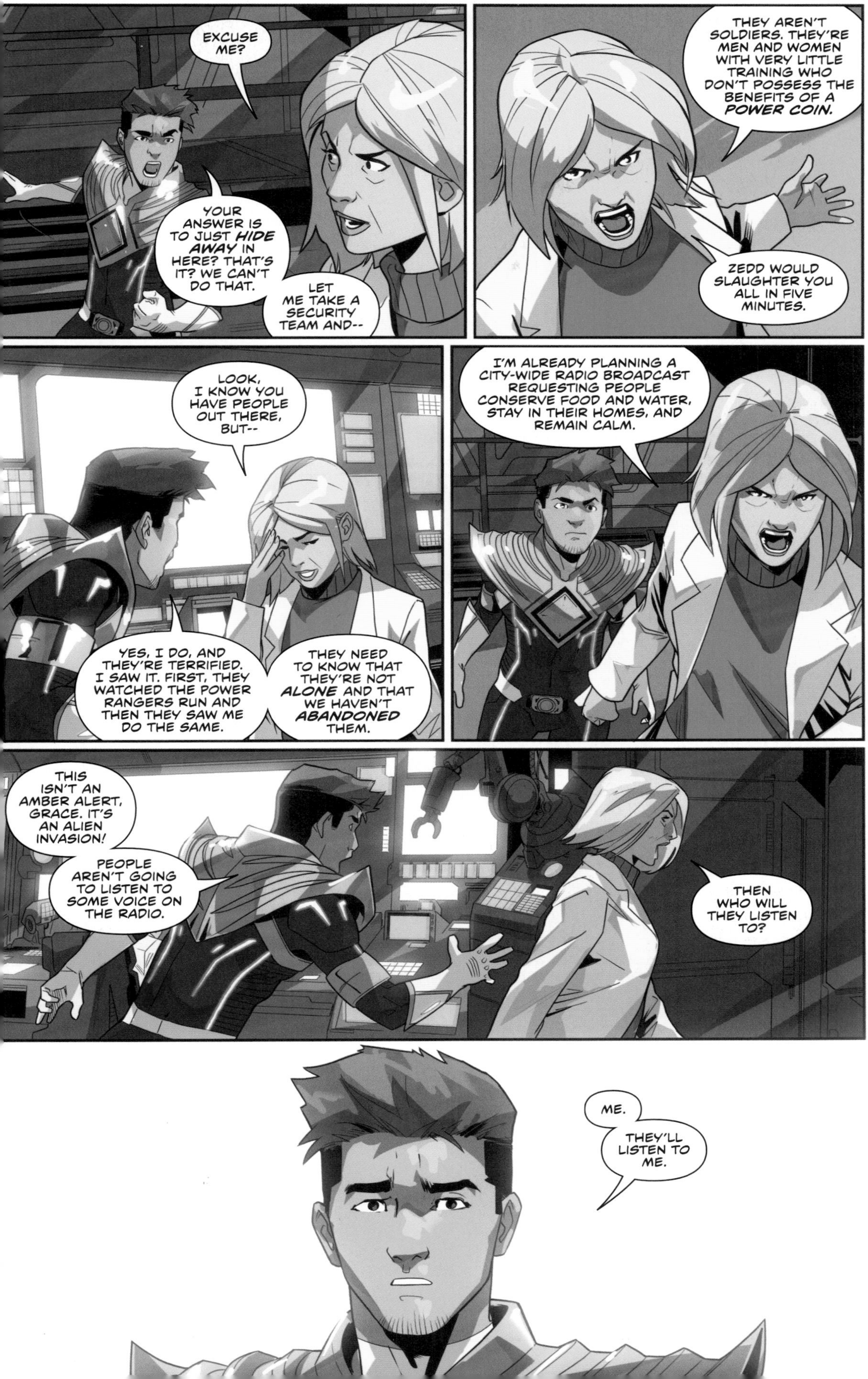
EXCUSE ME?
YOUR ANSWER IS TO JUST HIDE AWAY IN HERE? THAT'S IT? WE CAN'T DO THAT.
LET ME TAKE A SECURITY TEAM AND--
THEY AREN'T SOLDIERS. THEY'RE MEN AND WOMEN WITH VERY LITTLE TRAINING WHO DON'T POSSESS THE BENEFITS OF A POWER COIN.
ZEDD WOULD SLAUGHTER YOU ALL IN FIVE MINUTES.
LOOK, I KNOW YOU HAVE PEOPLE OUT THERE, BUT--
YES, I DO, AND THEY'RE TERRIFIED. I SAW IT. FIRST, THEY WATCHED THE POWER RANGERS RUN AND THEN THEY SAW ME DO THE SAME.
THEY NEED TO KNOW THAT THEY'RE NOT ALONE AND THAT WE HAVEN'T ABANDONED THEM.
I'M ALREADY PLANNING A CITY-WIDE RADIO BROADCAST REQUESTING PEOPLE CONSERVE FOOD AND WATER, STAY IN THEIR HOMES, AND REMAIN CALM.
THIS ISN'T AN AMBER ALERT, GRACE. IT'S AN ALIEN INVASION!
PEOPLE AREN'T GOING TO LISTEN TO SOME VOICE ON THE RADIO.
THEN WHO WILL THEY LISTEN TO?
ME.
THEY'LL LISTEN TO ME.

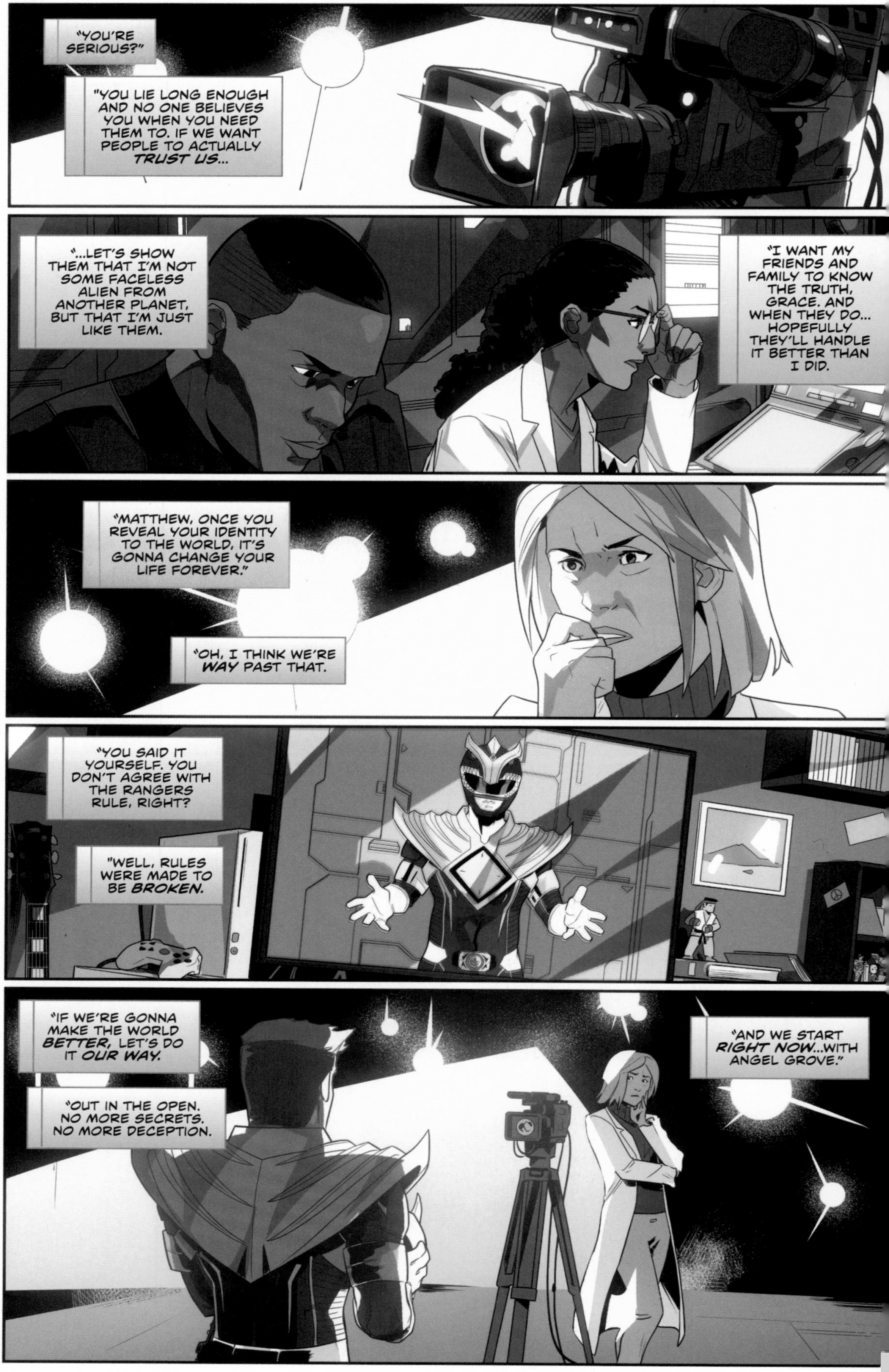
"YOU'RE SERIOUS?"
"YOU LIE LONG ENOUGH AND NO ONE BELIEVES YOU WHEN YOU NEED THEM TO. IF WE WANT PEOPLE TO ACTUALLY *TRUST US*...
"...LET'S SHOW THEM THAT I'M NOT SOME FACELESS ALIEN FROM ANOTHER PLANET, BUT THAT I'M JUST LIKE THEM.
"I WANT MY FRIENDS AND FAMILY TO KNOW THE TRUTH, GRACE. AND WHEN THEY DO... HOPEFULLY THEY'LL HANDLE IT BETTER THAN I DID.
"MATTHEW, ONCE YOU REVEAL YOUR IDENTITY TO THE WORLD, IT'S GONNA CHANGE YOUR LIFE FOREVER."
"OH, I THINK WE'RE *WAY* PAST THAT.
"YOU SAID IT YOURSELF. YOU DON'T AGREE WITH THE RANGERS RULE, RIGHT?
"WELL, RULES WERE MADE TO BE *BROKEN*.
"IF WE'RE GONNA MAKE THE WORLD *BETTER*, LET'S DO IT *OUR WAY*.
"OUT IN THE OPEN. NO MORE SECRETS. NO MORE DECEPTION.
"AND WE START *RIGHT NOW*...WITH ANGEL GROVE."

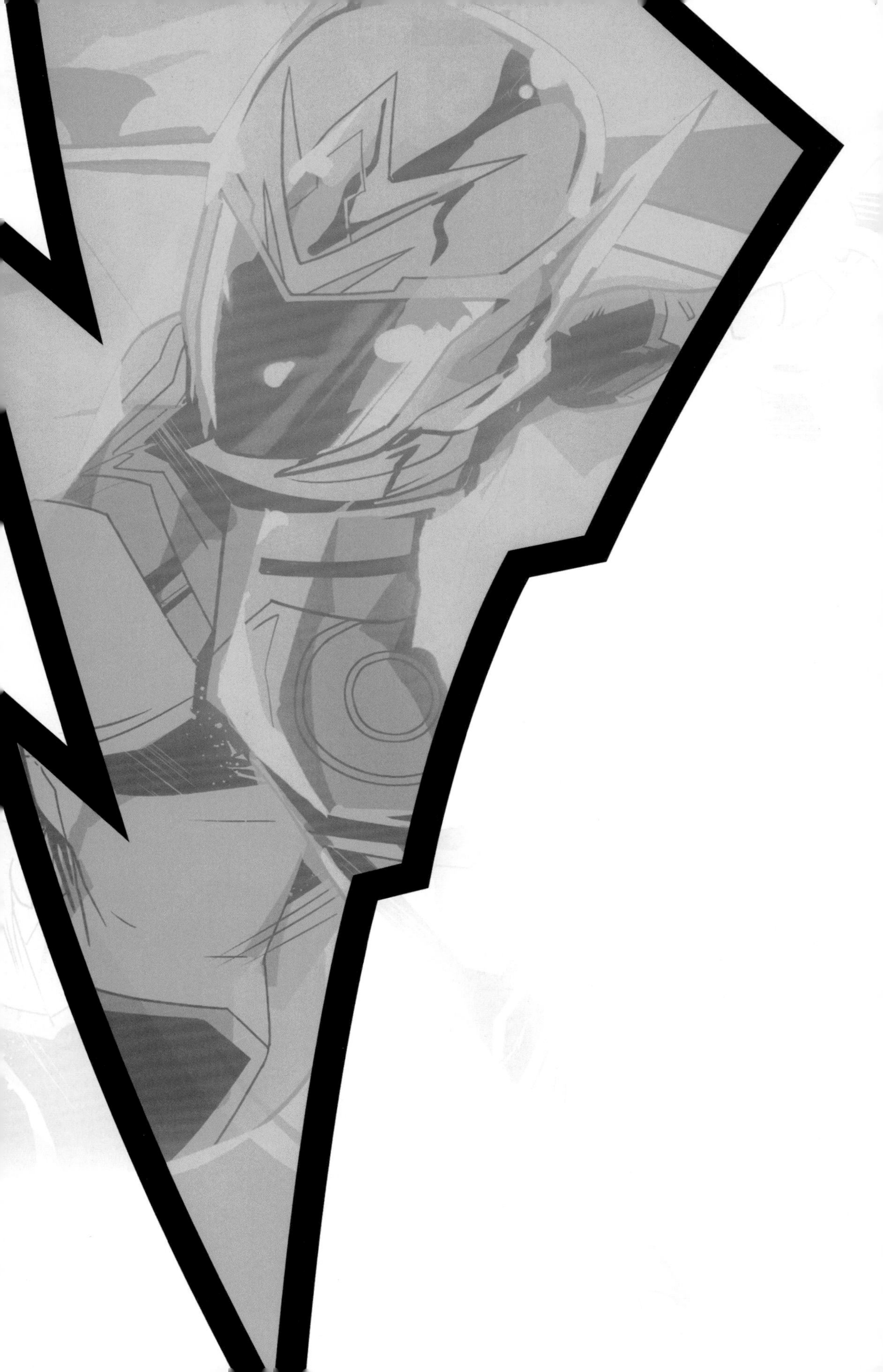

CHAPTER SIX

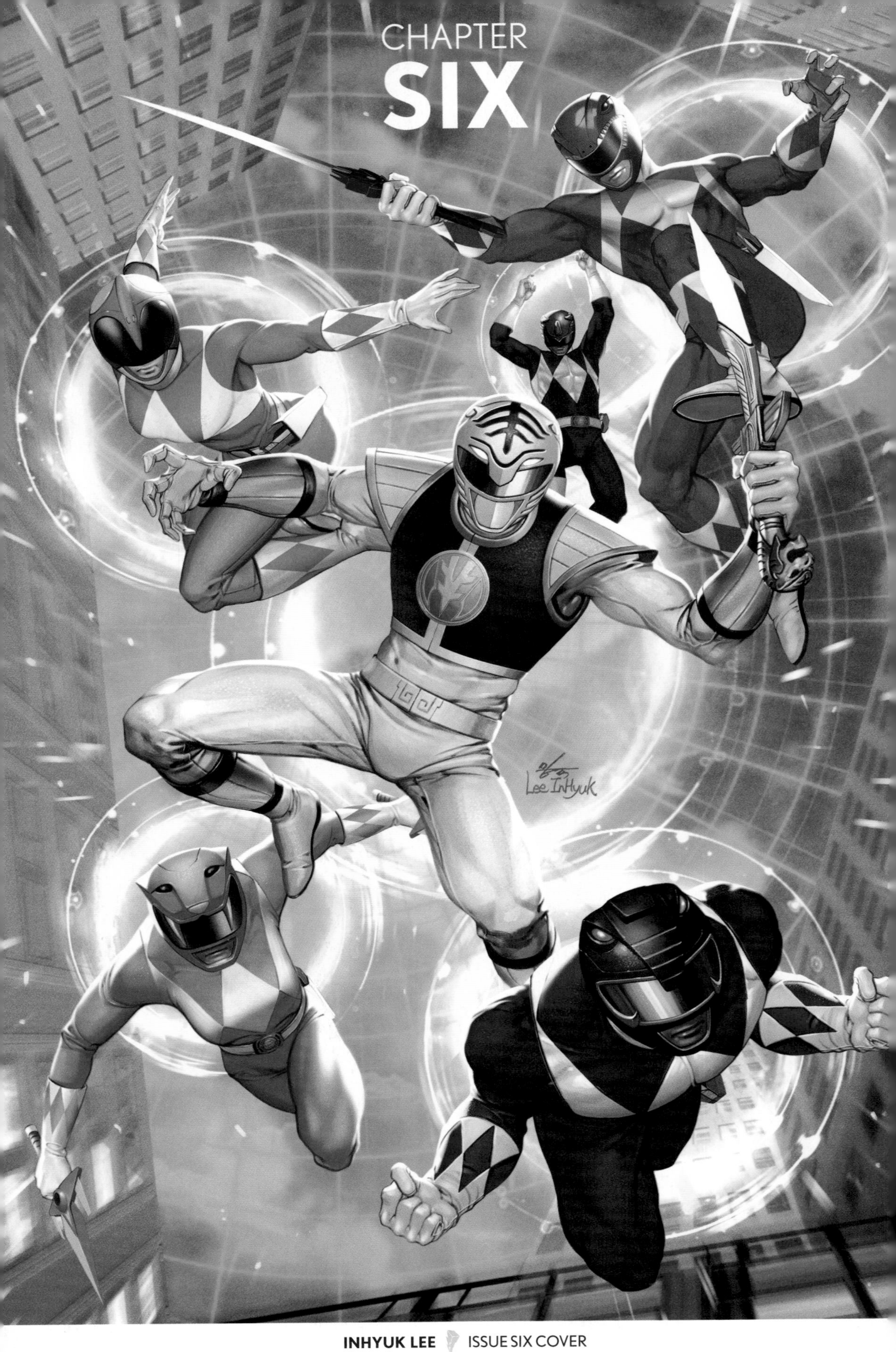
Lee InHyuk

INHYUK LEE | ISSUE SIX COVER

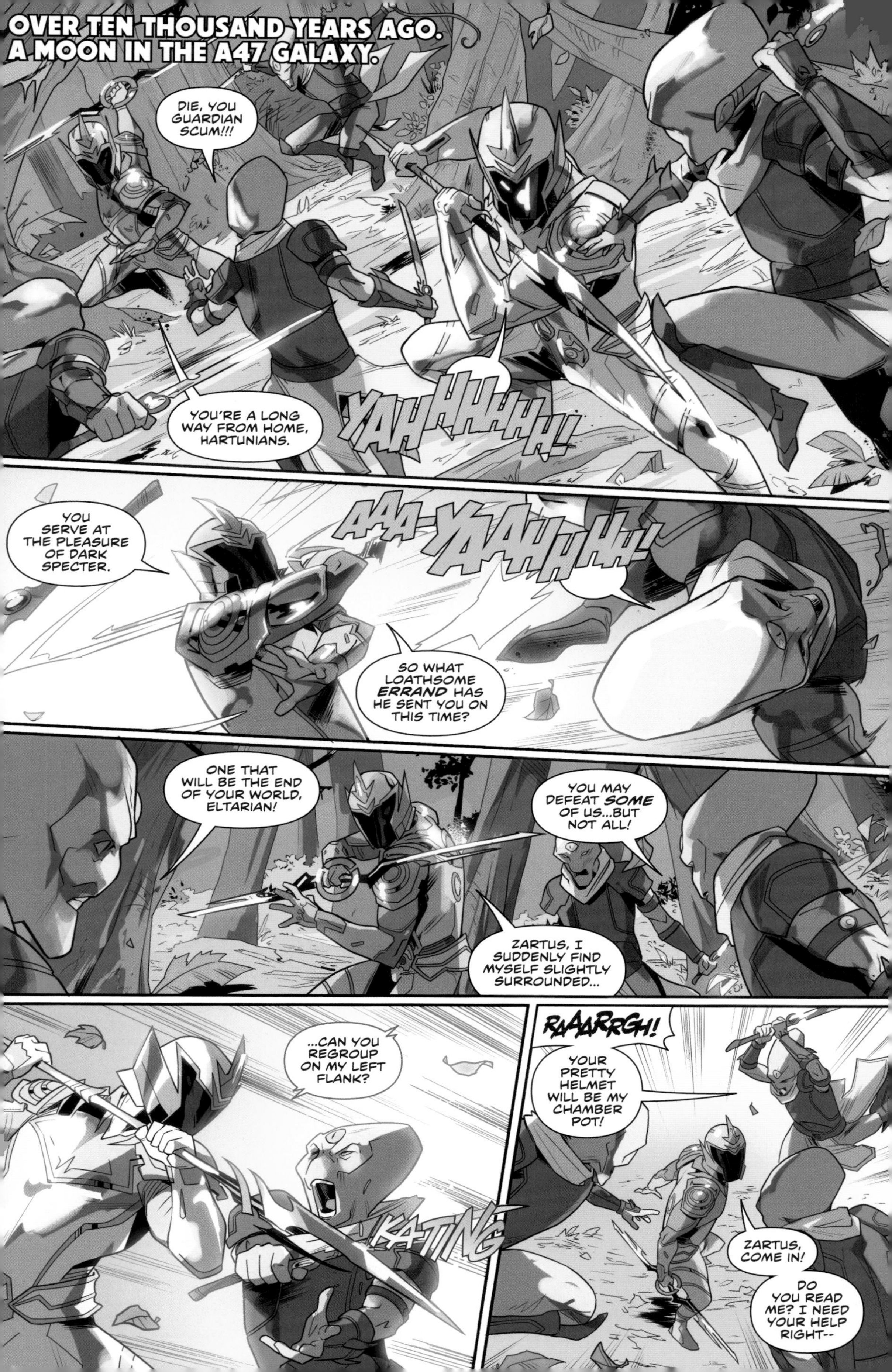

OVER TEN THOUSAND YEARS AGO. A MOON IN THE A47 GALAXY.
DIE, YOU GUARDIAN SCUM!!!
YOU'RE A LONG WAY FROM HOME, HARTUNIANS.
YAHHHHHH!
YOU SERVE AT THE PLEASURE OF DARK SPECTER.
AAA-YAAHHHH!
SO WHAT LOATHSOME *ERRAND* HAS HE SENT YOU ON THIS TIME?
ONE THAT WILL BE THE END OF YOUR WORLD, ELTARIAN!
YOU MAY DEFEAT *SOME* OF US...BUT NOT ALL!
ZARTUS, I SUDDENLY FIND MYSELF SLIGHTLY SURROUNDED...
...CAN YOU REGROUP ON MY LEFT FLANK?
KATING
RAAARRGH!
YOUR PRETTY HELMET WILL BE MY CHAMBER POT!
ZARTUS, COME IN!
DO YOU READ ME? I NEED YOUR HELP RIGHT--

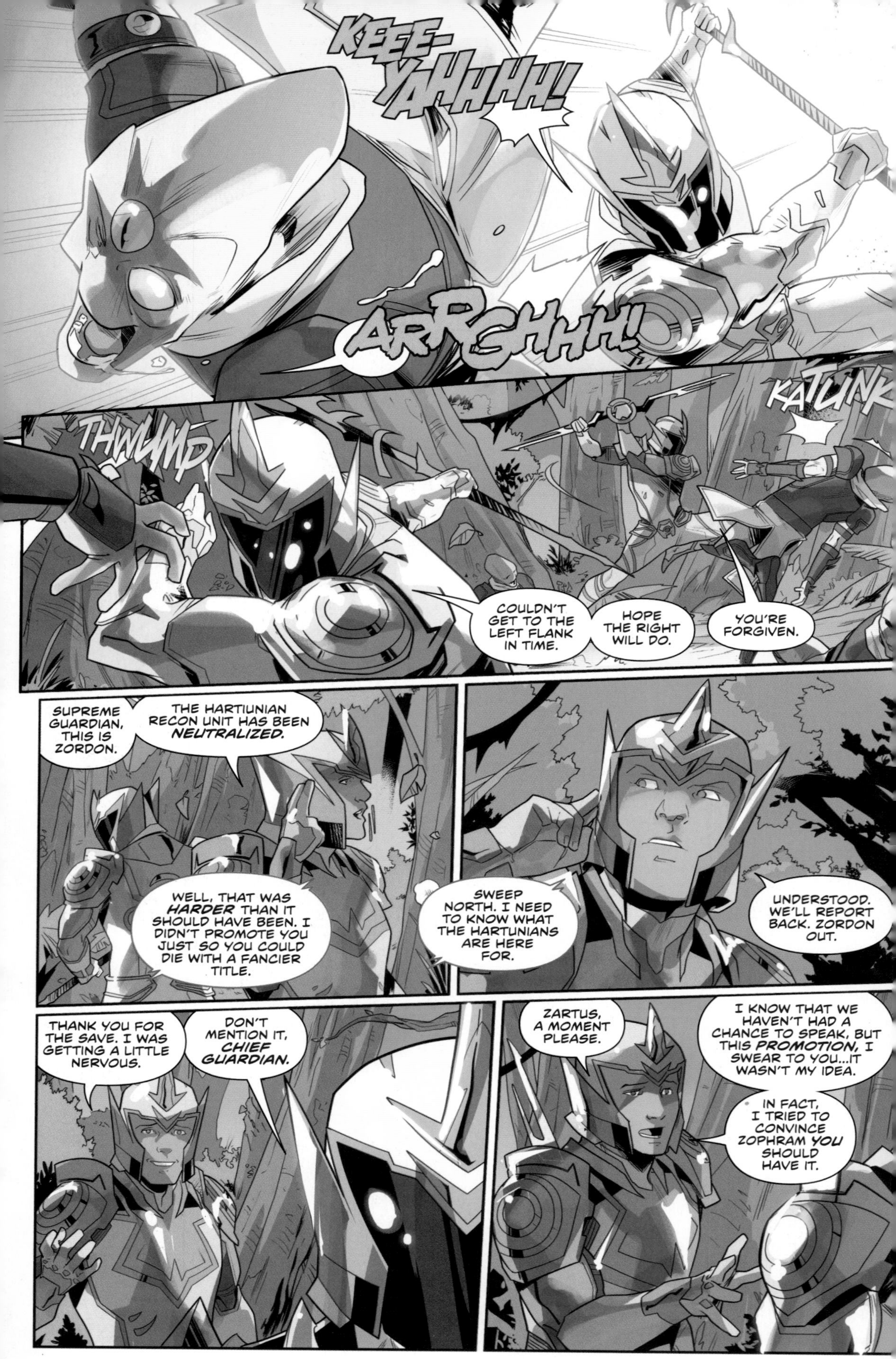
KEEE-YAHHHH!
ARRGHHH!
THWUMP
KATUNK
COULDN'T GET TO THE LEFT FLANK IN TIME.
HOPE THE RIGHT WILL DO.
YOU'RE FORGIVEN.
SUPREME GUARDIAN, THIS IS ZORDON.
THE HARTIUNIAN RECON UNIT HAS BEEN NEUTRALIZED.
WELL, THAT WAS HARDER THAN IT SHOULD HAVE BEEN. I DIDN'T PROMOTE YOU JUST SO YOU COULD DIE WITH A FANCIER TITLE.
SWEEP NORTH. I NEED TO KNOW WHAT THE HARTUNIANS ARE HERE FOR.
UNDERSTOOD. WE'LL REPORT BACK. ZORDON OUT.
THANK YOU FOR THE SAVE. I WAS GETTING A LITTLE NERVOUS.
DON'T MENTION IT, CHIEF GUARDIAN.
ZARTUS, A MOMENT PLEASE.
I KNOW THAT WE HAVEN'T HAD A CHANCE TO SPEAK, BUT THIS PROMOTION, I SWEAR TO YOU...IT WASN'T MY IDEA.
IN FACT, I TRIED TO CONVINCE ZOPHRAM YOU SHOULD HAVE IT.

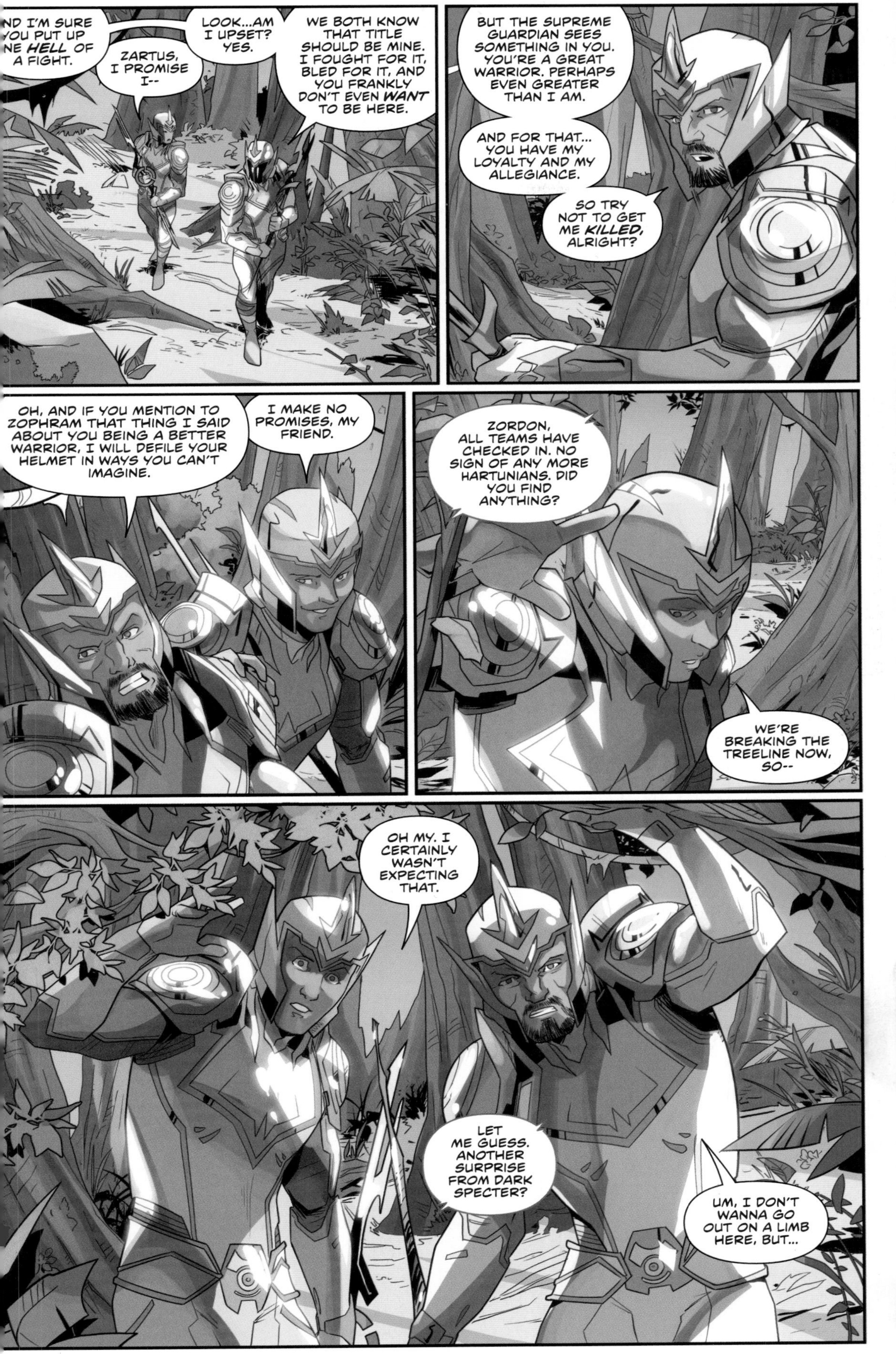
ND I'M SURE YOU PUT UP NE *HELL* OF A FIGHT.
ZARTUS, I PROMISE I--
LOOK...AM I UPSET? YES.
WE BOTH KNOW THAT TITLE SHOULD BE MINE. I FOUGHT FOR IT, BLED FOR IT, AND YOU FRANKLY DON'T EVEN *WANT* TO BE HERE.
BUT THE SUPREME GUARDIAN SEES SOMETHING IN YOU. YOU'RE A GREAT WARRIOR. PERHAPS EVEN GREATER THAN I AM.
AND FOR THAT... YOU HAVE MY LOYALTY AND MY ALLEGIANCE.
SO TRY NOT TO GET ME *KILLED,* ALRIGHT?
OH, AND IF YOU MENTION TO ZOPHRAM THAT THING I SAID ABOUT YOU BEING A BETTER WARRIOR, I WILL DEFILE YOUR HELMET IN WAYS YOU CAN'T IMAGINE.
I MAKE NO PROMISES, MY FRIEND.
ZORDON, ALL TEAMS HAVE CHECKED IN. NO SIGN OF ANY MORE HARTUNIANS. DID YOU FIND ANYTHING?
WE'RE BREAKING THE TREELINE NOW, SO--
OH MY. I CERTAINLY WASN'T EXPECTING THAT.
LET ME GUESS. ANOTHER SURPRISE FROM DARK SPECTER?
UM, I DON'T WANNA GO OUT ON A LIMB HERE, BUT...

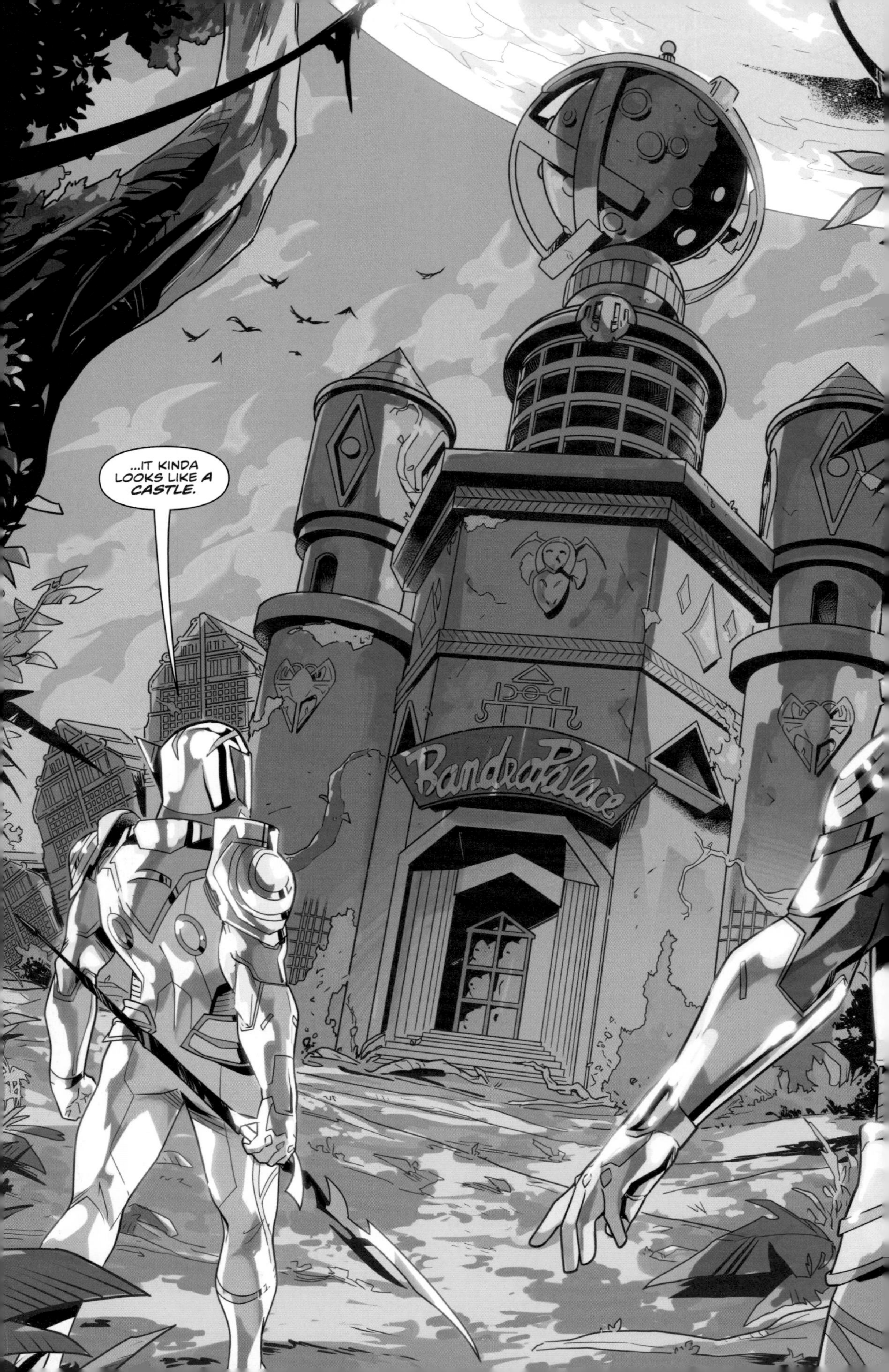
...IT KINDA LOOKS LIKE A CASTLE.
BandraPalace

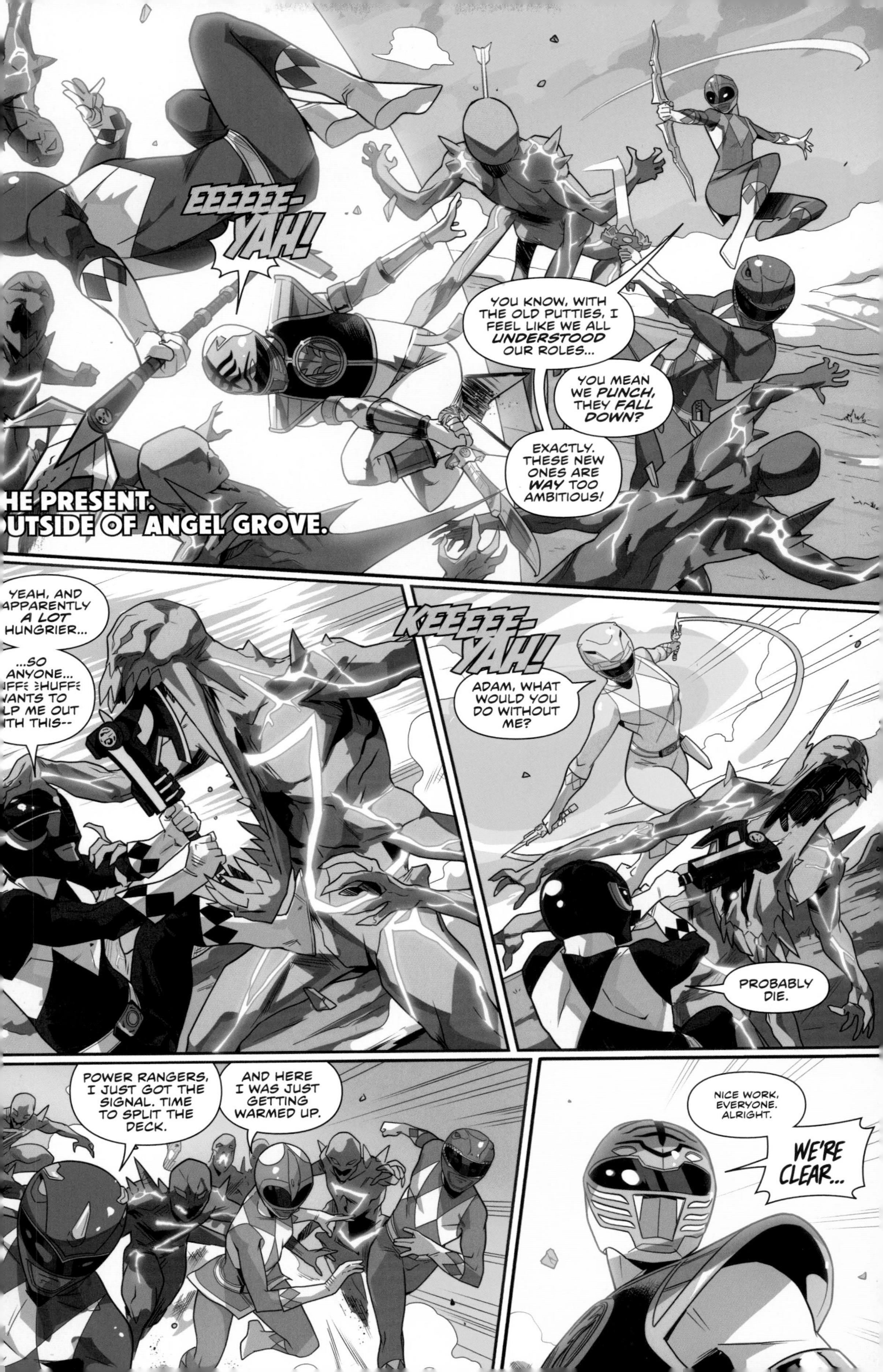

EEEEEE-YAH!
YOU KNOW, WITH THE OLD PUTTIES, I FEEL LIKE WE ALL UNDERSTOOD OUR ROLES...
YOU MEAN WE PUNCH, THEY FALL DOWN?
EXACTLY. THESE NEW ONES ARE WAY TOO AMBITIOUS!
HE PRESENT.
UTSIDE OF ANGEL GROVE.
YEAH, AND APPARENTLY A LOT HUNGRIER...
...SO ANYONE... UFF• SHUFF• VANTS TO LP ME OUT ITH THIS--
KEEEEE-YAH!
ADAM, WHAT WOULD YOU DO WITHOUT ME?
PROBABLY DIE.
POWER RANGERS, I JUST GOT THE SIGNAL. TIME TO SPLIT THE DECK.
AND HERE I WAS JUST GETTING WARMED UP.
NICE WORK, EVERYONE. ALRIGHT.
WE'RE CLEAR...

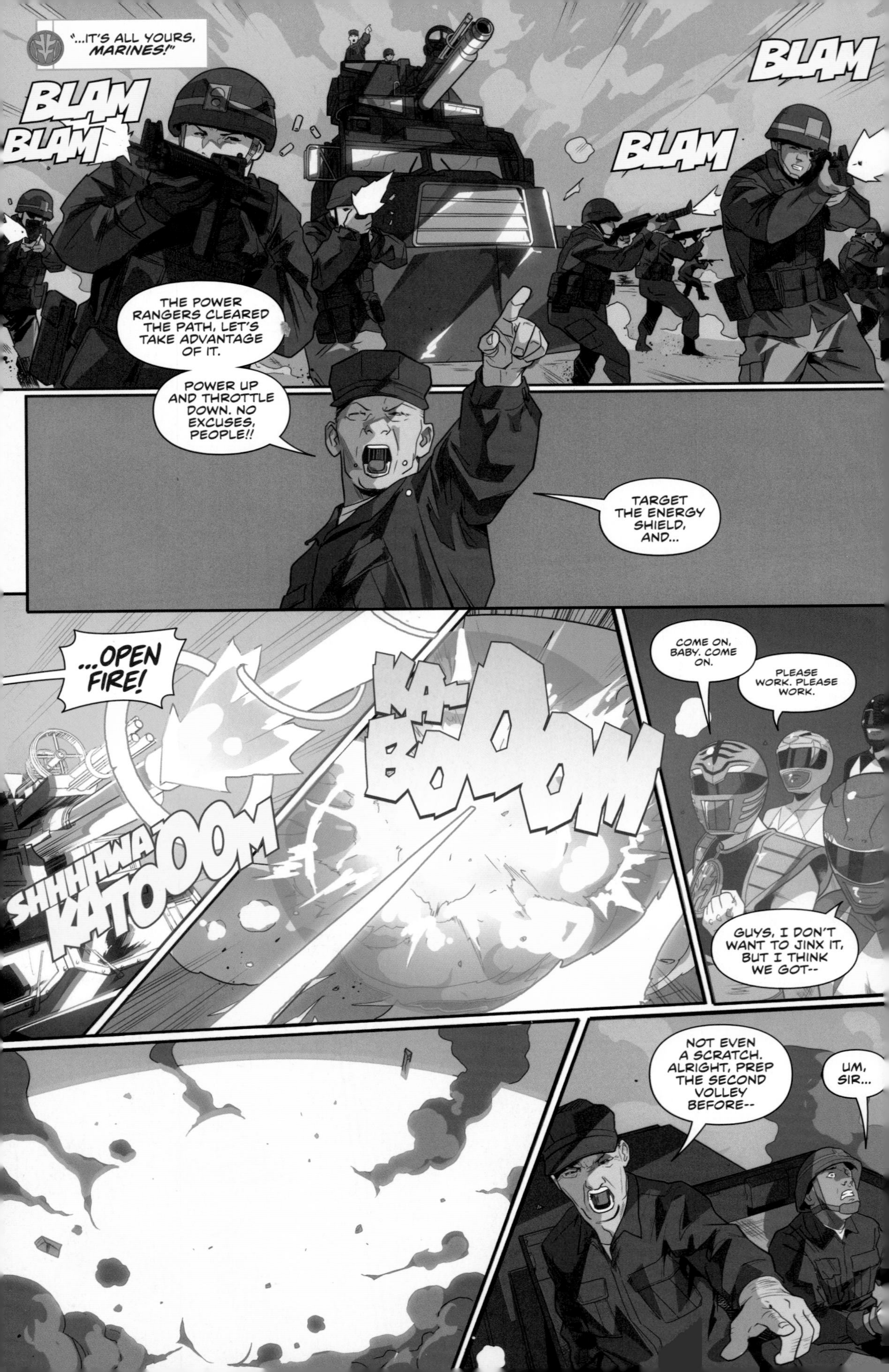
"...IT'S ALL YOURS, MARINES!"
BLAM BLAM
BLAM
BLAM
THE POWER RANGERS CLEARED THE PATH, LET'S TAKE ADVANTAGE OF IT.
POWER UP AND THROTTLE DOWN. NO EXCUSES, PEOPLE!!
TARGET THE ENERGY SHIELD, AND...
...OPEN FIRE!
SHHHHWA KATOOOOM
KA-BOOOOM
COME ON, BABY. COME ON.
PLEASE WORK. PLEASE WORK.
GUYS, I DON'T WANT TO JINX IT, BUT I THINK WE GOT--
NOT EVEN A SCRATCH. ALRIGHT, PREP THE SECOND VOLLEY BEFORE--
UM, SIR...

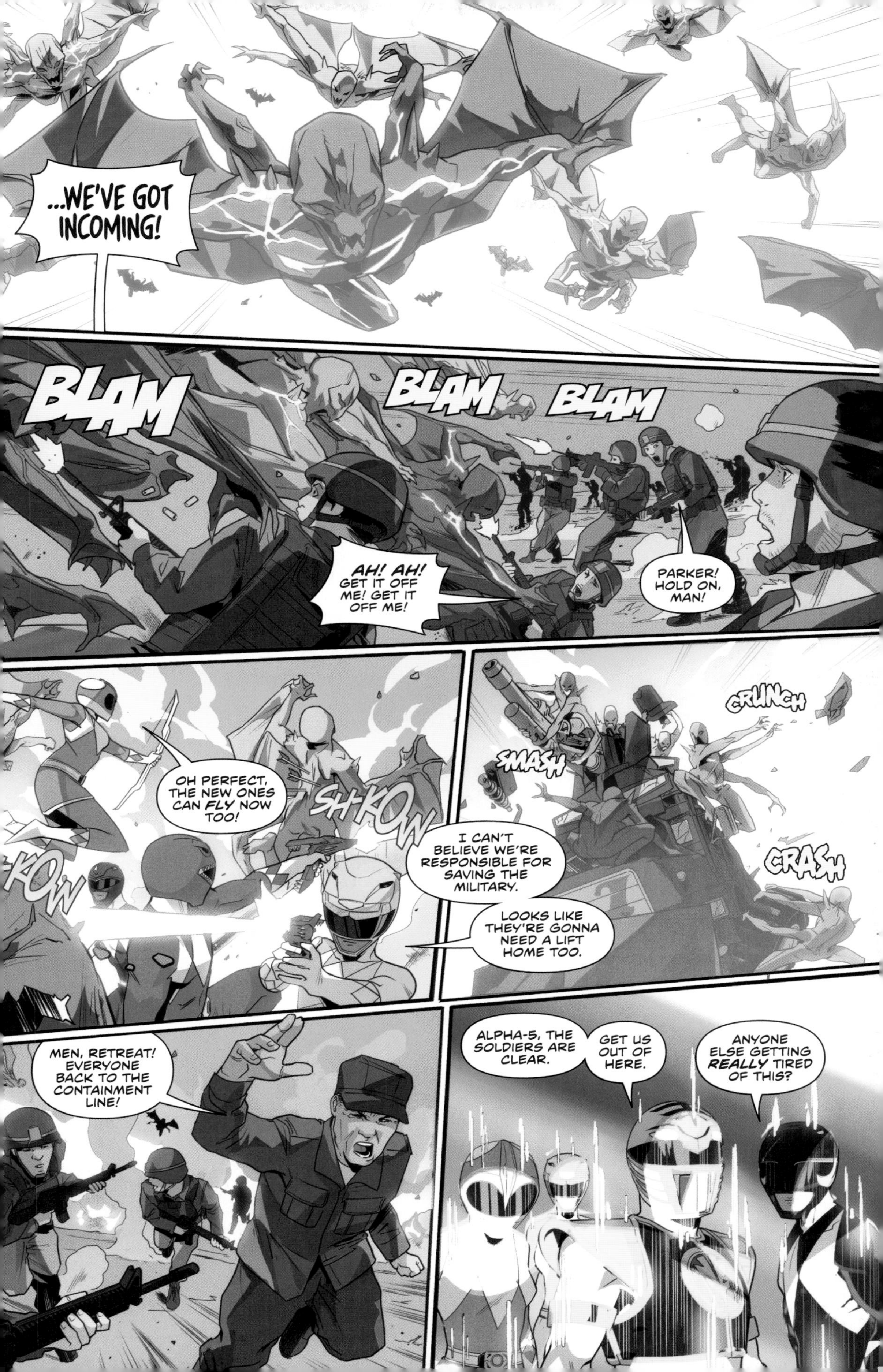
...WE'VE GOT INCOMING!
BLAM
BLAM
BLAM
AH! AH! GET IT OFF ME! GET IT OFF ME!
PARKER! HOLD ON, MAN!
OH PERFECT, THE NEW ONES CAN FLY NOW TOO!
SH-KOW
KOW
I CAN'T BELIEVE WE'RE RESPONSIBLE FOR SAVING THE MILITARY.
LOOKS LIKE THEY'RE GONNA NEED A LIFT HOME TOO.
CRUNCH
SMASH
CRASH
MEN, RETREAT! EVERYONE BACK TO THE CONTAINMENT LINE!
ALPHA-5, THE SOLDIERS ARE CLEAR.
GET US OUT OF HERE.
ANYONE ELSE GETTING REALLY TIRED OF THIS?

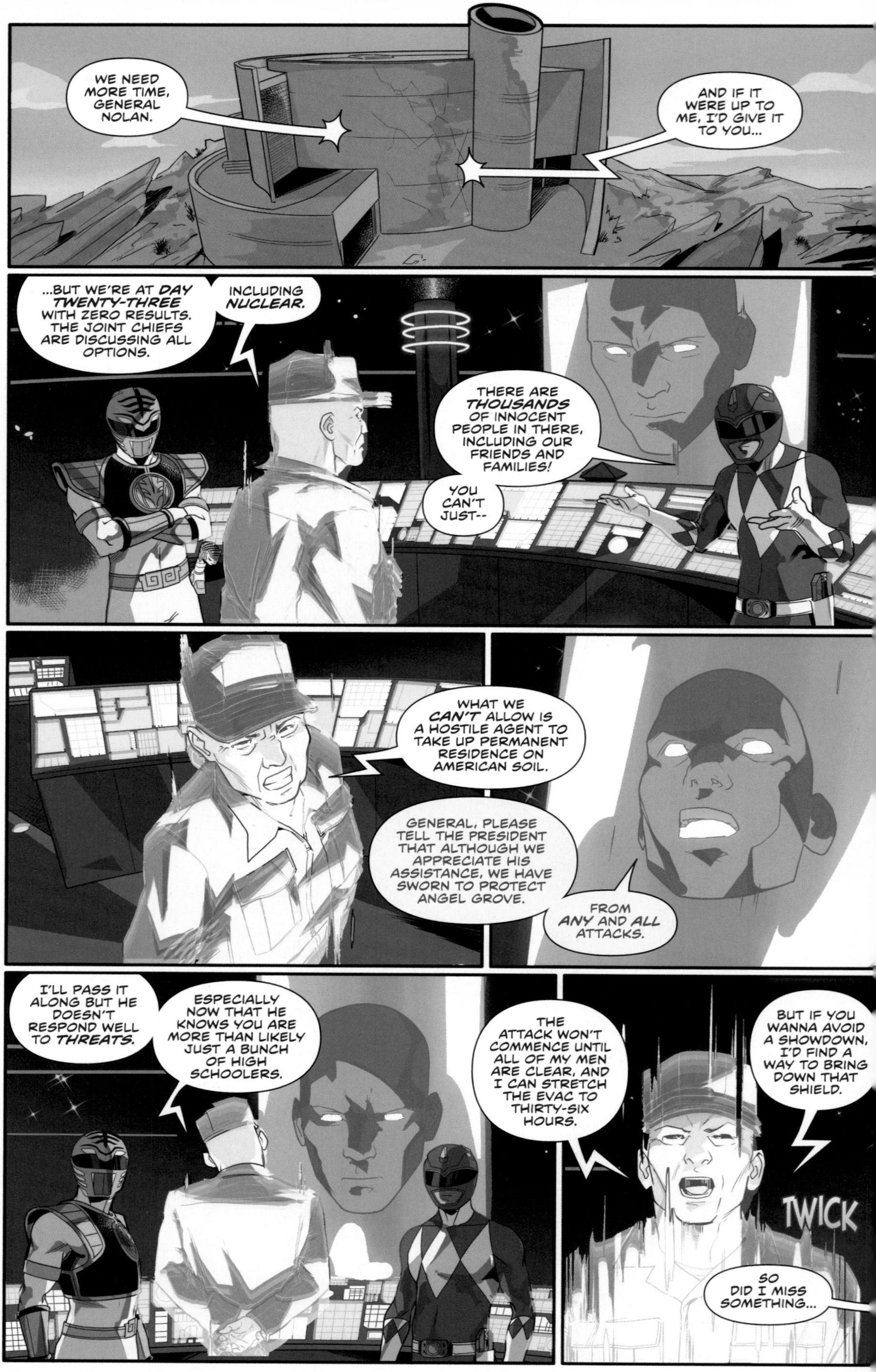
WE NEED MORE TIME, GENERAL NOLAN.
AND IF IT WERE UP TO ME, I'D GIVE IT TO YOU...
...BUT WE'RE AT DAY TWENTY-THREE WITH ZERO RESULTS. THE JOINT CHIEFS ARE DISCUSSING ALL OPTIONS.
INCLUDING NUCLEAR.
THERE ARE THOUSANDS OF INNOCENT PEOPLE IN THERE, INCLUDING OUR FRIENDS AND FAMILIES!
YOU CAN'T JUST--
WHAT WE CAN'T ALLOW IS A HOSTILE AGENT TO TAKE UP PERMANENT RESIDENCE ON AMERICAN SOIL.
GENERAL, PLEASE TELL THE PRESIDENT THAT ALTHOUGH WE APPRECIATE HIS ASSISTANCE, WE HAVE SWORN TO PROTECT ANGEL GROVE.
FROM ANY AND ALL ATTACKS.
I'LL PASS IT ALONG BUT HE DOESN'T RESPOND WELL TO THREATS.
ESPECIALLY NOW THAT HE KNOWS YOU ARE MORE THAN LIKELY JUST A BUNCH OF HIGH SCHOOLERS.
THE ATTACK WON'T COMMENCE UNTIL ALL OF MY MEN ARE CLEAR, AND I CAN STRETCH THE EVAC TO THIRTY-SIX HOURS.
BUT IF YOU WANNA AVOID A SHOWDOWN, I'D FIND A WAY TO BRING DOWN THAT SHIELD.
TWICK
SO DID I MISS SOMETHING...

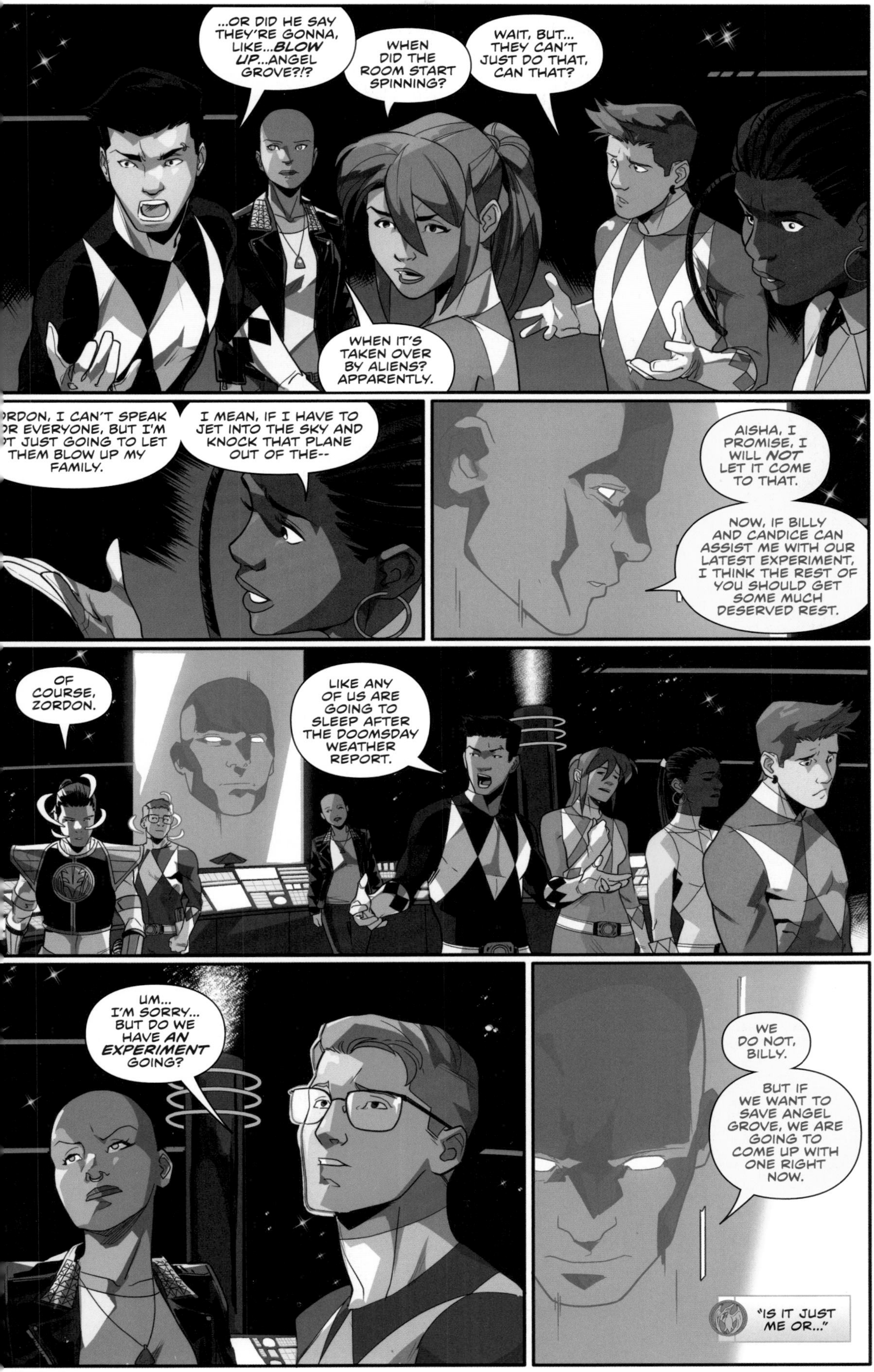
...OR DID HE SAY THEY'RE GONNA, LIKE...BLOW UP...ANGEL GROVE?!?
WHEN DID THE ROOM START SPINNING?
WAIT, BUT... THEY CAN'T JUST DO THAT, CAN THAT?
WHEN IT'S TAKEN OVER BY ALIENS? APPARENTLY.
RDON, I CAN'T SPEAK R EVERYONE, BUT I'M T JUST GOING TO LET THEM BLOW UP MY FAMILY.
I MEAN, IF I HAVE TO JET INTO THE SKY AND KNOCK THAT PLANE OUT OF THE--
AISHA, I PROMISE, I WILL NOT LET IT COME TO THAT.
NOW, IF BILLY AND CANDICE CAN ASSIST ME WITH OUR LATEST EXPERIMENT, I THINK THE REST OF YOU SHOULD GET SOME MUCH DESERVED REST.
OF COURSE, ZORDON.
LIKE ANY OF US ARE GOING TO SLEEP AFTER THE DOOMSDAY WEATHER REPORT.
UM... I'M SORRY... BUT DO WE HAVE AN EXPERIMENT GOING?
WE DO NOT, BILLY.
BUT IF WE WANT TO SAVE ANGEL GROVE, WE ARE GOING TO COME UP WITH ONE RIGHT NOW.
"IS IT JUST ME OR..."

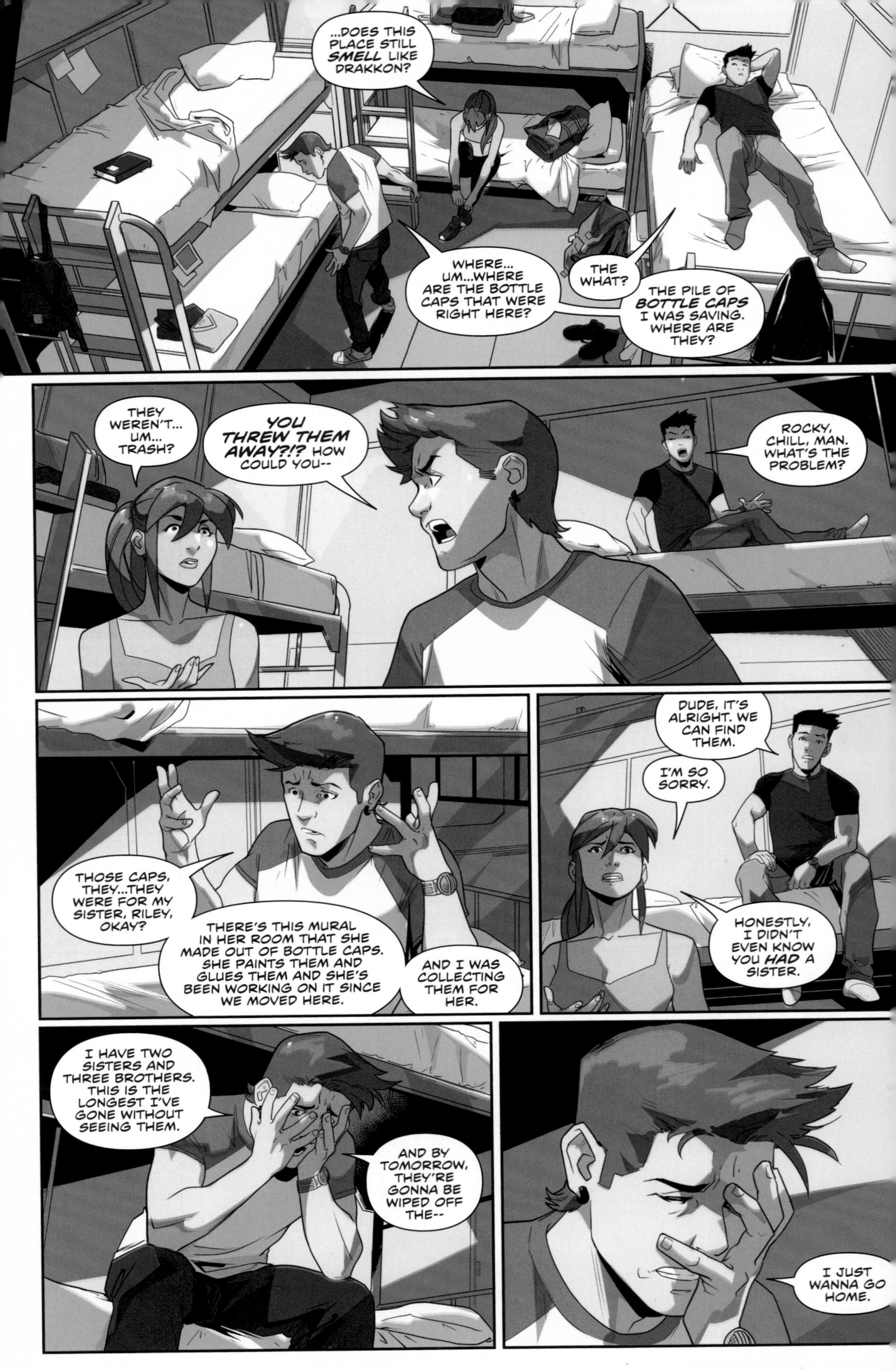
...DOES THIS PLACE STILL SMELL LIKE DRAKKON?
WHERE... UM...WHERE ARE THE BOTTLE CAPS THAT WERE RIGHT HERE?
THE WHAT?
THE PILE OF BOTTLE CAPS I WAS SAVING. WHERE ARE THEY?
THEY WEREN'T... UM... TRASH?
YOU THREW THEM AWAY?!? HOW COULD YOU--
ROCKY, CHILL, MAN. WHAT'S THE PROBLEM?
THOSE CAPS, THEY...THEY WERE FOR MY SISTER, RILEY, OKAY?
THERE'S THIS MURAL IN HER ROOM THAT SHE MADE OUT OF BOTTLE CAPS. SHE PAINTS THEM AND GLUES THEM AND SHE'S BEEN WORKING ON IT SINCE WE MOVED HERE.
AND I WAS COLLECTING THEM FOR HER.
DUDE, IT'S ALRIGHT. WE CAN FIND THEM.
I'M SO SORRY.
HONESTLY, I DIDN'T EVEN KNOW YOU HAD A SISTER.
I HAVE TWO SISTERS AND THREE BROTHERS. THIS IS THE LONGEST I'VE GONE WITHOUT SEEING THEM.
AND BY TOMORROW, THEY'RE GONNA BE WIPED OFF THE--
I JUST WANNA GO HOME.

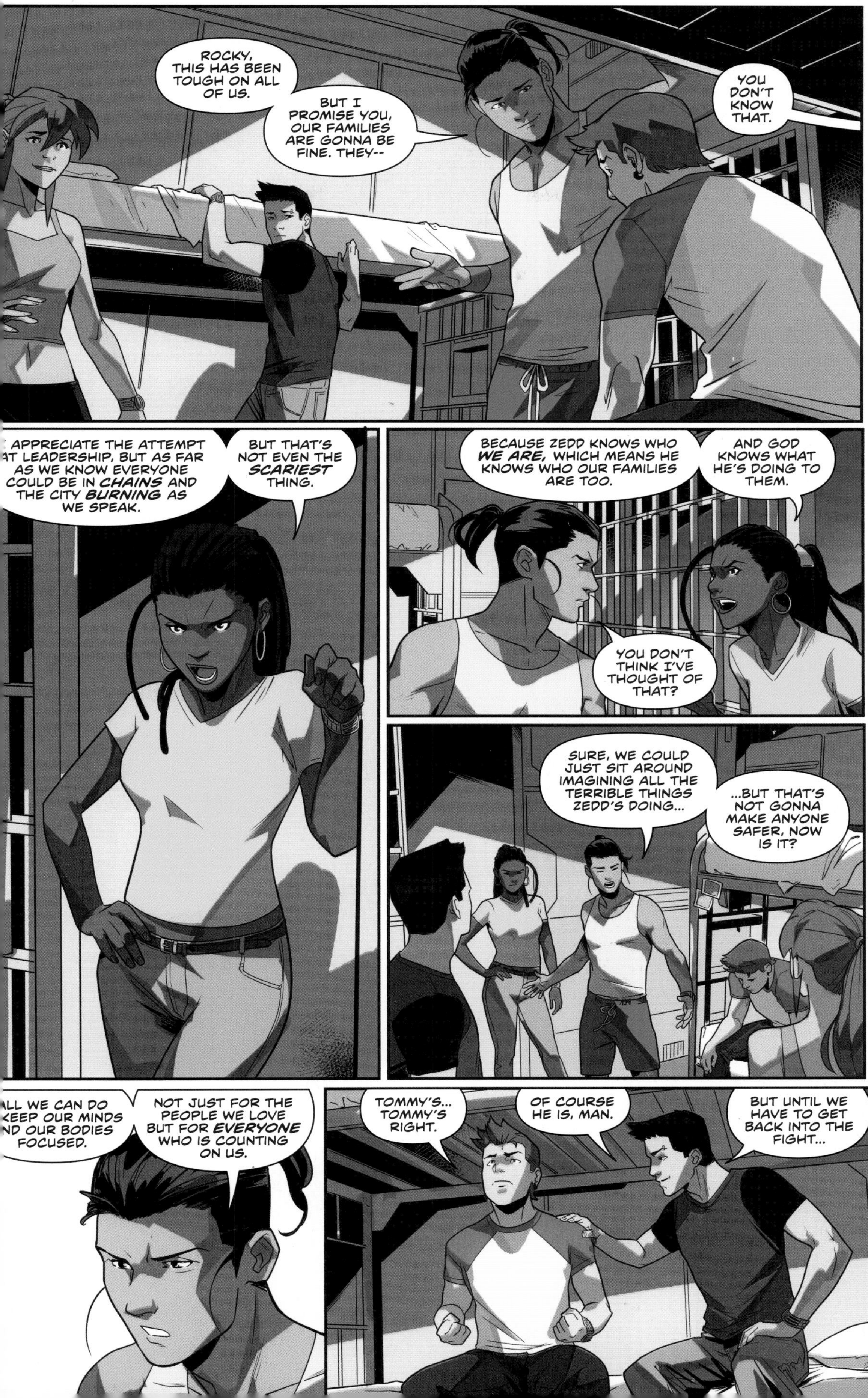
ROCKY, THIS HAS BEEN TOUGH ON ALL OF US.
BUT I PROMISE YOU, OUR FAMILIES ARE GONNA BE FINE. THEY--
YOU DON'T KNOW THAT.
I APPRECIATE THE ATTEMPT AT LEADERSHIP, BUT AS FAR AS WE KNOW EVERYONE COULD BE IN CHAINS AND THE CITY BURNING AS WE SPEAK.
BUT THAT'S NOT EVEN THE SCARIEST THING.
BECAUSE ZEDD KNOWS WHO WE ARE, WHICH MEANS HE KNOWS WHO OUR FAMILIES ARE TOO.
AND GOD KNOWS WHAT HE'S DOING TO THEM.
YOU DON'T THINK I'VE THOUGHT OF THAT?
SURE, WE COULD JUST SIT AROUND IMAGINING ALL THE TERRIBLE THINGS ZEDD'S DOING...
...BUT THAT'S NOT GONNA MAKE ANYONE SAFER, NOW IS IT?
ALL WE CAN DO KEEP OUR MINDS AND OUR BODIES FOCUSED.
NOT JUST FOR THE PEOPLE WE LOVE BUT FOR EVERYONE WHO IS COUNTING ON US.
TOMMY'S... TOMMY'S RIGHT.
OF COURSE HE IS, MAN.
BUT UNTIL WE HAVE TO GET BACK INTO THE FIGHT...

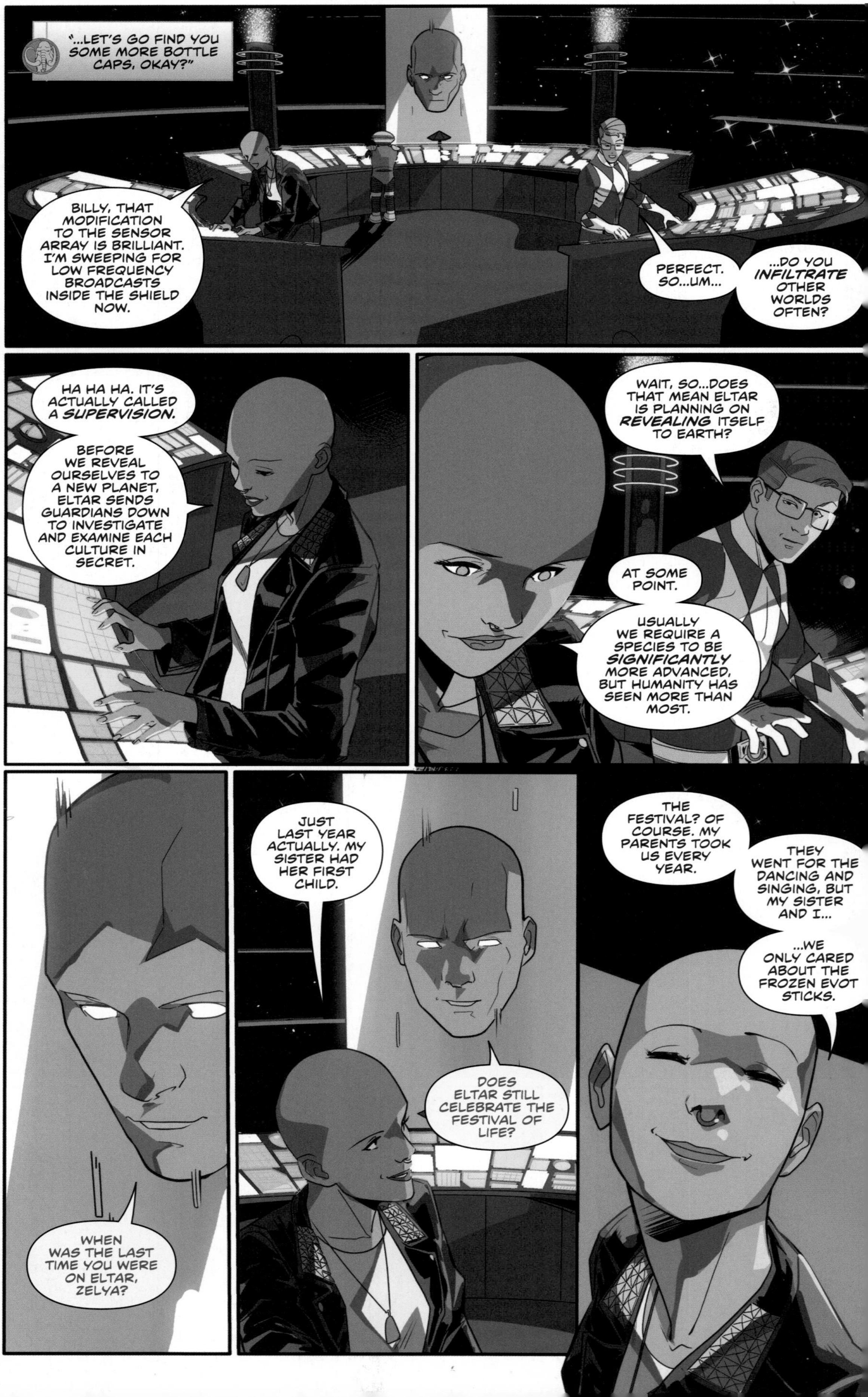
"...LET'S GO FIND YOU SOME MORE BOTTLE CAPS, OKAY?"
BILLY, THAT MODIFICATION TO THE SENSOR ARRAY IS BRILLIANT. I'M SWEEPING FOR LOW FREQUENCY BROADCASTS INSIDE THE SHIELD NOW.
PERFECT. SO...UM...
...DO YOU INFILTRATE OTHER WORLDS OFTEN?
HA HA HA. IT'S ACTUALLY CALLED A SUPERVISION.
BEFORE WE REVEAL OURSELVES TO A NEW PLANET, ELTAR SENDS GUARDIANS DOWN TO INVESTIGATE AND EXAMINE EACH CULTURE IN SECRET.
WAIT, SO...DOES THAT MEAN ELTAR IS PLANNING ON REVEALING ITSELF TO EARTH?
AT SOME POINT.
USUALLY WE REQUIRE A SPECIES TO BE SIGNIFICANTLY MORE ADVANCED, BUT HUMANITY HAS SEEN MORE THAN MOST.
WHEN WAS THE LAST TIME YOU WERE ON ELTAR, ZELYA?
JUST LAST YEAR ACTUALLY. MY SISTER HAD HER FIRST CHILD.
DOES ELTAR STILL CELEBRATE THE FESTIVAL OF LIFE?
THE FESTIVAL? OF COURSE. MY PARENTS TOOK US EVERY YEAR.
THEY WENT FOR THE DANCING AND SINGING, BUT MY SISTER AND I...
...WE ONLY CARED ABOUT THE FROZEN EVOT STICKS.

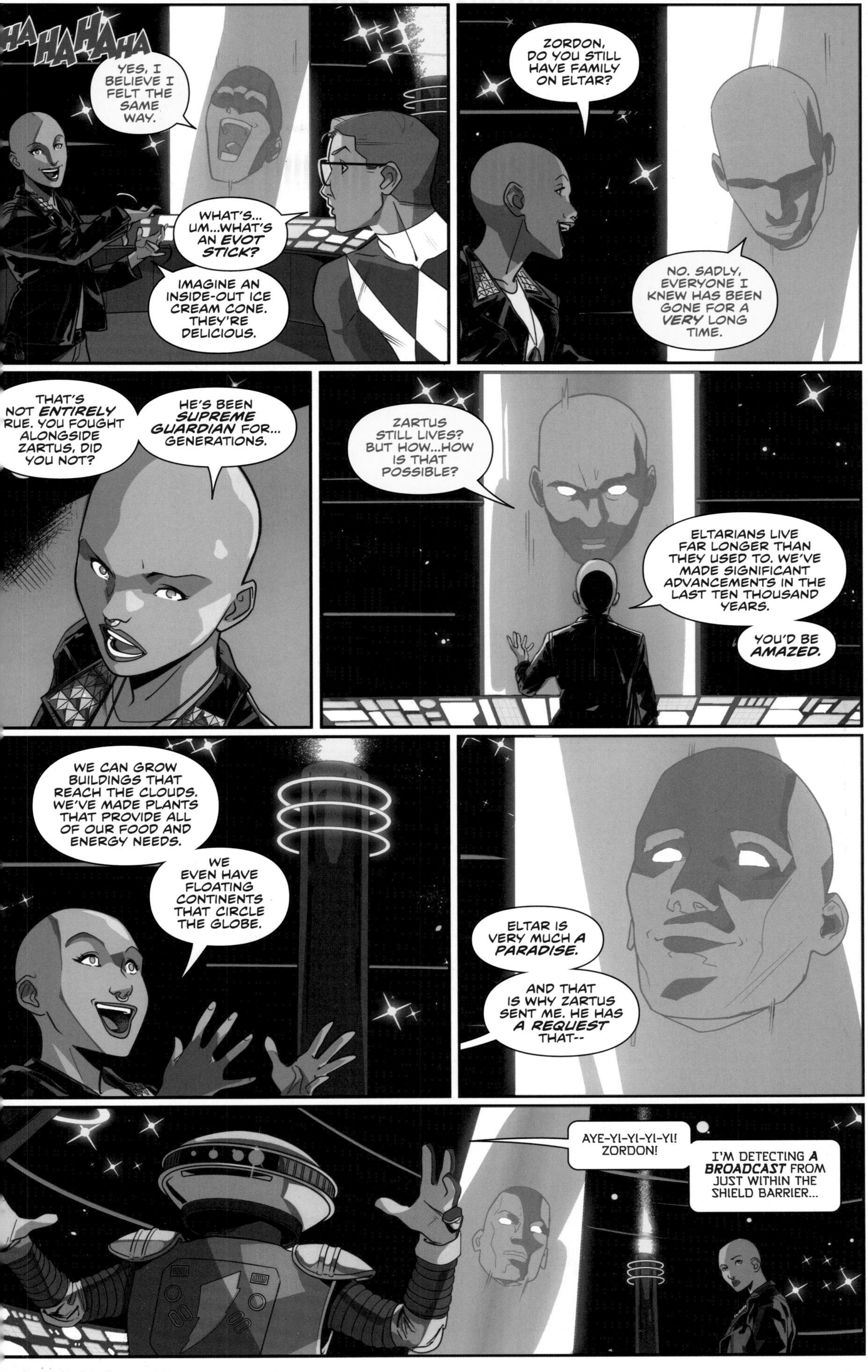
HAHAHAHAHA
YES, I BELIEVE I FELT THE SAME WAY.
WHAT'S... UM...WHAT'S AN *EVOT STICK?*
IMAGINE AN INSIDE-OUT ICE CREAM CONE. THEY'RE DELICIOUS.
ZORDON, DO YOU STILL HAVE FAMILY ON ELTAR?
NO. SADLY, EVERYONE I KNEW HAS BEEN GONE FOR A *VERY* LONG TIME.
THAT'S NOT *ENTIRELY* RUE. YOU FOUGHT ALONGSIDE ZARTUS, DID YOU NOT?
HE'S BEEN *SUPREME GUARDIAN* FOR... GENERATIONS.
ZARTUS STILL LIVES? BUT HOW...HOW IS THAT POSSIBLE?
ELTARIANS LIVE FAR LONGER THAN THEY USED TO. WE'VE MADE SIGNIFICANT ADVANCEMENTS IN THE LAST TEN THOUSAND YEARS.
YOU'D BE *AMAZED.*
WE CAN GROW BUILDINGS THAT REACH THE CLOUDS. WE'VE MADE PLANTS THAT PROVIDE ALL OF OUR FOOD AND ENERGY NEEDS.
WE EVEN HAVE FLOATING CONTINENTS THAT CIRCLE THE GLOBE.
ELTAR IS VERY MUCH *A PARADISE.*
AND THAT IS WHY ZARTUS SENT ME. HE HAS *A REQUEST* THAT--
AYE-YI-YI-YI-YI! ZORDON!
I'M DETECTING *A BROADCAST* FROM JUST WITHIN THE SHIELD BARRIER...

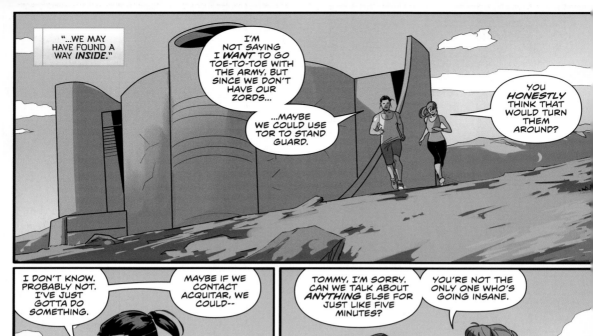

"...WE MAY HAVE FOUND A WAY *INSIDE*."

I'M NOT SAYING I *WANT* TO GO TOE-TO-TOE WITH THE ARMY, BUT SINCE WE DON'T HAVE OUR ZORDS...

...MAYBE WE COULD USE TOR TO STAND GUARD.

YOU *HONESTLY* THINK THAT WOULD TURN THEM AROUND?

I DON'T KNOW. PROBABLY NOT. I'VE JUST GOTTA DO SOMETHING.

MAYBE IF WE CONTACT ACQUITAR, WE COULD--

TOMMY, I'M SORRY. CAN WE TALK ABOUT *ANYTHING* ELSE FOR JUST LIKE FIVE MINUTES?

YOU'RE NOT THE ONLY ONE WHO'S GOING INSANE.

OKAY...

THEN LET'S TALK ABOUT *MATT*.

...

PLEASE DON'T DO THIS RIGHT NOW.

DID YOU *KNOW* HE WAS THE GREEN RANGER?

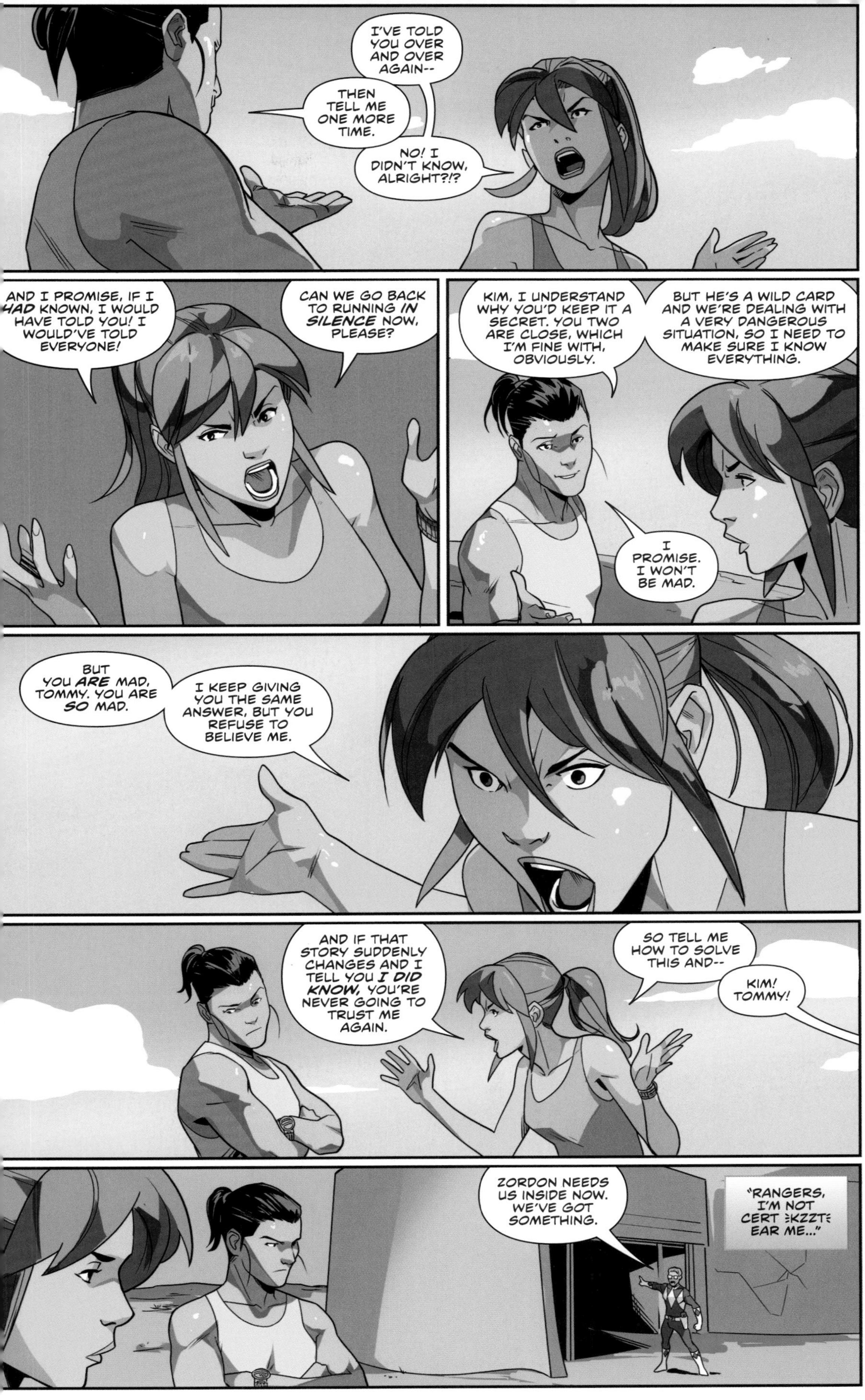
I'VE TOLD YOU OVER AND OVER AGAIN--
THEN TELL ME ONE MORE TIME.
NO! I DIDN'T KNOW, ALRIGHT?!?
AND I PROMISE, IF I HAD KNOWN, I WOULD HAVE TOLD YOU! I WOULD'VE TOLD EVERYONE!
CAN WE GO BACK TO RUNNING IN SILENCE NOW, PLEASE?
KIM, I UNDERSTAND WHY YOU'D KEEP IT A SECRET. YOU TWO ARE CLOSE, WHICH I'M FINE WITH, OBVIOUSLY.
BUT HE'S A WILD CARD AND WE'RE DEALING WITH A VERY DANGEROUS SITUATION, SO I NEED TO MAKE SURE I KNOW EVERYTHING.
I PROMISE. I WON'T BE MAD.
BUT YOU ARE MAD, TOMMY. YOU ARE SO MAD.
I KEEP GIVING YOU THE SAME ANSWER, BUT YOU REFUSE TO BELIEVE ME.
AND IF THAT STORY SUDDENLY CHANGES AND I TELL YOU I DID KNOW, YOU'RE NEVER GOING TO TRUST ME AGAIN.
SO TELL ME HOW TO SOLVE THIS AND--
KIM! TOMMY!
ZORDON NEEDS US INSIDE NOW. WE'VE GOT SOMETHING.
"RANGERS, I'M NOT CERT ƸKZZTƷ EAR ME..."

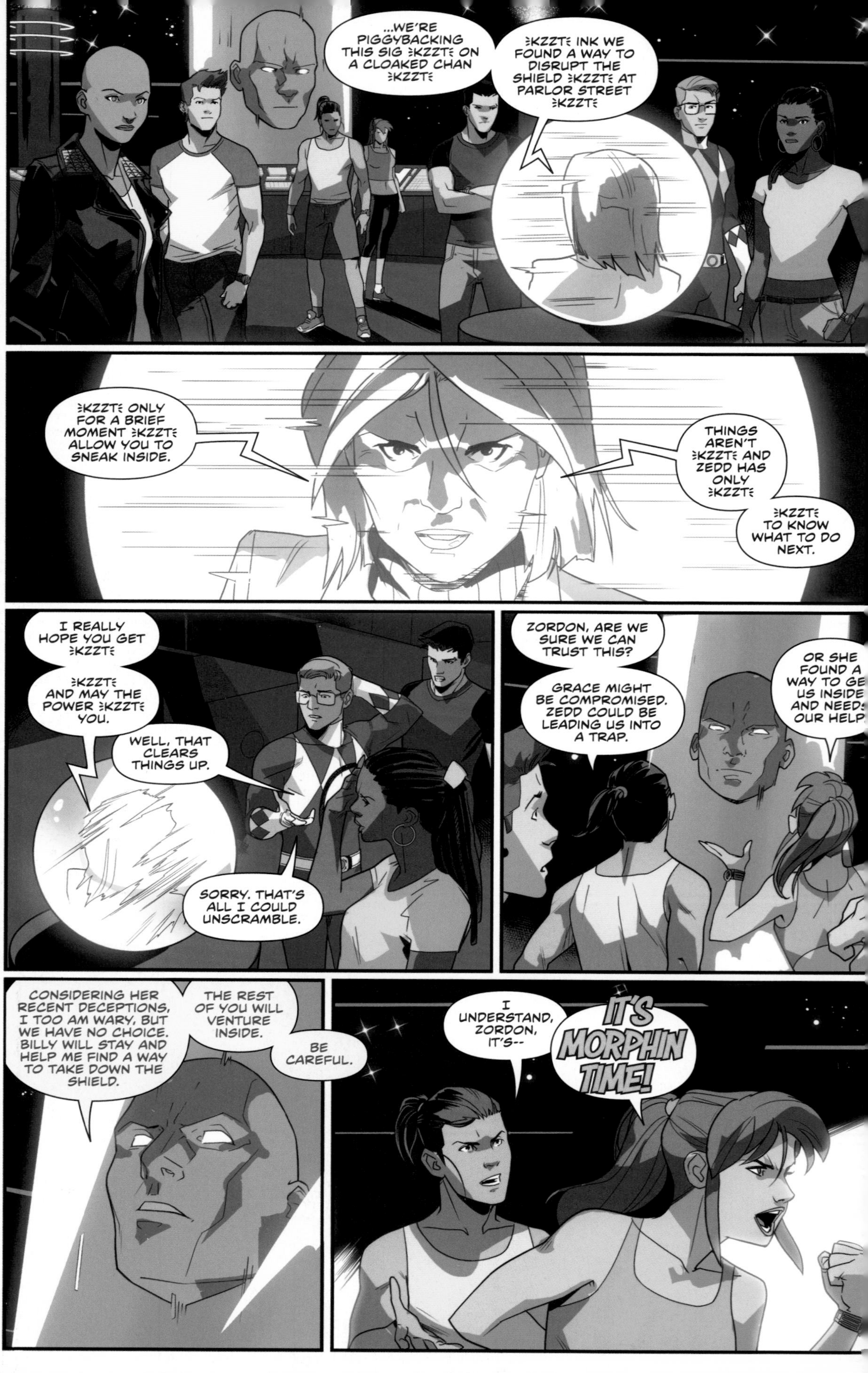
...WE'RE PIGGYBACKING THIS SIG ƎKZZTƐ ON A CLOAKED CHAN ƎKZZTƐ
ƎKZZTƐ INK WE FOUND A WAY TO DISRUPT THE SHIELD ƎKZZTƐ AT PARLOR STREET ƎKZZTƐ
ƎKZZTƐ ONLY FOR A BRIEF MOMENT ƎKZZTƐ ALLOW YOU TO SNEAK INSIDE.
THINGS AREN'T ƎKZZTƐ AND ZEDD HAS ONLY ƎKZZTƐ
ƎKZZTƐ TO KNOW WHAT TO DO NEXT.
I REALLY HOPE YOU GET ƎKZZTƐ
ƎKZZTƐ AND MAY THE POWER ƎKZZTƐ YOU.
WELL, THAT CLEARS THINGS UP.
SORRY. THAT'S ALL I COULD UNSCRAMBLE.
ZORDON, ARE WE SURE WE CAN TRUST THIS?
GRACE MIGHT BE COMPROMISED. ZEDD COULD BE LEADING US INTO A TRAP.
OR SHE FOUND A WAY TO GE US INSIDE AND NEED OUR HELP
CONSIDERING HER RECENT DECEPTIONS, I TOO AM WARY, BUT WE HAVE NO CHOICE. BILLY WILL STAY AND HELP ME FIND A WAY TO TAKE DOWN THE SHIELD.
THE REST OF YOU WILL VENTURE INSIDE.
BE CAREFUL.
I UNDERSTAND, ZORDON, IT'S--
IT'S MORPHIN TIME!

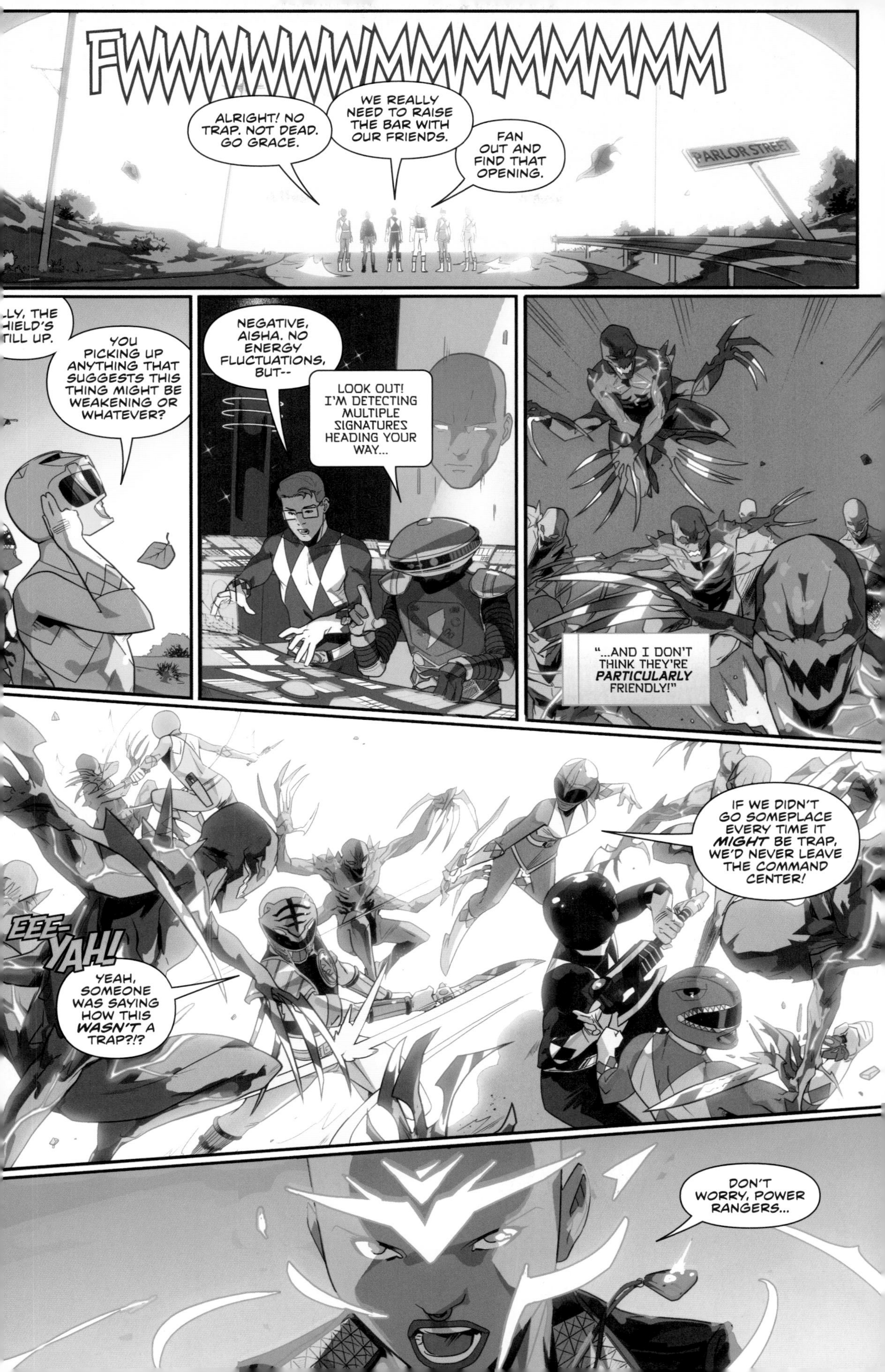
FWWWWWWMMMMMMMM
ALRIGHT! NO TRAP. NOT DEAD. GO GRACE.
WE REALLY NEED TO RAISE THE BAR WITH OUR FRIENDS.
FAN OUT AND FIND THAT OPENING.
PARLOR STREET
LY, THE HIELD'S TILL UP.
YOU PICKING UP ANYTHING THAT SUGGESTS THIS THING MIGHT BE WEAKENING OR WHATEVER?
NEGATIVE, AISHA. NO ENERGY FLUCTUATIONS, BUT--
LOOK OUT! I'M DETECTING MULTIPLE SIGNATURES HEADING YOUR WAY...
"...AND I DON'T THINK THEY'RE PARTICULARLY FRIENDLY!"
IF WE DIDN'T GO SOMEPLACE EVERY TIME IT MIGHT BE TRAP, WE'D NEVER LEAVE THE COMMAND CENTER!
EEE-YAH!
YEAH, SOMEONE WAS SAYING HOW THIS WASN'T A TRAP?!?
DON'T WORRY, POWER RANGERS...

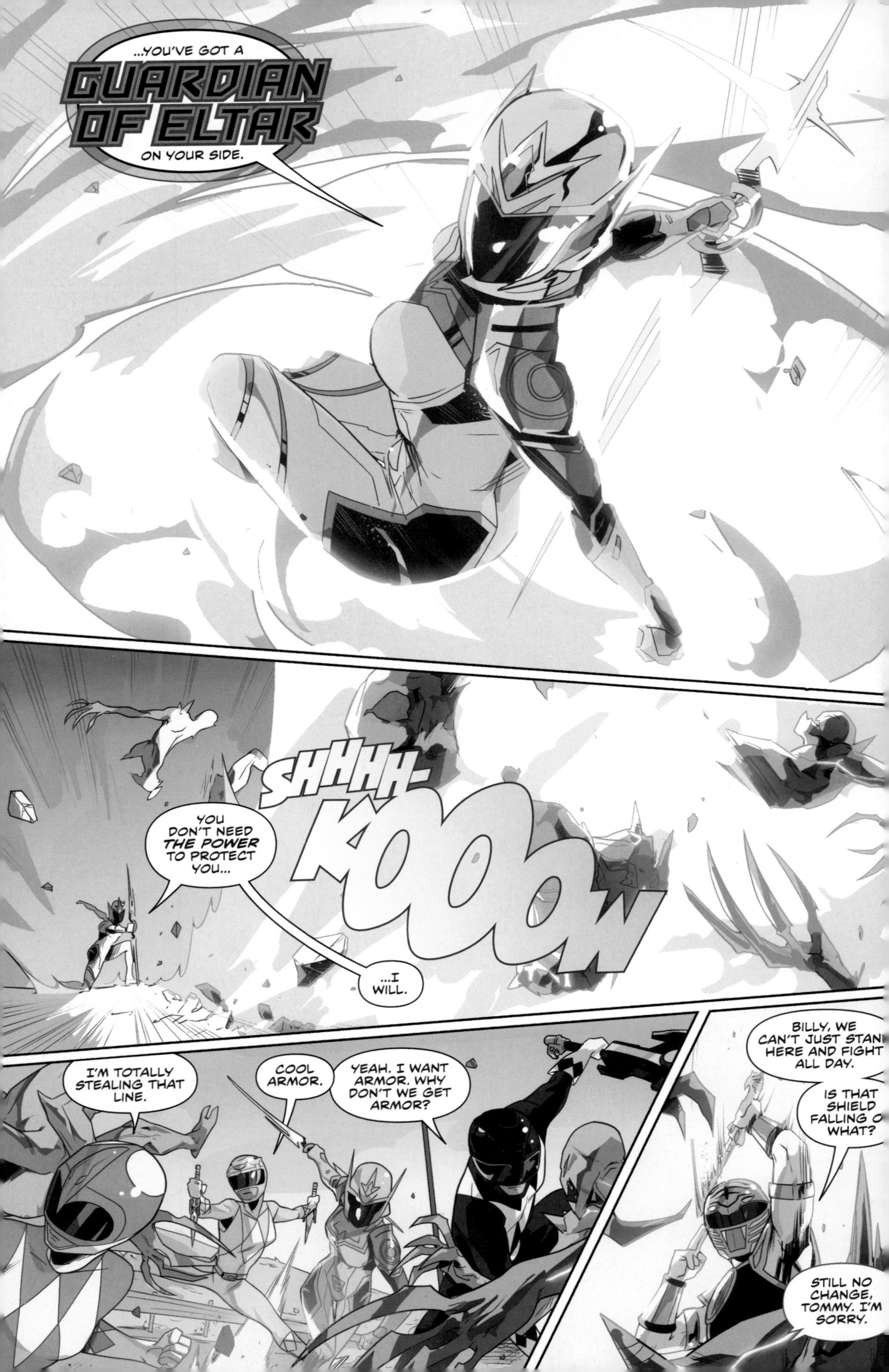
...YOU'VE GOT A GUARDIAN OF ELTAR ON YOUR SIDE.
SHHHH-KOOOM
YOU DON'T NEED THE POWER TO PROTECT YOU...
...I WILL.
I'M TOTALLY STEALING THAT LINE.
COOL ARMOR.
YEAH. I WANT ARMOR. WHY DON'T WE GET ARMOR?
BILLY, WE CAN'T JUST STAN HERE AND FIGHT ALL DAY.
IS THAT SHIELD FALLING O WHAT?
STILL NO CHANGE, TOMMY. I'M SORRY.

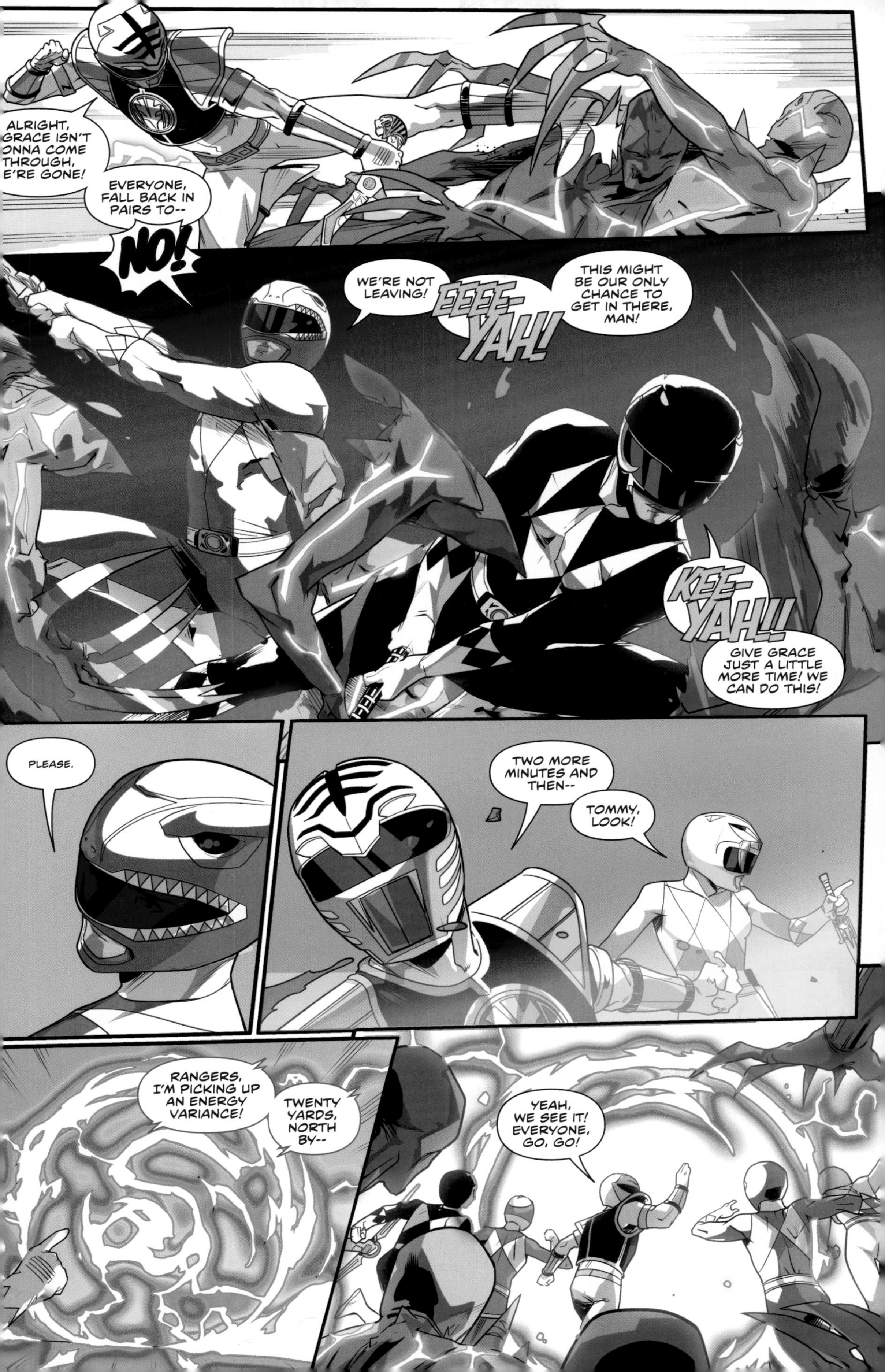

ALRIGHT, GRACE ISN'T ONNA COME THROUGH, E'RE GONE!
EVERYONE, FALL BACK IN PAIRS TO--
NO!
WE'RE NOT LEAVING!
EEEE-YAH!
THIS MIGHT BE OUR ONLY CHANCE TO GET IN THERE, MAN!
KEE-YAH!!
GIVE GRACE JUST A LITTLE MORE TIME! WE CAN DO THIS!
PLEASE.
TWO MORE MINUTES AND THEN--
TOMMY, LOOK!
RANGERS, I'M PICKING UP AN ENERGY VARIANCE!
TWENTY YARDS, NORTH BY--
YEAH, WE SEE IT! EVERYONE, GO, GO!

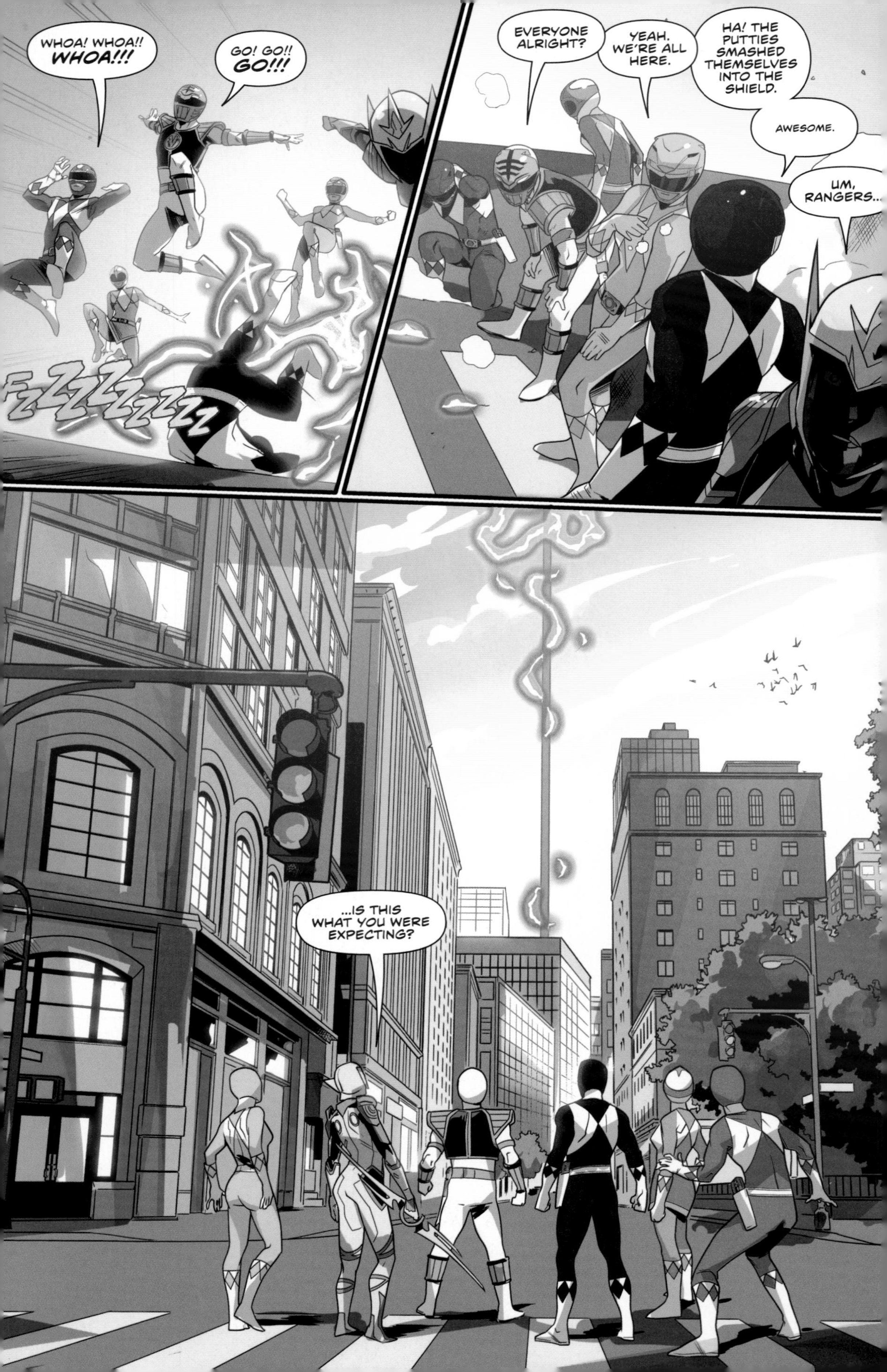
WHOA! WHOA!! WHOA!!!
GO! GO!! GO!!!
FZZZZZZZZZZZ
EVERYONE ALRIGHT?
YEAH. WE'RE ALL HERE.
HA! THE PUTTIES SMASHED THEMSELVES INTO THE SHIELD.
AWESOME.
UM, RANGERS...
...IS THIS WHAT YOU WERE EXPECTING?

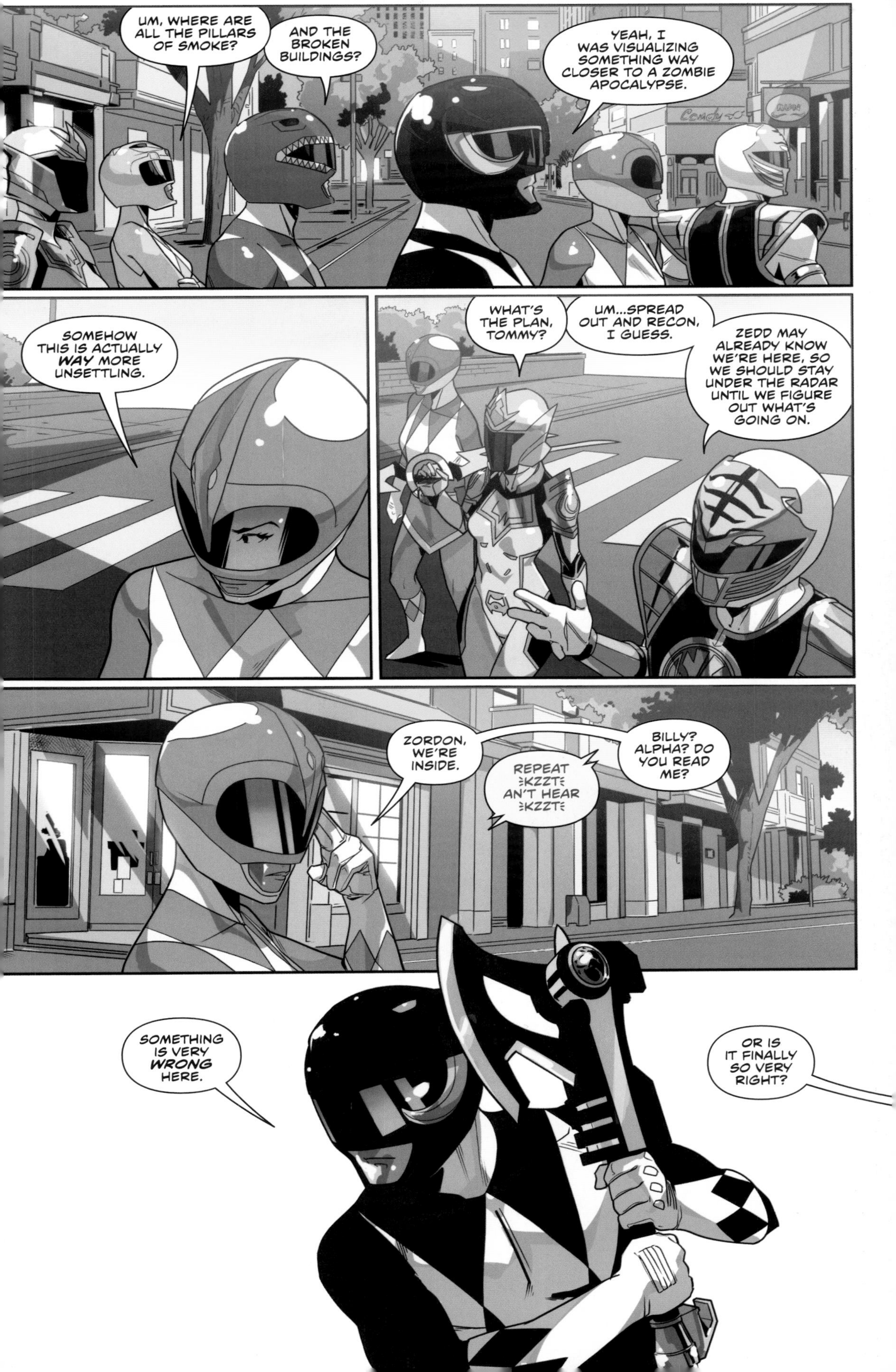
UM, WHERE ARE ALL THE PILLARS OF SMOKE?
AND THE BROKEN BUILDINGS?
YEAH, I WAS VISUALIZING SOMETHING WAY CLOSER TO A ZOMBIE APOCALYPSE.
SOMEHOW THIS IS ACTUALLY WAY MORE UNSETTLING.
WHAT'S THE PLAN, TOMMY?
UM...SPREAD OUT AND RECON, I GUESS.
ZEDD MAY ALREADY KNOW WE'RE HERE, SO WE SHOULD STAY UNDER THE RADAR UNTIL WE FIGURE OUT WHAT'S GOING ON.
ZORDON, WE'RE INSIDE.
BILLY? ALPHA? DO YOU READ ME?
REPEAT KZZT AN'T HEAR KZZT
SOMETHING IS VERY WRONG HERE.
OR IS IT FINALLY SO VERY RIGHT?

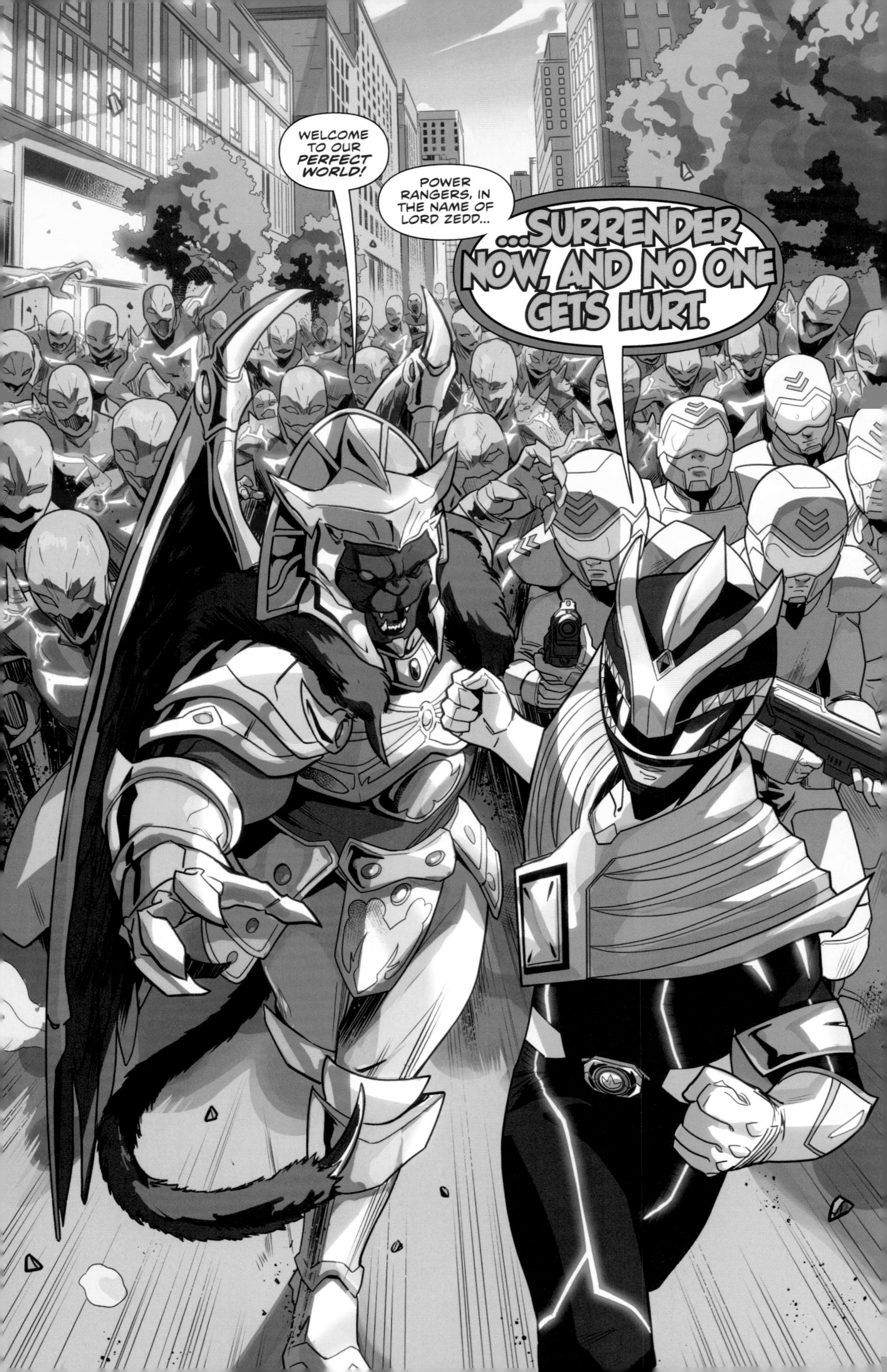
WELCOME TO OUR PERFECT WORLD!
POWER RANGERS, IN THE NAME OF LORD ZEDD...
...SURRENDER NOW, AND NO ONE GETS HURT.

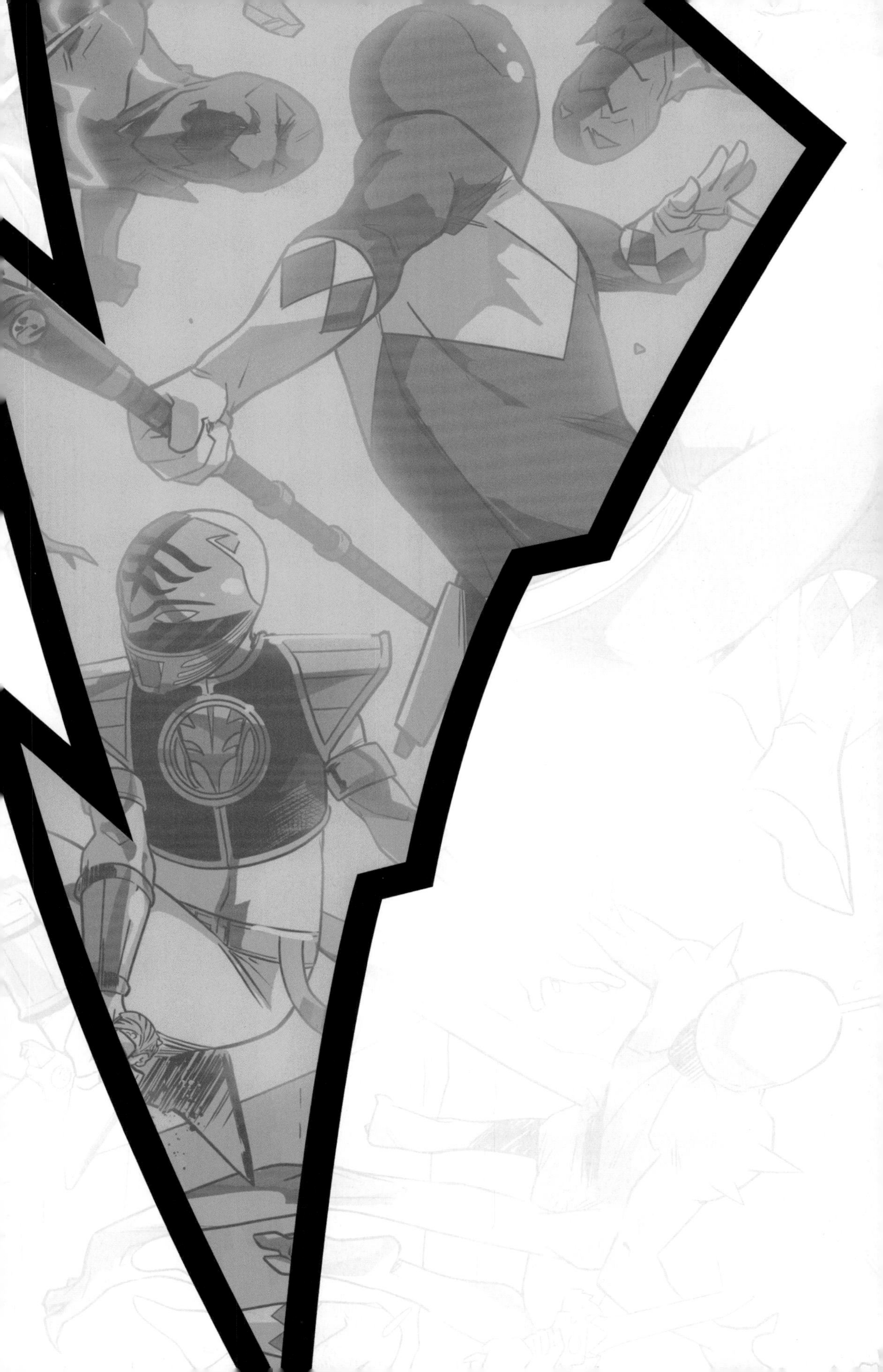

CHAPTER SEVEN

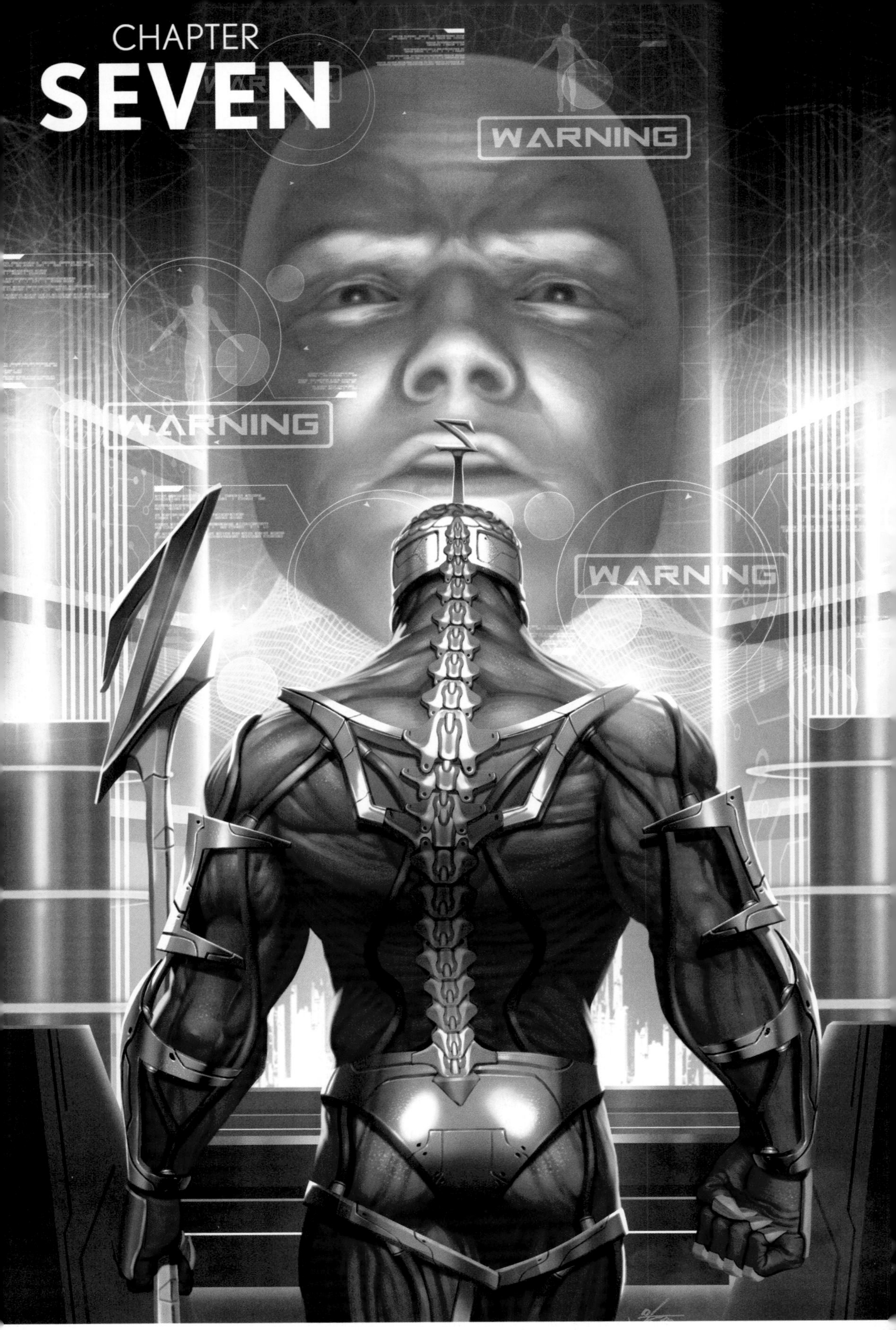
WARNING
WARNING
WARNING

INHYUK LEE | ISSUE SEVEN COVER

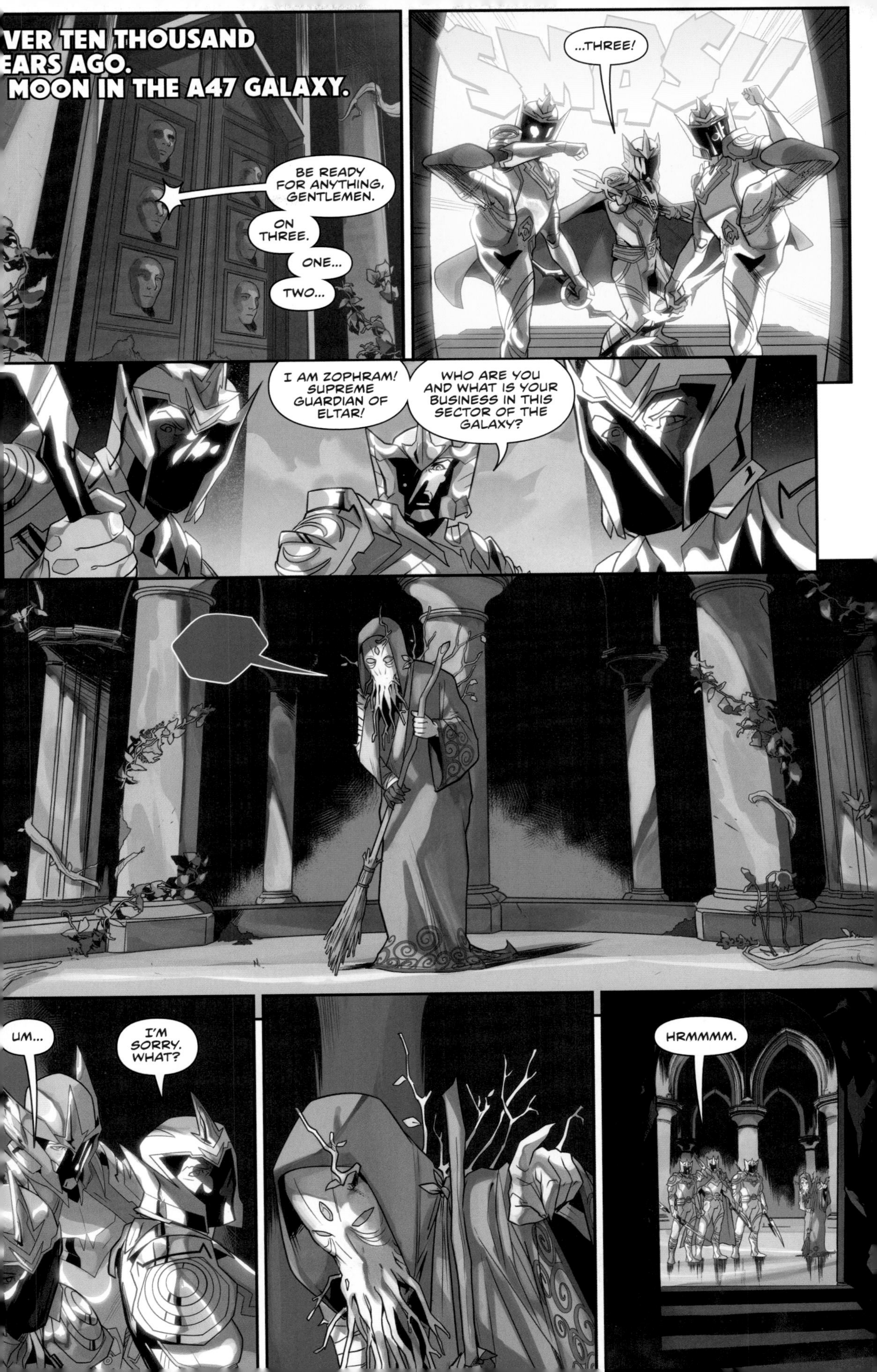
VER TEN THOUSAND
EARS AGO.
MOON IN THE A47 GALAXY.
BE READY FOR ANYTHING, GENTLEMEN.
ON THREE.
ONE...
TWO...
SMASH
...THREE!
I AM ZOPHRAM! SUPREME GUARDIAN OF ELTAR!
WHO ARE YOU AND WHAT IS YOUR BUSINESS IN THIS SECTOR OF THE GALAXY?
UM...
I'M SORRY. WHAT?
HRMMMM.

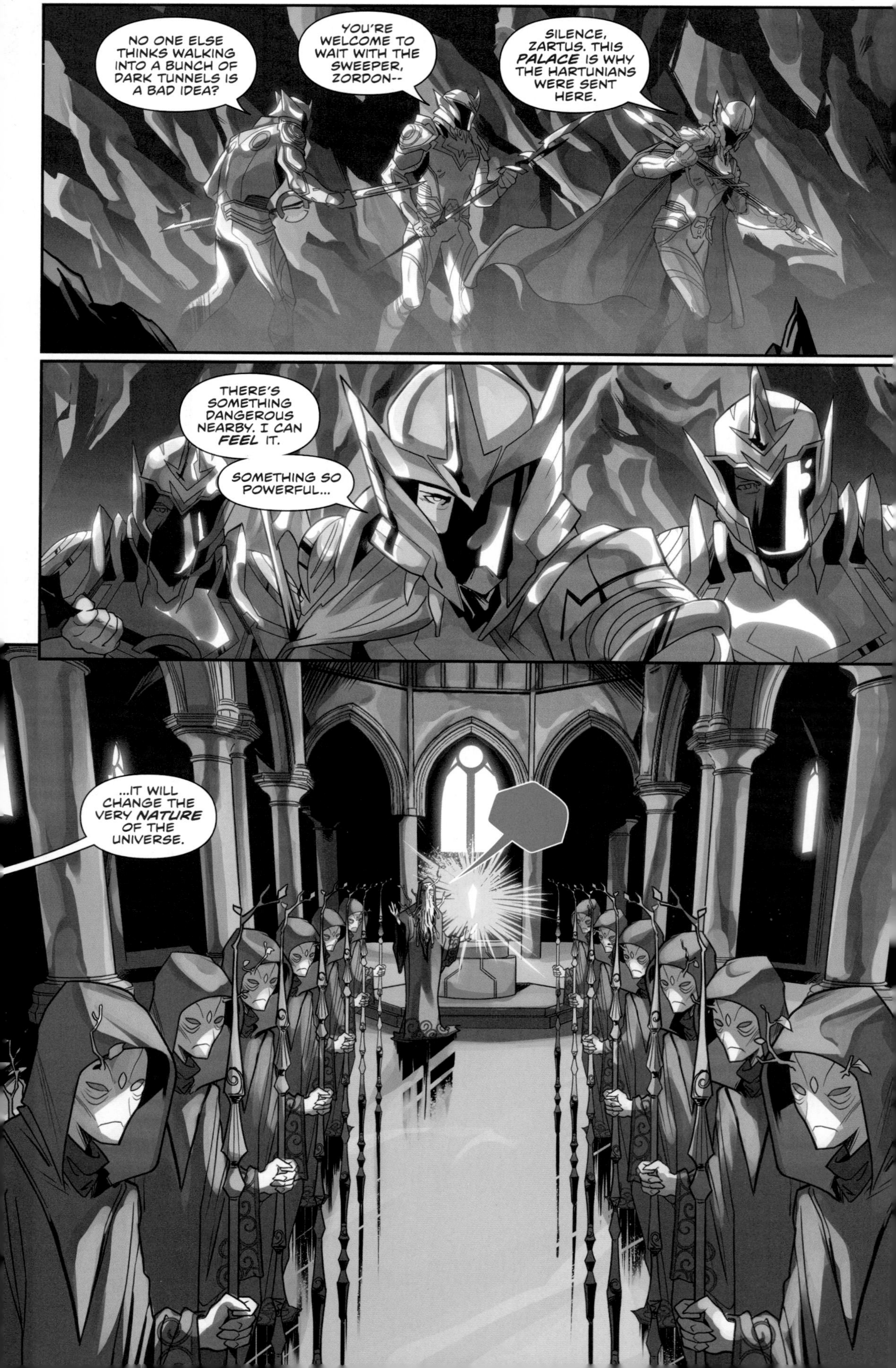
NO ONE ELSE THINKS WALKING INTO A BUNCH OF DARK TUNNELS IS A BAD IDEA?
YOU'RE WELCOME TO WAIT WITH THE SWEEPER, ZORDON--
SILENCE, ZARTUS. THIS PALACE IS WHY THE HARTUNIANS WERE SENT HERE.
THERE'S SOMETHING DANGEROUS NEARBY. I CAN FEEL IT.
SOMETHING SO POWERFUL...
...IT WILL CHANGE THE VERY NATURE OF THE UNIVERSE.

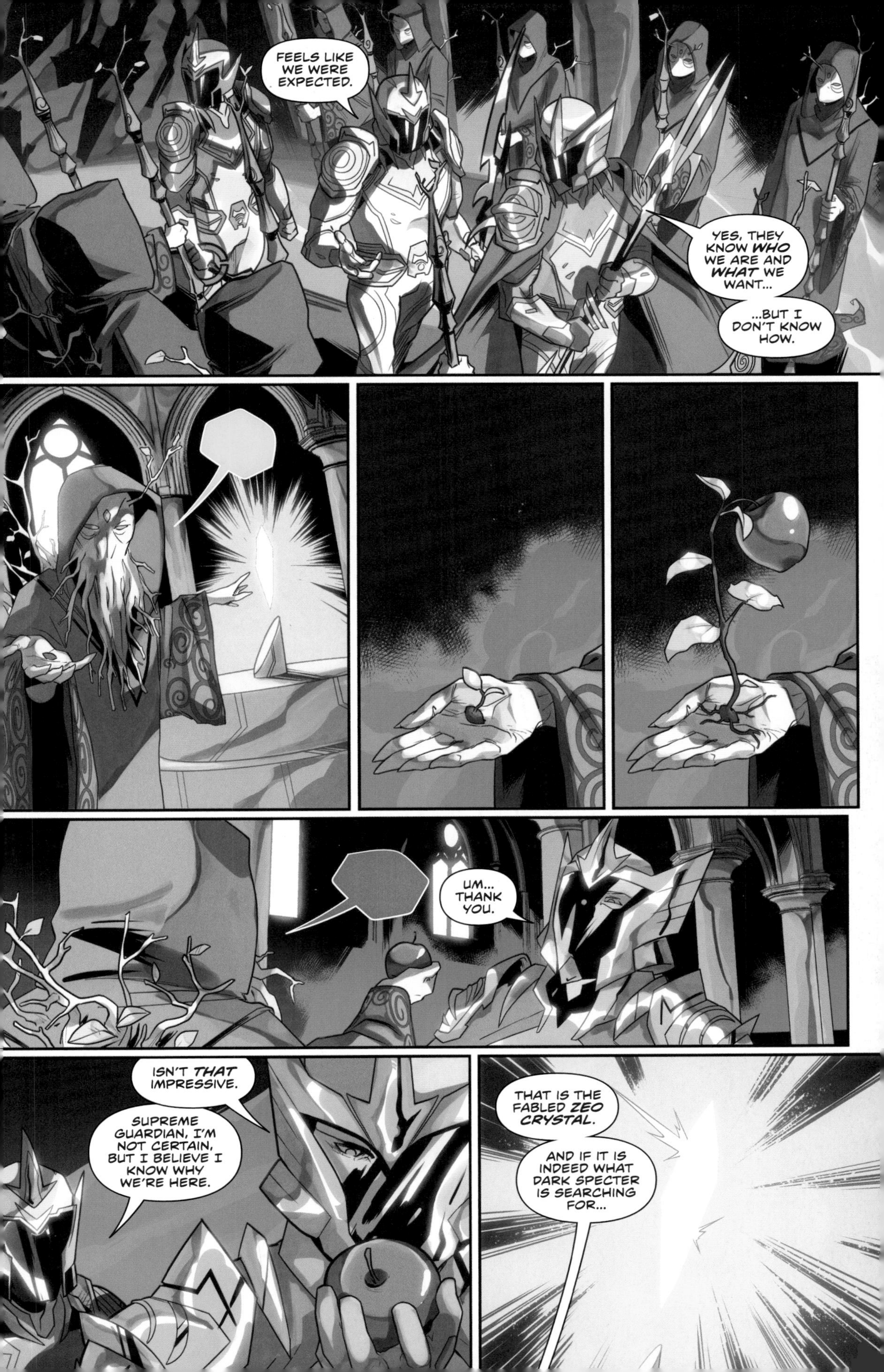

FEELS LIKE WE WERE EXPECTED.
YES, THEY KNOW *WHO* WE ARE AND *WHAT* WE WANT...
...BUT I DON'T KNOW HOW.
UM... THANK YOU.
ISN'T *THAT* IMPRESSIVE.
SUPREME GUARDIAN, I'M NOT CERTAIN, BUT I BELIEVE I KNOW WHY WE'RE HERE.
THAT IS THE FABLED *ZEO CRYSTAL*.
AND IF IT IS INDEED WHAT DARK SPECTER IS SEARCHING FOR...

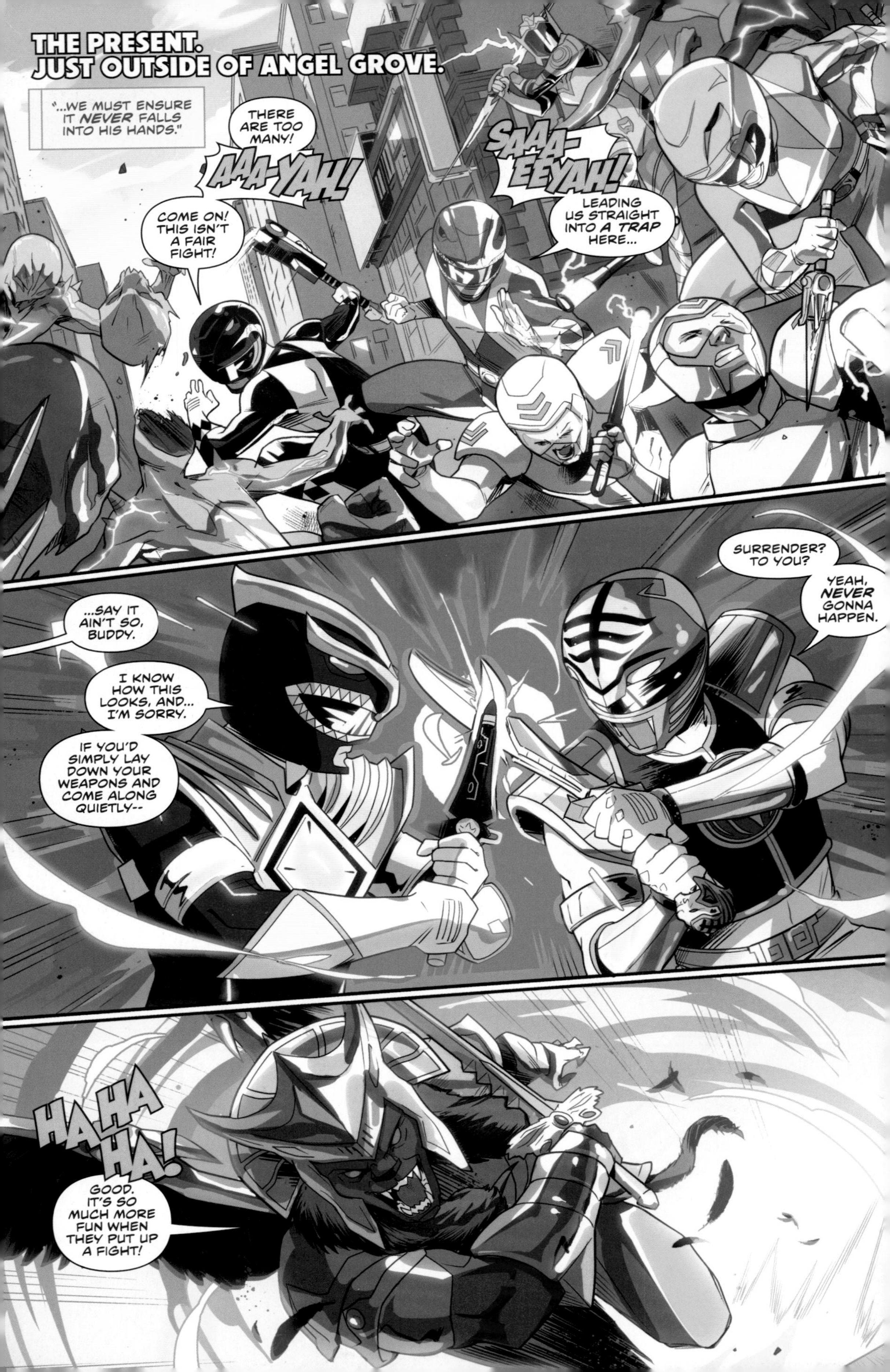
THE PRESENT.
JUST OUTSIDE OF ANGEL GROVE.
"...WE MUST ENSURE IT NEVER FALLS INTO HIS HANDS."
THERE ARE TOO MANY!
AAA-YAH!
COME ON! THIS ISN'T A FAIR FIGHT!
SAAA-EEYAH!
LEADING US STRAIGHT INTO A TRAP HERE...
...SAY IT AIN'T SO, BUDDY.
I KNOW HOW THIS LOOKS, AND... I'M SORRY.
IF YOU'D SIMPLY LAY DOWN YOUR WEAPONS AND COME ALONG QUIETLY--
SURRENDER? TO YOU?
YEAH, NEVER GONNA HAPPEN.
HA HA HA HA!
GOOD. IT'S SO MUCH MORE FUN WHEN THEY PUT UP A FIGHT!

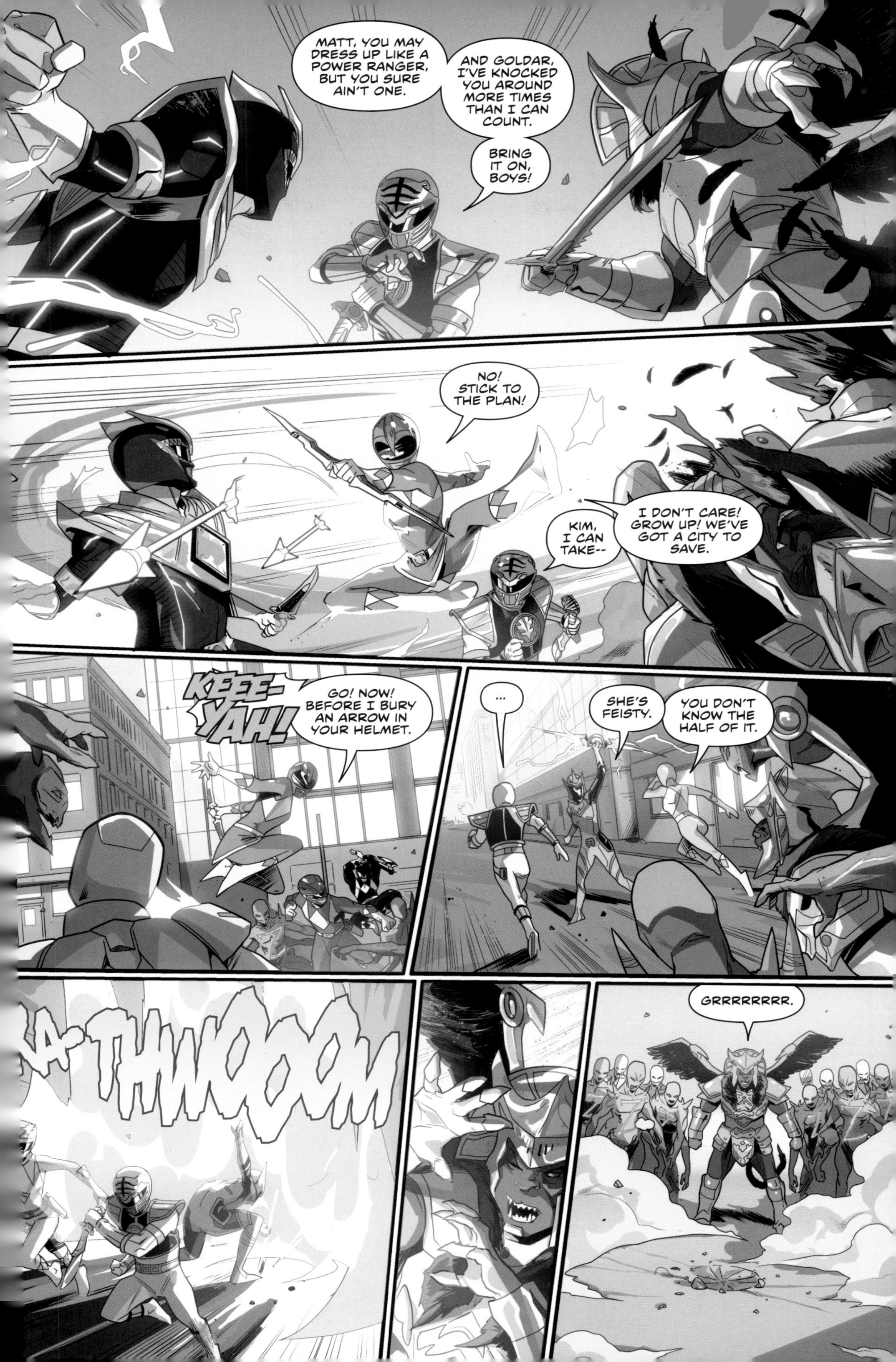
MATT, YOU MAY DRESS UP LIKE A POWER RANGER, BUT YOU SURE AIN'T ONE.
AND GOLDAR, I'VE KNOCKED YOU AROUND MORE TIMES THAN I CAN COUNT.
BRING IT ON, BOYS!
NO! STICK TO THE PLAN!
KIM, I CAN TAKE--
I DON'T CARE! GROW UP! WE'VE GOT A CITY TO SAVE.
KEEE-YAH!
GO! NOW! BEFORE I BURY AN ARROW IN YOUR HELMET.
...
SHE'S FEISTY.
YOU DON'T KNOW THE HALF OF IT.
KA-THWOOOM
GRRRRRRRR.

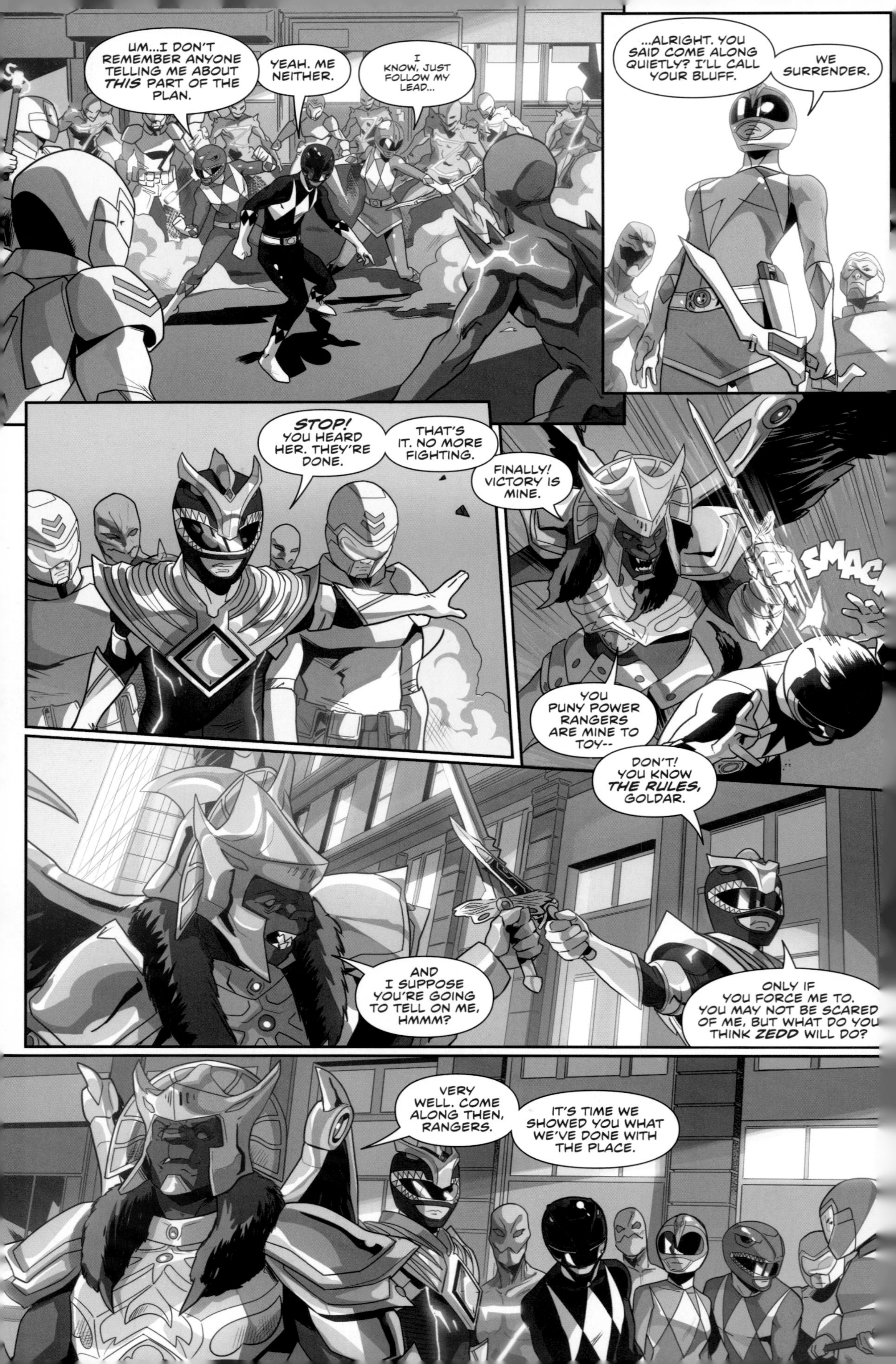
UM...I DON'T REMEMBER ANYONE TELLING ME ABOUT THIS PART OF THE PLAN.
YEAH. ME NEITHER.
I KNOW, JUST FOLLOW MY LEAD...
...ALRIGHT. YOU SAID COME ALONG QUIETLY? I'LL CALL YOUR BLUFF.
WE SURRENDER.
STOP! YOU HEARD HER. THEY'RE DONE.
THAT'S IT. NO MORE FIGHTING.
FINALLY! VICTORY IS MINE.
SMAC
YOU PUNY POWER RANGERS ARE MINE TO TOY--
DON'T! YOU KNOW THE RULES, GOLDAR.
AND I SUPPOSE YOU'RE GOING TO TELL ON ME, HMMM?
ONLY IF YOU FORCE ME TO. YOU MAY NOT BE SCARED OF ME, BUT WHAT DO YOU THINK ZEDD WILL DO?
VERY WELL. COME ALONG THEN, RANGERS.
IT'S TIME WE SHOWED YOU WHAT WE'VE DONE WITH THE PLACE.

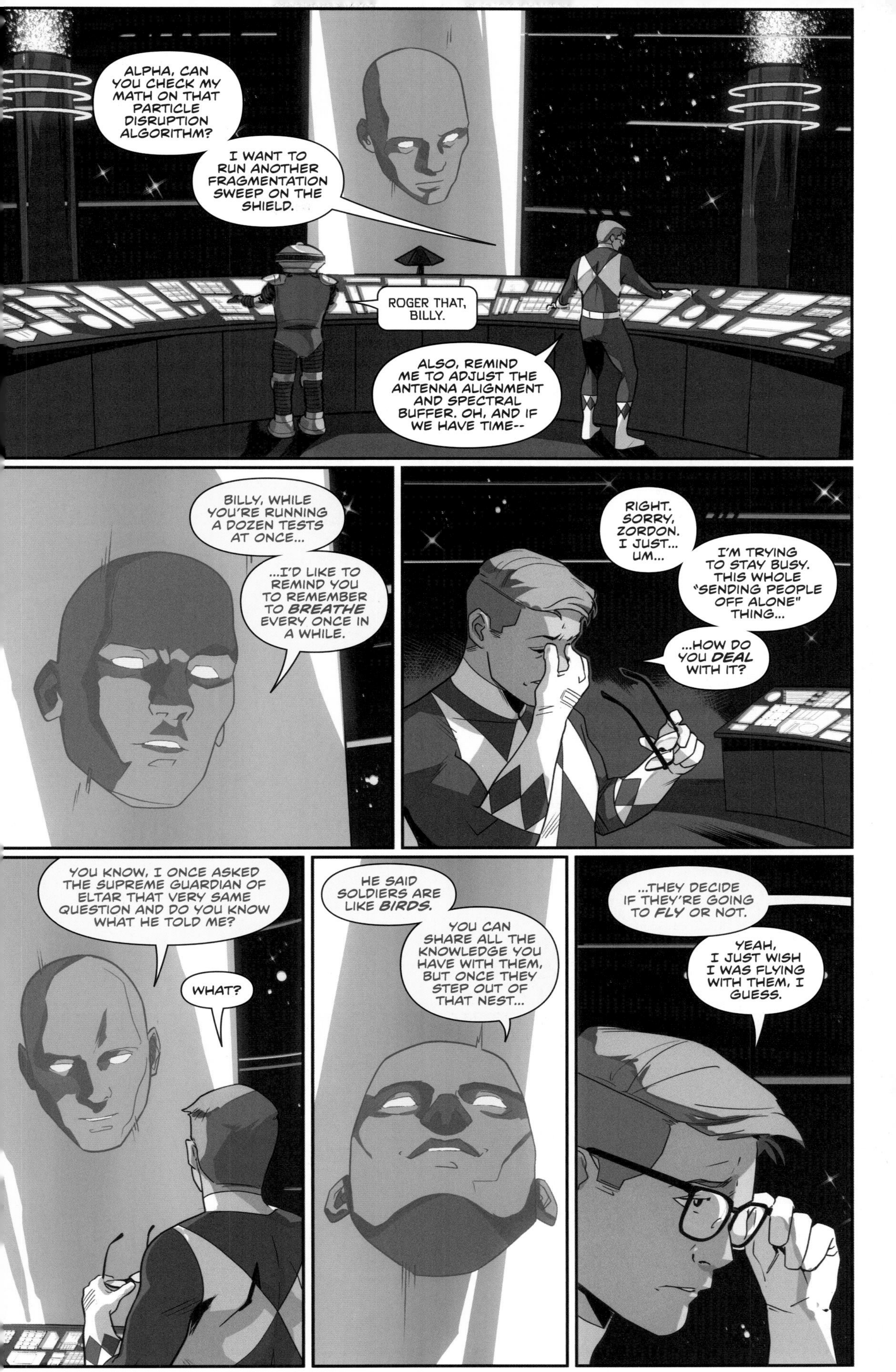
ALPHA, CAN YOU CHECK MY MATH ON THAT PARTICLE DISRUPTION ALGORITHM?
I WANT TO RUN ANOTHER FRAGMENTATION SWEEP ON THE SHIELD.
ROGER THAT, BILLY.
ALSO, REMIND ME TO ADJUST THE ANTENNA ALIGNMENT AND SPECTRAL BUFFER. OH, AND IF WE HAVE TIME--
BILLY, WHILE YOU'RE RUNNING A DOZEN TESTS AT ONCE...
...I'D LIKE TO REMIND YOU TO REMEMBER TO BREATHE EVERY ONCE IN A WHILE.
RIGHT. SORRY, ZORDON. I JUST... UM...
I'M TRYING TO STAY BUSY. THIS WHOLE "SENDING PEOPLE OFF ALONE" THING...
...HOW DO YOU DEAL WITH IT?
YOU KNOW, I ONCE ASKED THE SUPREME GUARDIAN OF ELTAR THAT VERY SAME QUESTION AND DO YOU KNOW WHAT HE TOLD ME?
WHAT?
HE SAID SOLDIERS ARE LIKE BIRDS.
YOU CAN SHARE ALL THE KNOWLEDGE YOU HAVE WITH THEM, BUT ONCE THEY STEP OUT OF THAT NEST...
...THEY DECIDE IF THEY'RE GOING TO FLY OR NOT.
YEAH, I JUST WISH I WAS FLYING WITH THEM, I GUESS.

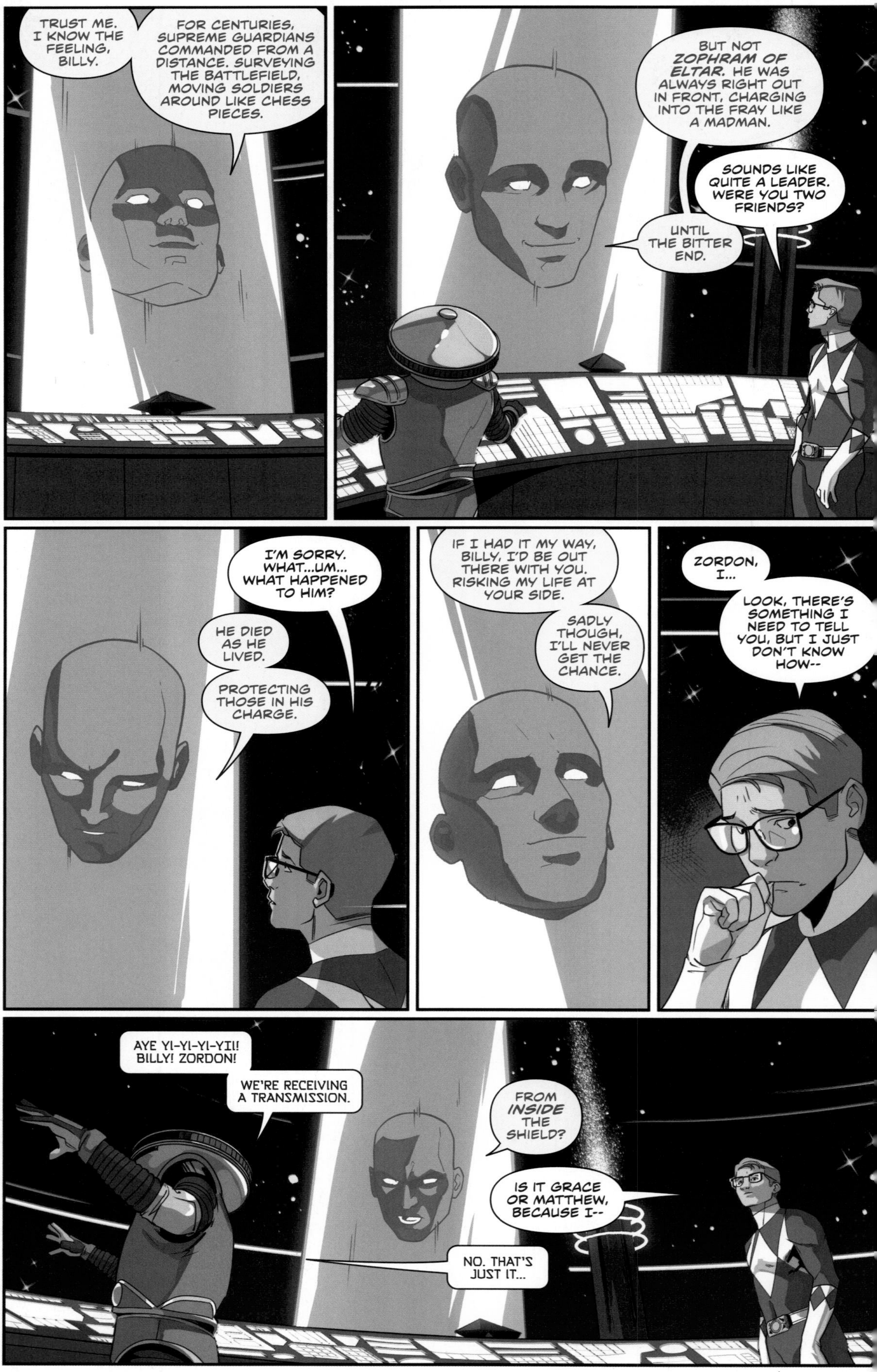
TRUST ME. I KNOW THE FEELING, BILLY.
FOR CENTURIES, SUPREME GUARDIANS COMMANDED FROM A DISTANCE. SURVEYING THE BATTLEFIELD, MOVING SOLDIERS AROUND LIKE CHESS PIECES.
BUT NOT *ZOPHRAM OF ELTAR.* HE WAS ALWAYS RIGHT OUT IN FRONT, CHARGING INTO THE FRAY LIKE A MADMAN.
SOUNDS LIKE QUITE A LEADER. WERE YOU TWO FRIENDS?
UNTIL THE BITTER END.
I'M SORRY. WHAT...UM... WHAT HAPPENED TO HIM?
HE DIED AS HE LIVED.
PROTECTING THOSE IN HIS CHARGE.
IF I HAD IT MY WAY, BILLY, I'D BE OUT THERE WITH YOU. RISKING MY LIFE AT YOUR SIDE.
SADLY THOUGH, I'LL NEVER GET THE CHANCE.
ZORDON, I...
LOOK, THERE'S SOMETHING I NEED TO TELL YOU, BUT I JUST DON'T KNOW HOW--
AYE YI-YI-YI-YII! BILLY! ZORDON!
WE'RE RECEIVING A TRANSMISSION.
FROM *INSIDE* THE SHIELD?
IS IT GRACE OR MATTHEW, BECAUSE I--
NO. THAT'S JUST IT...

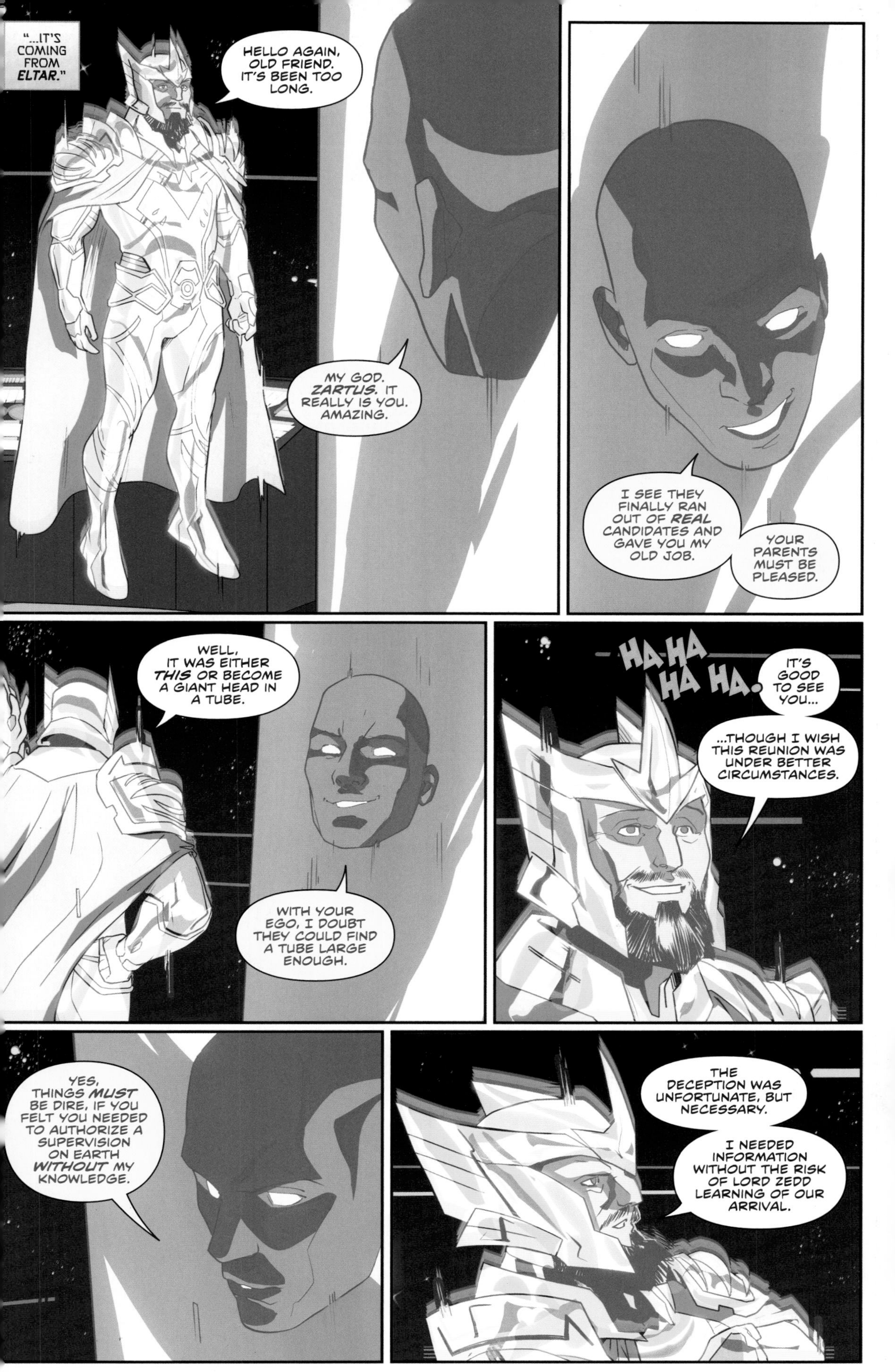
"...IT'S COMING FROM *ELTAR*."
HELLO AGAIN, OLD FRIEND. IT'S BEEN TOO LONG.
MY GOD. *ZARTUS.* IT REALLY IS YOU. AMAZING.
I SEE THEY FINALLY RAN OUT OF *REAL* CANDIDATES AND GAVE YOU MY OLD JOB.
YOUR PARENTS MUST BE PLEASED.
WELL, IT WAS EITHER *THIS* OR BECOME A GIANT HEAD IN A TUBE.
WITH YOUR EGO, I DOUBT THEY COULD FIND A TUBE LARGE ENOUGH.
HA HA HA HA.
IT'S GOOD TO SEE YOU...
...THOUGH I WISH THIS REUNION WAS UNDER BETTER CIRCUMSTANCES.
YES, THINGS *MUST* BE DIRE, IF YOU FELT YOU NEEDED TO AUTHORIZE A SUPERVISION ON EARTH *WITHOUT* MY KNOWLEDGE.
THE DECEPTION WAS UNFORTUNATE, BUT NECESSARY.
I NEEDED INFORMATION WITHOUT THE RISK OF LORD ZEDD LEARNING OF OUR ARRIVAL.

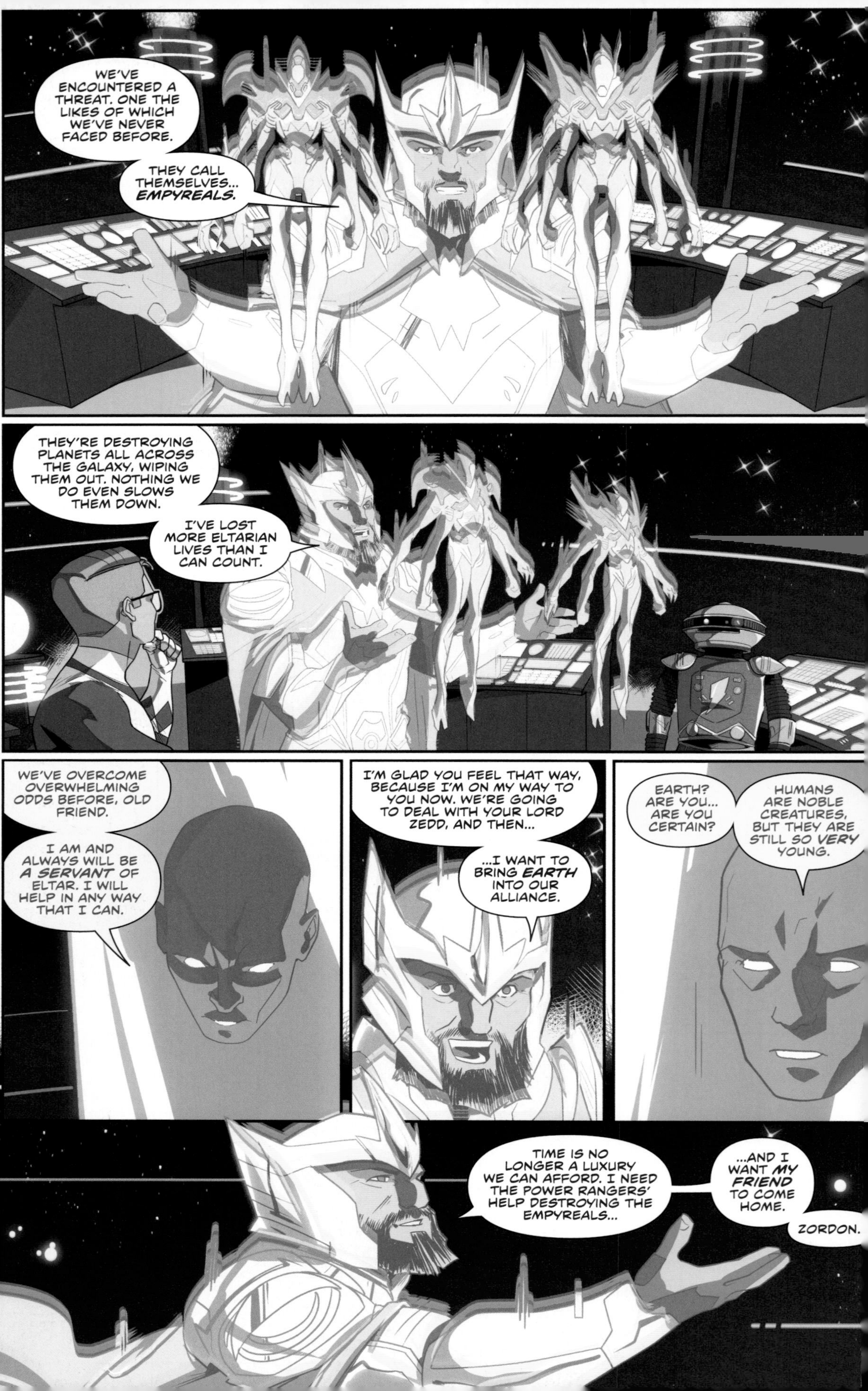
WE'VE ENCOUNTERED A THREAT. ONE THE LIKES OF WHICH WE'VE NEVER FACED BEFORE.
THEY CALL THEMSELVES... EMPYREALS.
THEY'RE DESTROYING PLANETS ALL ACROSS THE GALAXY, WIPING THEM OUT. NOTHING WE DO EVEN SLOWS THEM DOWN.
I'VE LOST MORE ELTARIAN LIVES THAN I CAN COUNT.
WE'VE OVERCOME OVERWHELMING ODDS BEFORE, OLD FRIEND.
I AM AND ALWAYS WILL BE A SERVANT OF ELTAR. I WILL HELP IN ANY WAY THAT I CAN.
I'M GLAD YOU FEEL THAT WAY, BECAUSE I'M ON MY WAY TO YOU NOW. WE'RE GOING TO DEAL WITH YOUR LORD ZEDD, AND THEN...
...I WANT TO BRING EARTH INTO OUR ALLIANCE.
EARTH? ARE YOU... ARE YOU CERTAIN?
HUMANS ARE NOBLE CREATURES, BUT THEY ARE STILL SO VERY YOUNG.
TIME IS NO LONGER A LUXURY WE CAN AFFORD. I NEED THE POWER RANGERS' HELP DESTROYING THE EMPYREALS...
...AND I WANT MY FRIEND TO COME HOME.
ZORDON.

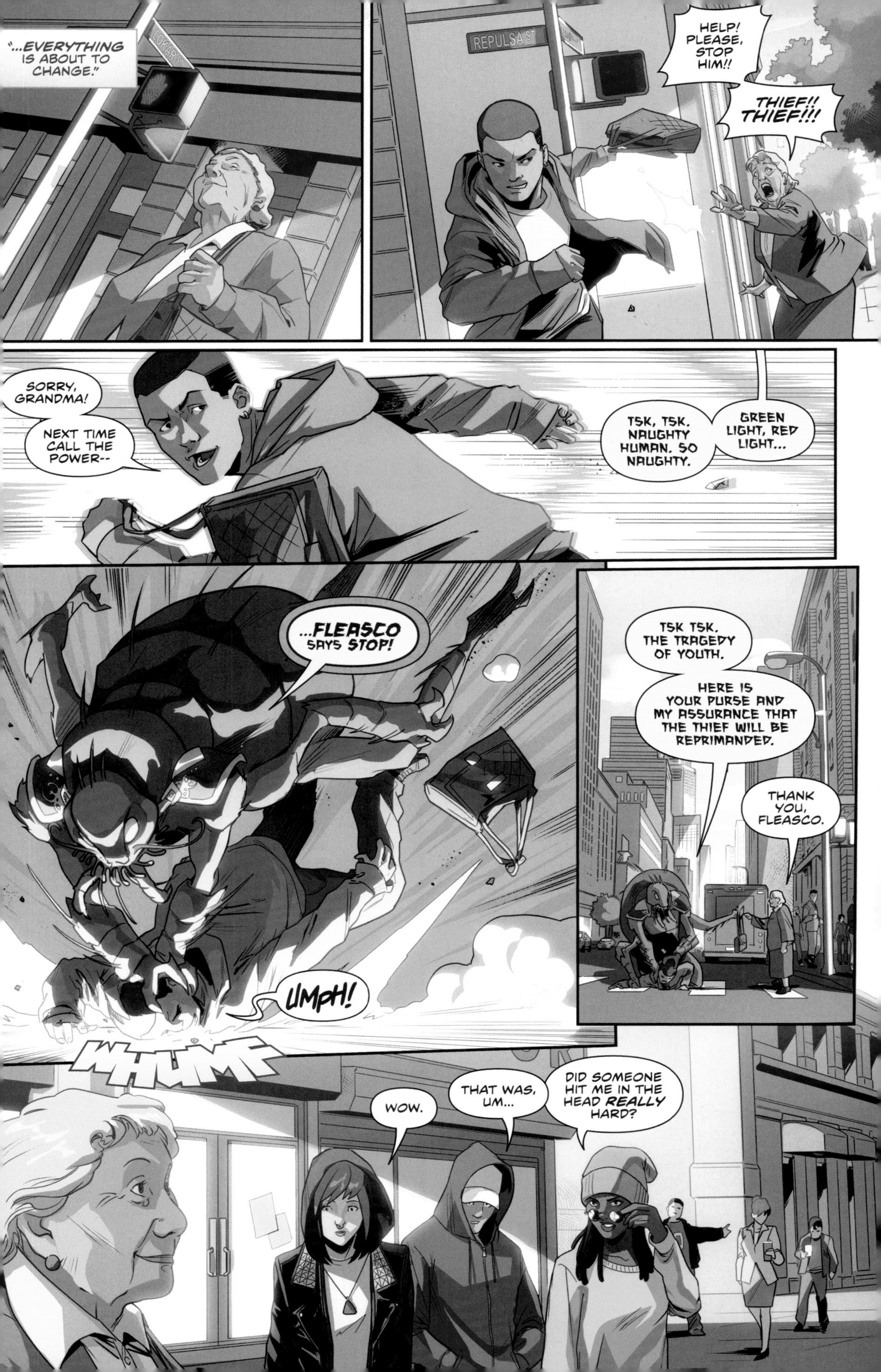
"...EVERYTHING IS ABOUT TO CHANGE."
LOKAR ST
REPULSA ST
HELP! PLEASE, STOP HIM!!
THIEF!! THIEF!!!
SORRY, GRANDMA!
NEXT TIME CALL THE POWER--
TSK, TSK. NAUGHTY HUMAN. SO NAUGHTY.
GREEN LIGHT, RED LIGHT...
...FLEASCO SAYS STOP!
UMPH!
WHUMF
TSK TSK. THE TRAGEDY OF YOUTH.
HERE IS YOUR PURSE AND MY ASSURANCE THAT THE THIEF WILL BE REPRIMANDED.
THANK YOU, FLEASCO.
WOW.
THAT WAS, UM...
DID SOMEONE HIT ME IN THE HEAD REALLY HARD?

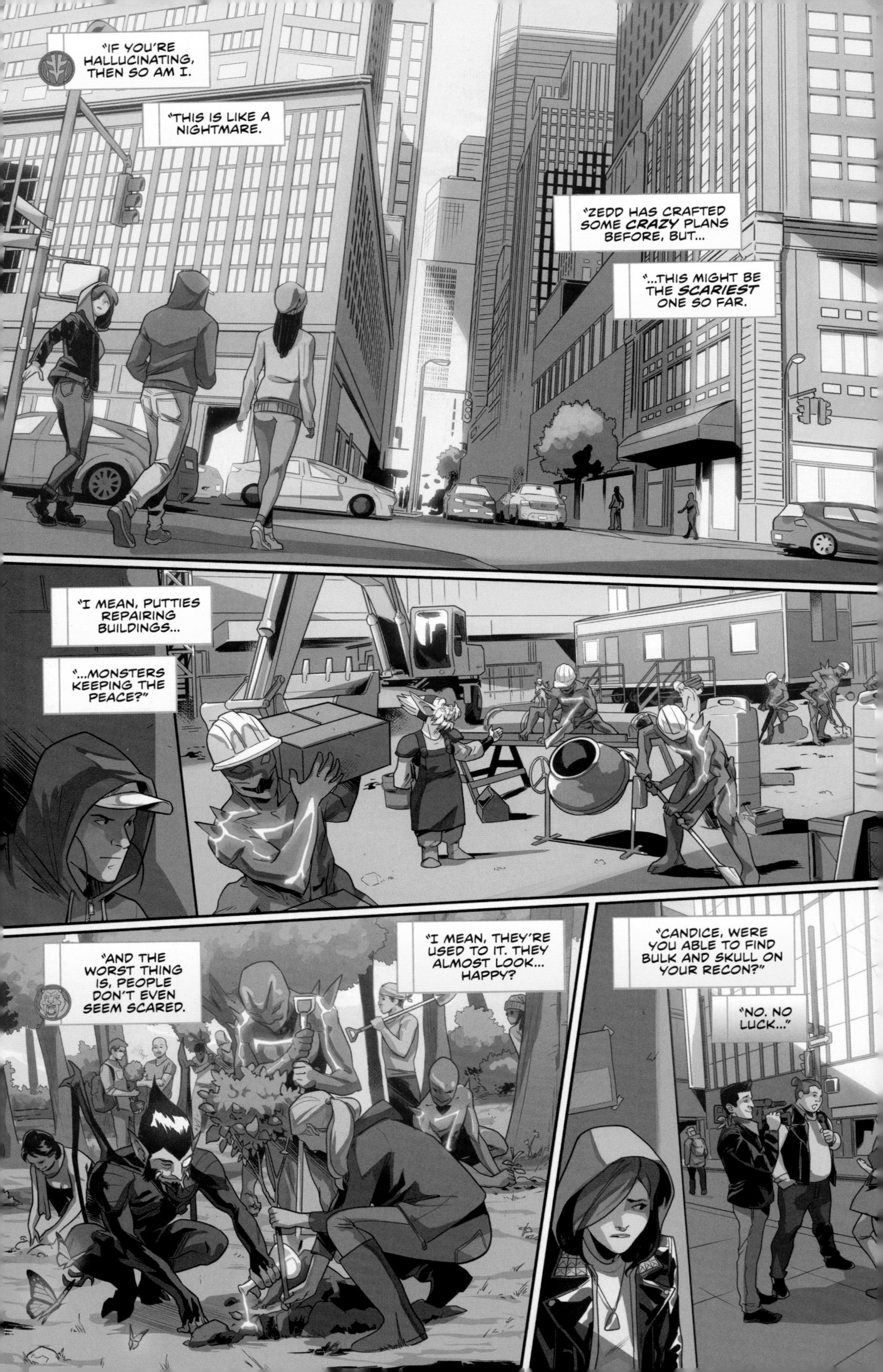
"IF YOU'RE HALLUCINATING, THEN SO AM I.
"THIS IS LIKE A NIGHTMARE.
"ZEDD HAS CRAFTED SOME CRAZY PLANS BEFORE, BUT...
"...THIS MIGHT BE THE SCARIEST ONE SO FAR.
"I MEAN, PUTTIES REPAIRING BUILDINGS...
"...MONSTERS KEEPING THE PEACE?"
"AND THE WORST THING IS, PEOPLE DON'T EVEN SEEM SCARED.
"I MEAN, THEY'RE USED TO IT. THEY ALMOST LOOK... HAPPY?
"CANDICE, WERE YOU ABLE TO FIND BULK AND SKULL ON YOUR RECON?"
"NO. NO LUCK..."

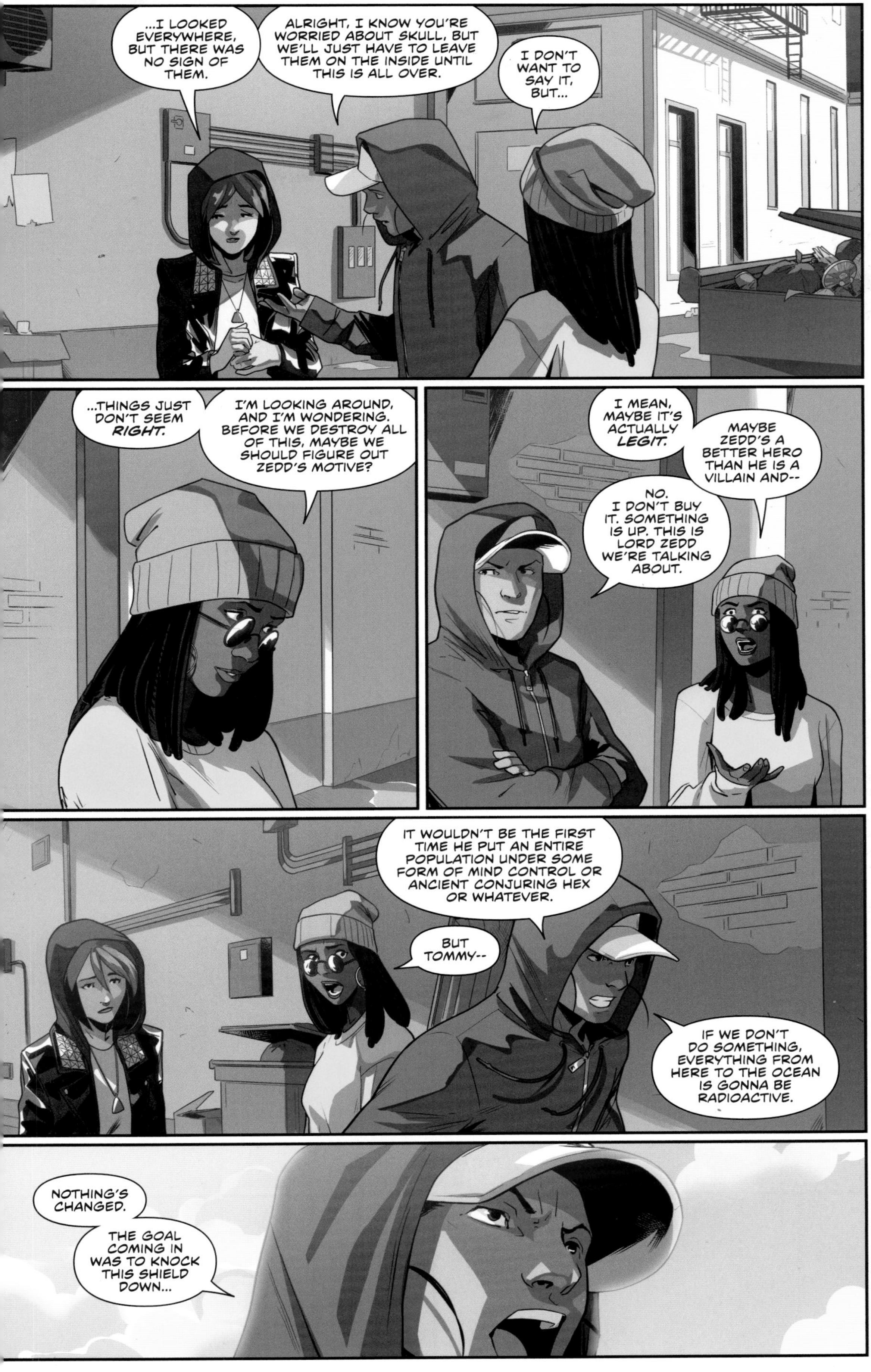
...I LOOKED EVERYWHERE, BUT THERE WAS NO SIGN OF THEM.
ALRIGHT, I KNOW YOU'RE WORRIED ABOUT SKULL, BUT WE'LL JUST HAVE TO LEAVE THEM ON THE INSIDE UNTIL THIS IS ALL OVER.
I DON'T WANT TO SAY IT, BUT...
...THINGS JUST DON'T SEEM RIGHT.
I'M LOOKING AROUND, AND I'M WONDERING. BEFORE WE DESTROY ALL OF THIS, MAYBE WE SHOULD FIGURE OUT ZEDD'S MOTIVE?
I MEAN, MAYBE IT'S ACTUALLY LEGIT.
MAYBE ZEDD'S A BETTER HERO THAN HE IS A VILLAIN AND--
NO. I DON'T BUY IT. SOMETHING IS UP. THIS IS LORD ZEDD WE'RE TALKING ABOUT.
IT WOULDN'T BE THE FIRST TIME HE PUT AN ENTIRE POPULATION UNDER SOME FORM OF MIND CONTROL OR ANCIENT CONJURING HEX OR WHATEVER.
BUT TOMMY--
IF WE DON'T DO SOMETHING, EVERYTHING FROM HERE TO THE OCEAN IS GONNA BE RADIOACTIVE.
NOTHING'S CHANGED.
THE GOAL COMING IN WAS TO KNOCK THIS SHIELD DOWN...

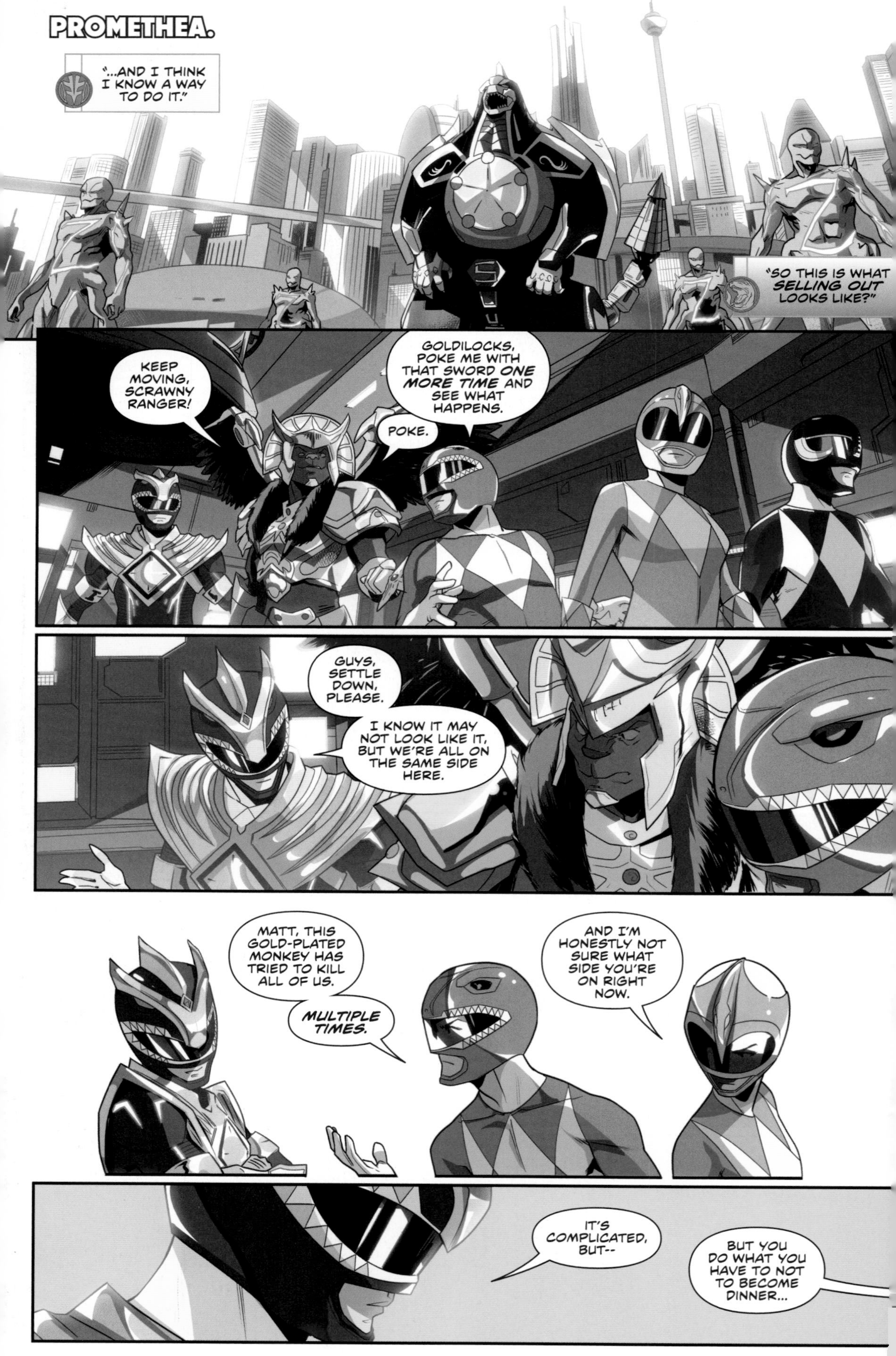
PROMETHEA.
"...AND I THINK I KNOW A WAY TO DO IT."
"SO THIS IS WHAT SELLING OUT LOOKS LIKE?"
KEEP MOVING, SCRAWNY RANGER!
GOLDILOCKS, POKE ME WITH THAT SWORD ONE MORE TIME AND SEE WHAT HAPPENS.
POKE.
GUYS, SETTLE DOWN, PLEASE.
I KNOW IT MAY NOT LOOK LIKE IT, BUT WE'RE ALL ON THE SAME SIDE HERE.
MATT, THIS GOLD-PLATED MONKEY HAS TRIED TO KILL ALL OF US.
MULTIPLE TIMES.
AND I'M HONESTLY NOT SURE WHAT SIDE YOU'RE ON RIGHT NOW.
IT'S COMPLICATED, BUT--
BUT YOU DO WHAT YOU HAVE TO NOT TO BECOME DINNER...

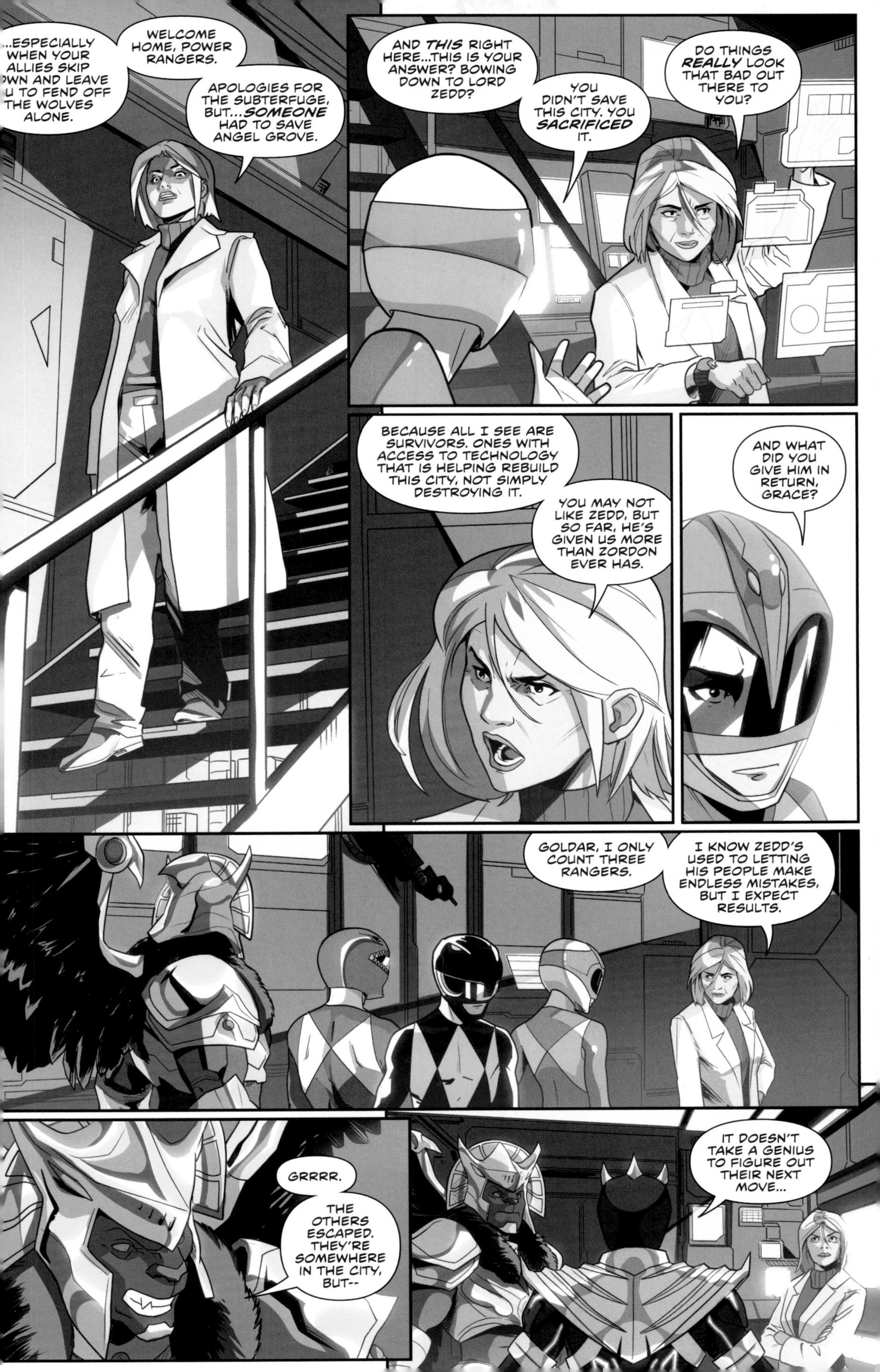

...ESPECIALLY WHEN YOUR ALLIES SKIP OWN AND LEAVE U TO FEND OFF THE WOLVES ALONE.
WELCOME HOME, POWER RANGERS.
APOLOGIES FOR THE SUBTERFUGE, BUT...SOMEONE HAD TO SAVE ANGEL GROVE.
AND THIS RIGHT HERE...THIS IS YOUR ANSWER? BOWING DOWN TO LORD ZEDD?
YOU DIDN'T SAVE THIS CITY. YOU SACRIFICED IT.
DO THINGS REALLY LOOK THAT BAD OUT THERE TO YOU?
BECAUSE ALL I SEE ARE SURVIVORS. ONES WITH ACCESS TO TECHNOLOGY THAT IS HELPING REBUILD THIS CITY, NOT SIMPLY DESTROYING IT.
YOU MAY NOT LIKE ZEDD, BUT SO FAR, HE'S GIVEN US MORE THAN ZORDON EVER HAS.
AND WHAT DID YOU GIVE HIM IN RETURN, GRACE?
GOLDAR, I ONLY COUNT THREE RANGERS.
I KNOW ZEDD'S USED TO LETTING HIS PEOPLE MAKE ENDLESS MISTAKES, BUT I EXPECT RESULTS.
GRRRR.
THE OTHERS ESCAPED. THEY'RE SOMEWHERE IN THE CITY, BUT--
IT DOESN'T TAKE A GENIUS TO FIGURE OUT THEIR NEXT MOVE...

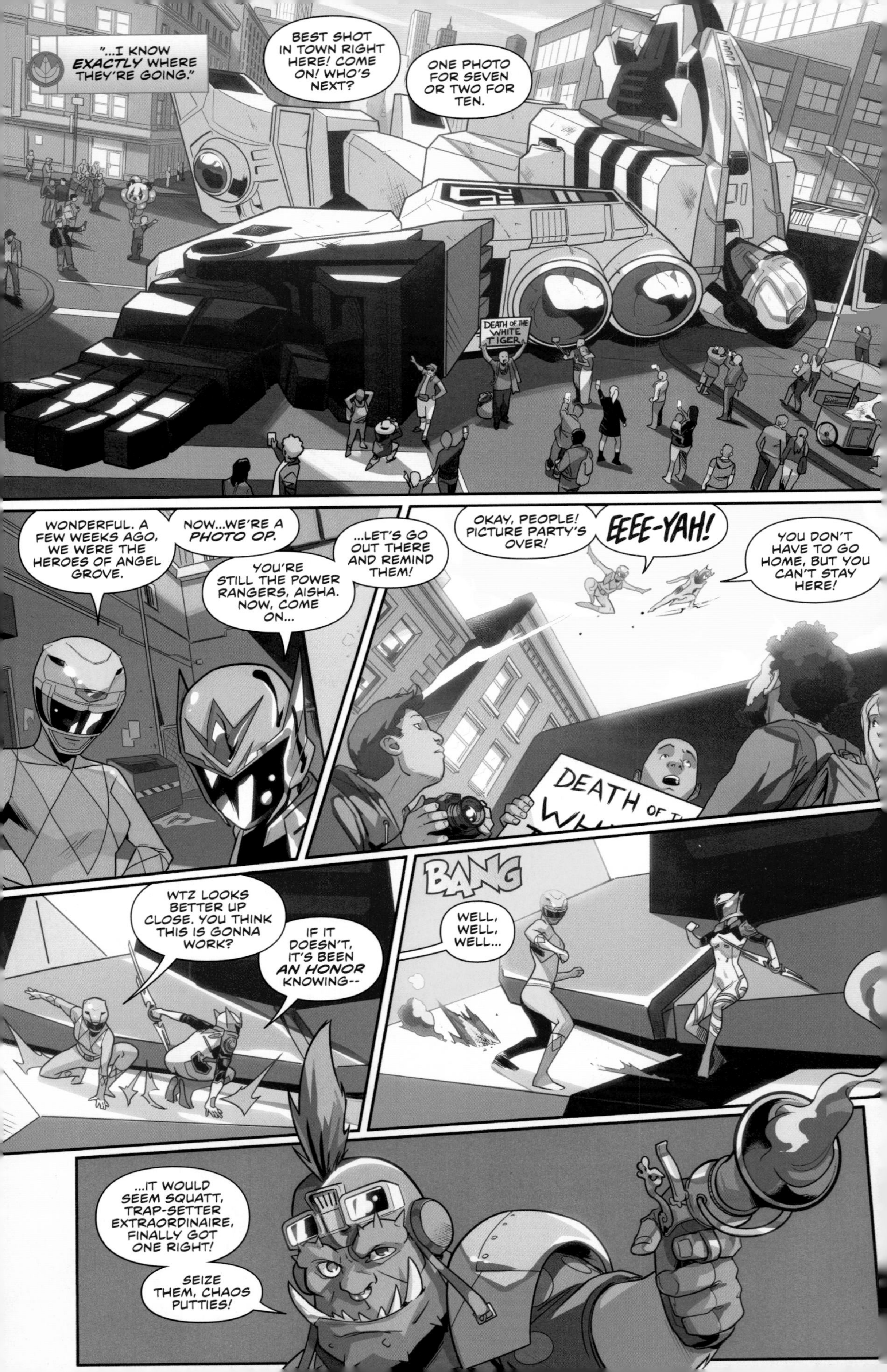
"...I KNOW EXACTLY WHERE THEY'RE GOING."
BEST SHOT IN TOWN RIGHT HERE! COME ON! WHO'S NEXT?
ONE PHOTO FOR SEVEN OR TWO FOR TEN.
DEATH OF THE WHITE TIGER
WONDERFUL. A FEW WEEKS AGO, WE WERE THE HEROES OF ANGEL GROVE.
NOW...WE'RE A PHOTO OP.
YOU'RE STILL THE POWER RANGERS, AISHA. NOW, COME ON...
...LET'S GO OUT THERE AND REMIND THEM!
OKAY, PEOPLE! PICTURE PARTY'S OVER!
EEEE-YAH!
YOU DON'T HAVE TO GO HOME, BUT YOU CAN'T STAY HERE!
WTZ LOOKS BETTER UP CLOSE. YOU THINK THIS IS GONNA WORK?
IF IT DOESN'T, IT'S BEEN AN HONOR KNOWING--
BANG
WELL, WELL, WELL...
...IT WOULD SEEM SQUATT, TRAP-SETTER EXTRAORDINAIRE, FINALLY GOT ONE RIGHT!
SEIZE THEM, CHAOS PUTTIES!

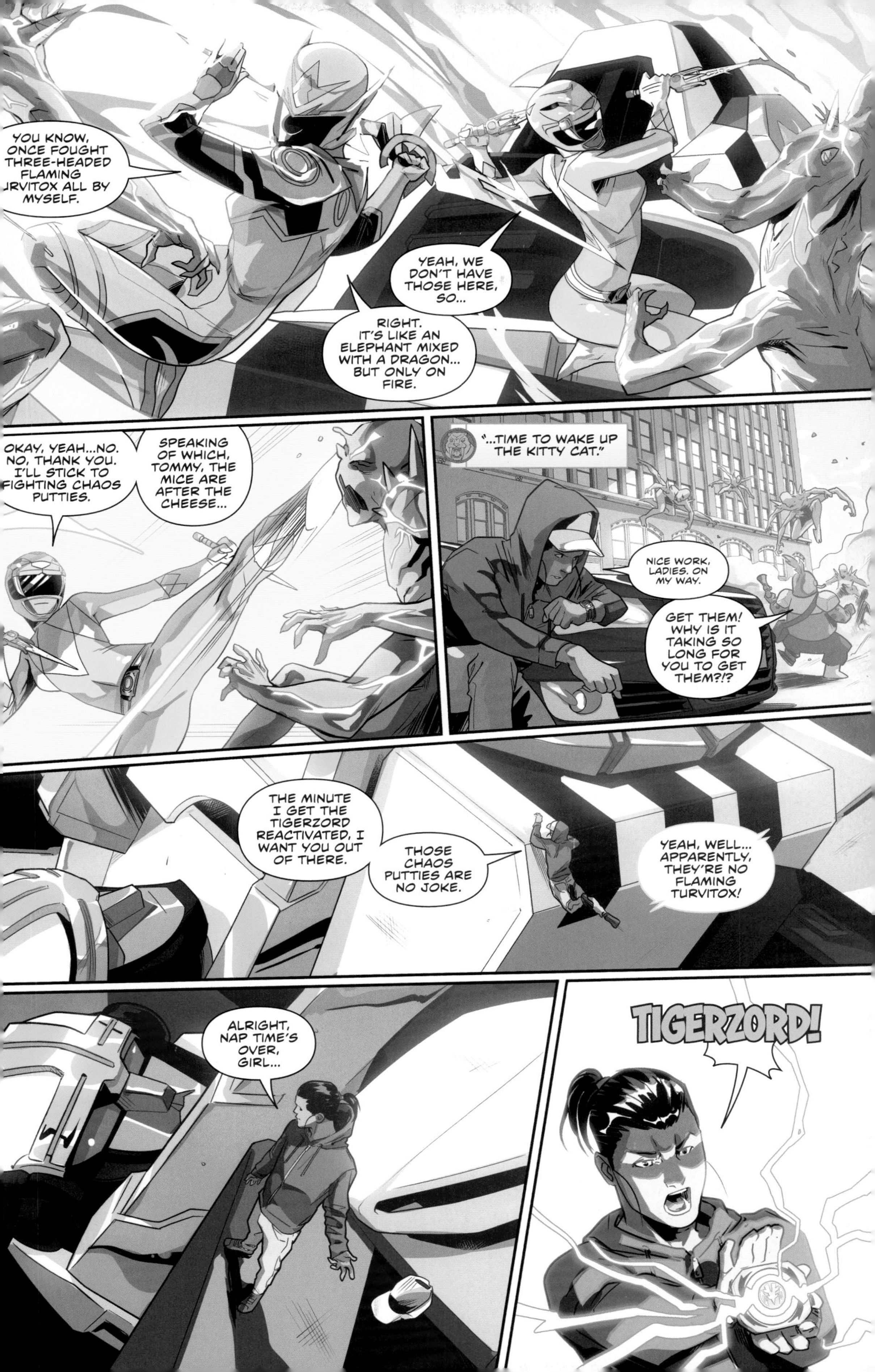
YOU KNOW, ONCE FOUGHT THREE-HEADED FLAMING URVITOX ALL BY MYSELF.
YEAH, WE DON'T HAVE THOSE HERE, SO...
RIGHT. IT'S LIKE AN ELEPHANT MIXED WITH A DRAGON... BUT ONLY ON FIRE.
OKAY, YEAH...NO. NO, THANK YOU. I'LL STICK TO FIGHTING CHAOS PUTTIES.
SPEAKING OF WHICH, TOMMY, THE MICE ARE AFTER THE CHEESE...
"...TIME TO WAKE UP THE KITTY CAT."
NICE WORK, LADIES. ON MY WAY.
GET THEM! WHY IS IT TAKING SO LONG FOR YOU TO GET THEM?!?
THE MINUTE I GET THE TIGERZORD REACTIVATED, I WANT YOU OUT OF THERE.
THOSE CHAOS PUTTIES ARE NO JOKE.
YEAH, WELL... APPARENTLY, THEY'RE NO FLAMING TURVITOX!
ALRIGHT, NAP TIME'S OVER, GIRL...
TIGERZORD!

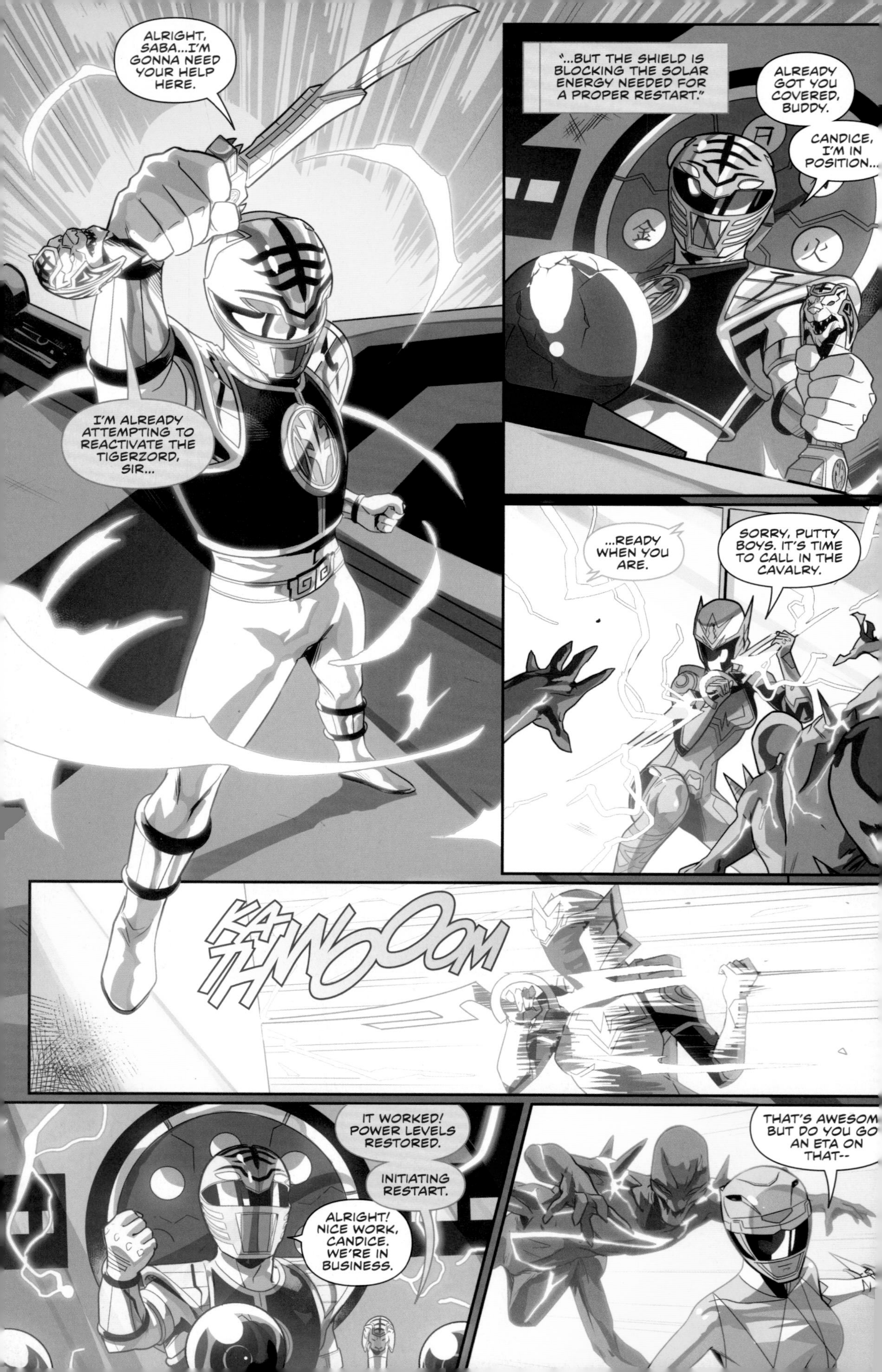
ALRIGHT, SABA...I'M GONNA NEED YOUR HELP HERE.
I'M ALREADY ATTEMPTING TO REACTIVATE THE TIGERZORD, SIR...
"...BUT THE SHIELD IS BLOCKING THE SOLAR ENERGY NEEDED FOR A PROPER RESTART."
ALREADY GOT YOU COVERED, BUDDY.
CANDICE, I'M IN POSITION...
...READY WHEN YOU ARE.
SORRY, PUTTY BOYS. IT'S TIME TO CALL IN THE CAVALRY.
KA-THWOOOM
IT WORKED! POWER LEVELS RESTORED.
INITIATING RESTART.
ALRIGHT! NICE WORK, CANDICE. WE'RE IN BUSINESS.
THAT'S AWESOM BUT DO YOU GO AN ETA ON THAT--

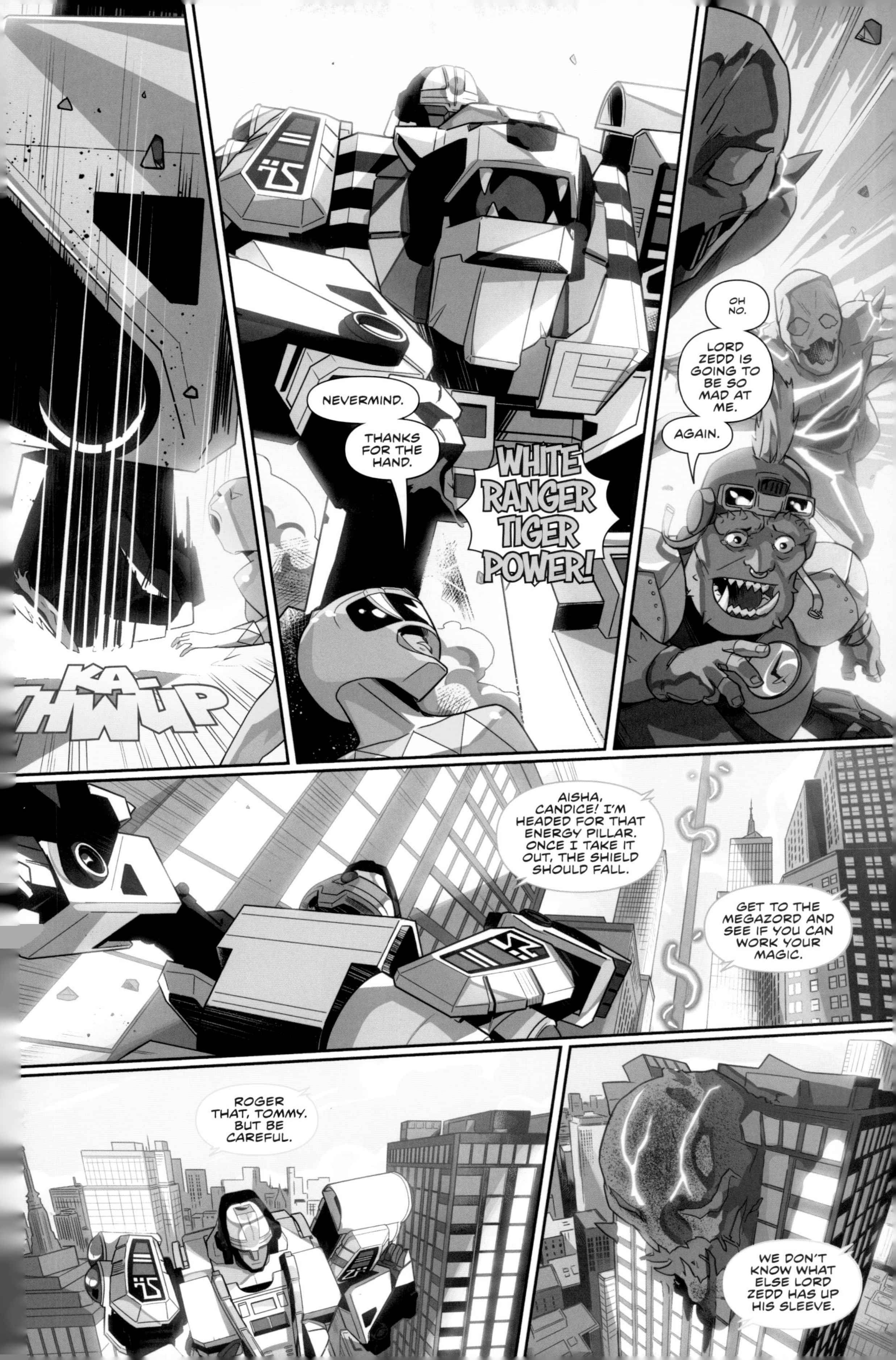
KA-THWUP
NEVERMIND.
THANKS FOR THE HAND.
WHITE RANGER TIGER POWER!
OH NO.
LORD ZEDD IS GOING TO BE SO MAD AT ME.
AGAIN.
AISHA, CANDICE! I'M HEADED FOR THAT ENERGY PILLAR. ONCE I TAKE IT OUT, THE SHIELD SHOULD FALL.
GET TO THE MEGAZORD AND SEE IF YOU CAN WORK YOUR MAGIC.
ROGER THAT, TOMMY. BUT BE CAREFUL.
WE DON'T KNOW WHAT ELSE LORD ZEDD HAS UP HIS SLEEVE.

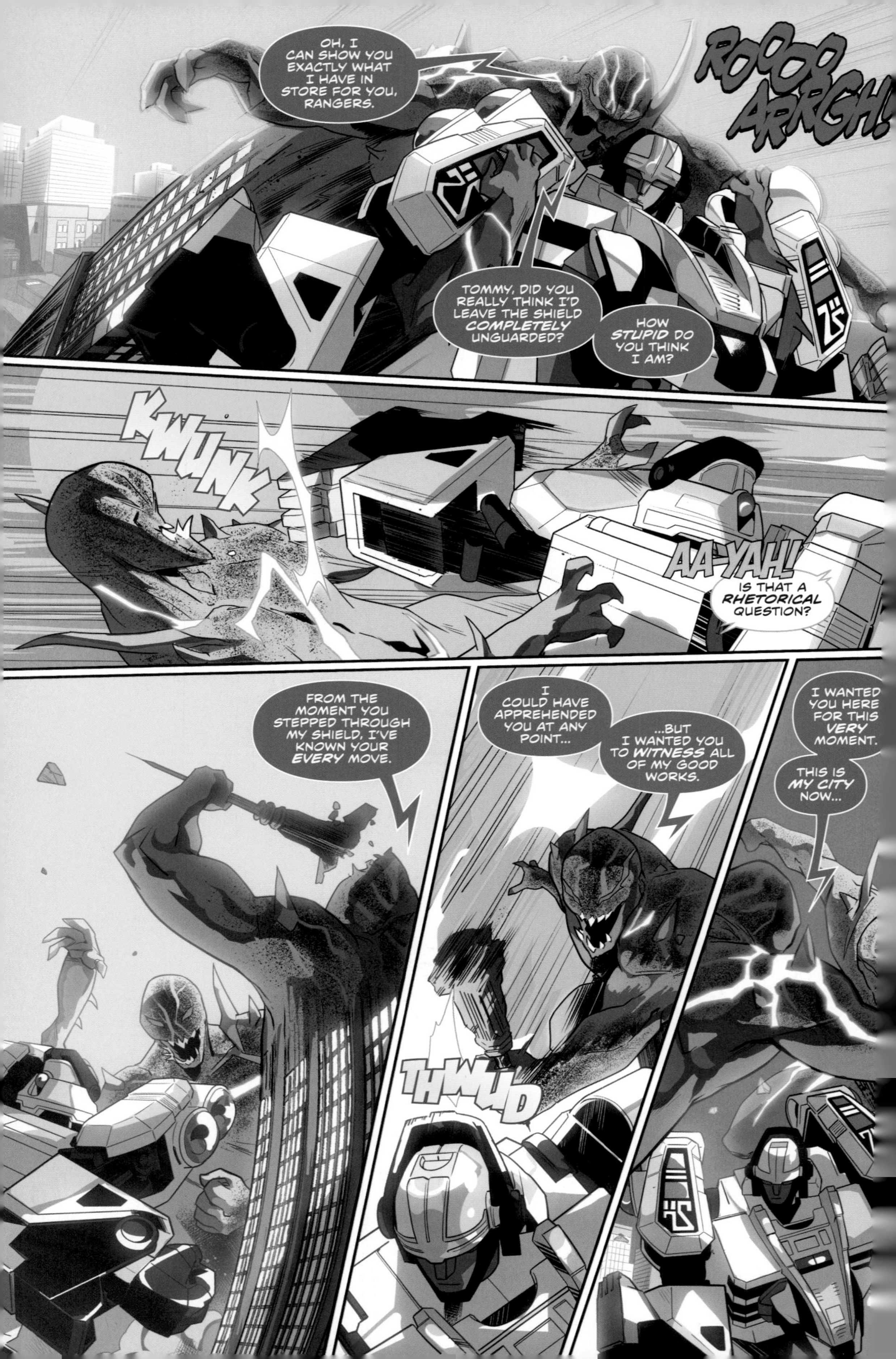
ROOOO ARRGH!
OH, I CAN SHOW YOU EXACTLY WHAT I HAVE IN STORE FOR YOU, RANGERS.
TOMMY, DID YOU REALLY THINK I'D LEAVE THE SHIELD COMPLETELY UNGUARDED?
HOW STUPID DO YOU THINK I AM?
KWUNK
AA YAH!
IS THAT A RHETORICAL QUESTION?
FROM THE MOMENT YOU STEPPED THROUGH MY SHIELD, I'VE KNOWN YOUR EVERY MOVE.
I COULD HAVE APPREHENDED YOU AT ANY POINT...
...BUT I WANTED YOU TO WITNESS ALL OF MY GOOD WORKS.
THWUD
I WANTED YOU HERE FOR THIS VERY MOMENT.
THIS IS MY CITY NOW...

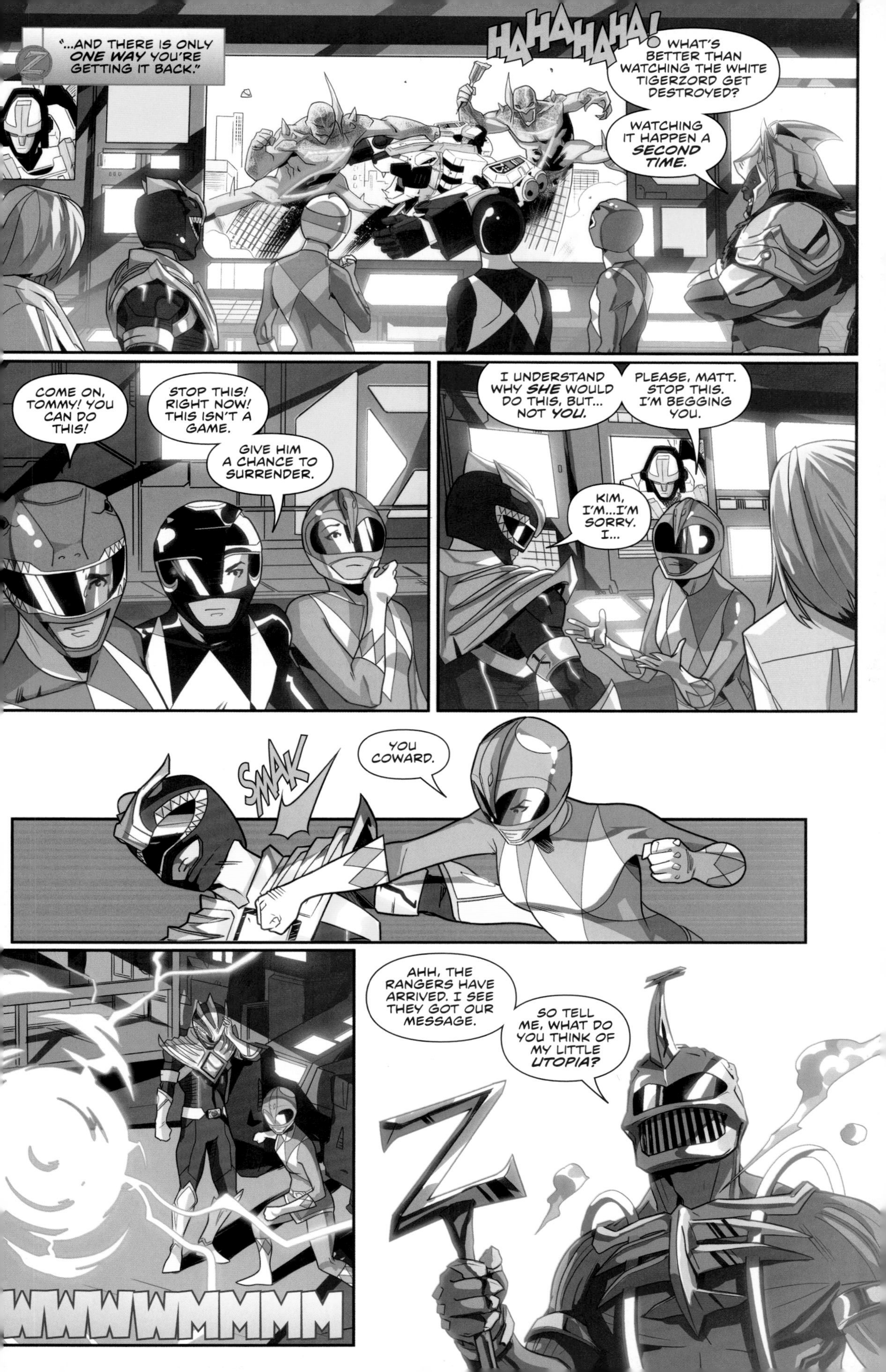

"...AND THERE IS ONLY ONE WAY YOU'RE GETTING IT BACK."
HAHAHAHA!
WHAT'S BETTER THAN WATCHING THE WHITE TIGERZORD GET DESTROYED?
WATCHING IT HAPPEN A SECOND TIME.
COME ON, TOMMY! YOU CAN DO THIS!
STOP THIS! RIGHT NOW! THIS ISN'T A GAME.
GIVE HIM A CHANCE TO SURRENDER.
I UNDERSTAND WHY SHE WOULD DO THIS, BUT... NOT YOU.
PLEASE, MATT. STOP THIS. I'M BEGGING YOU.
KIM, I'M...I'M SORRY. I...
SMAK
YOU COWARD.
WWWWMMMMM
AHH, THE RANGERS HAVE ARRIVED. I SEE THEY GOT OUR MESSAGE.
SO TELL ME, WHAT DO YOU THINK OF MY LITTLE UTOPIA?

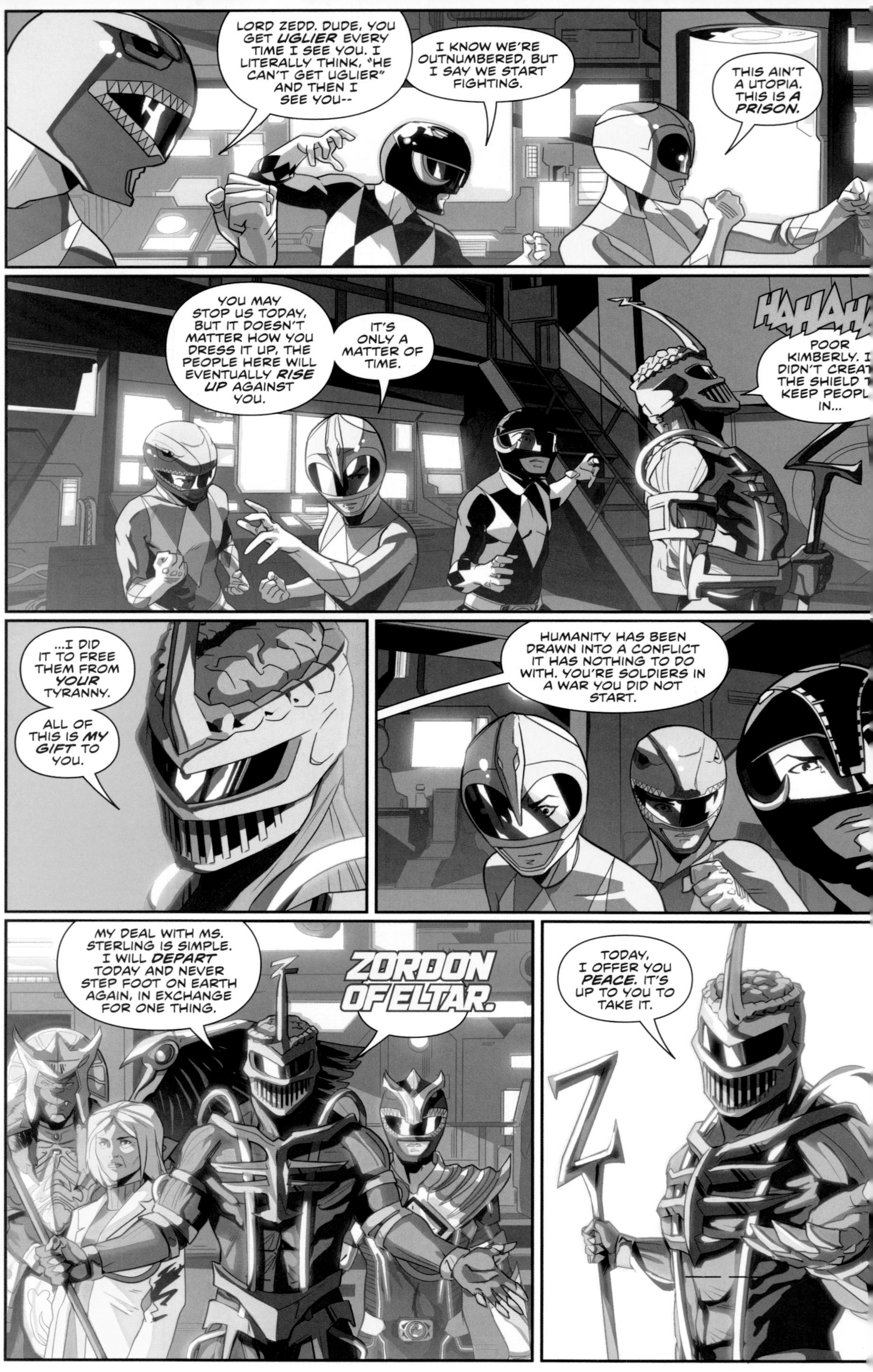

LORD ZEDD. DUDE, YOU GET UGLIER EVERY TIME I SEE YOU. I LITERALLY THINK, "HE CAN'T GET UGLIER" AND THEN I SEE YOU--
I KNOW WE'RE OUTNUMBERED, BUT I SAY WE START FIGHTING.
THIS AIN'T A UTOPIA. THIS IS A PRISON.
YOU MAY STOP US TODAY, BUT IT DOESN'T MATTER HOW YOU DRESS IT UP, THE PEOPLE HERE WILL EVENTUALLY RISE UP AGAINST YOU.
IT'S ONLY A MATTER OF TIME.
HAHAH
POOR KIMBERLY. I DIDN'T CREAT THE SHIELD T KEEP PEOPL IN...
...I DID IT TO FREE THEM FROM YOUR TYRANNY.
ALL OF THIS IS MY GIFT TO YOU.
HUMANITY HAS BEEN DRAWN INTO A CONFLICT IT HAS NOTHING TO DO WITH. YOU'RE SOLDIERS IN A WAR YOU DID NOT START.
MY DEAL WITH MS. STERLING IS SIMPLE. I WILL DEPART TODAY AND NEVER STEP FOOT ON EARTH AGAIN, IN EXCHANGE FOR ONE THING.
ZORDON OF ELTAR.
TODAY, I OFFER YOU PEACE. IT'S UP TO YOU TO TAKE IT.

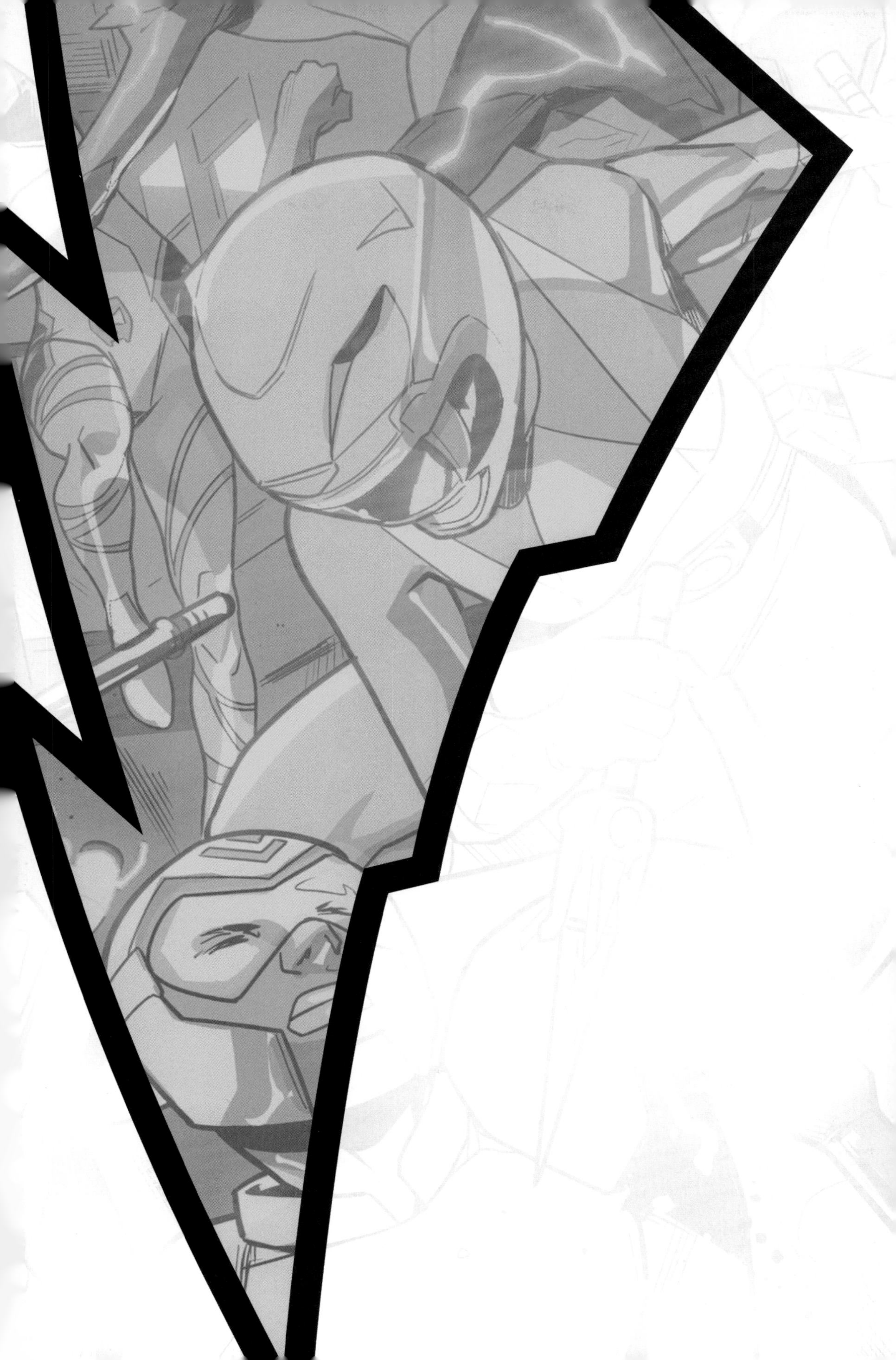

CHAPTER EIGHT

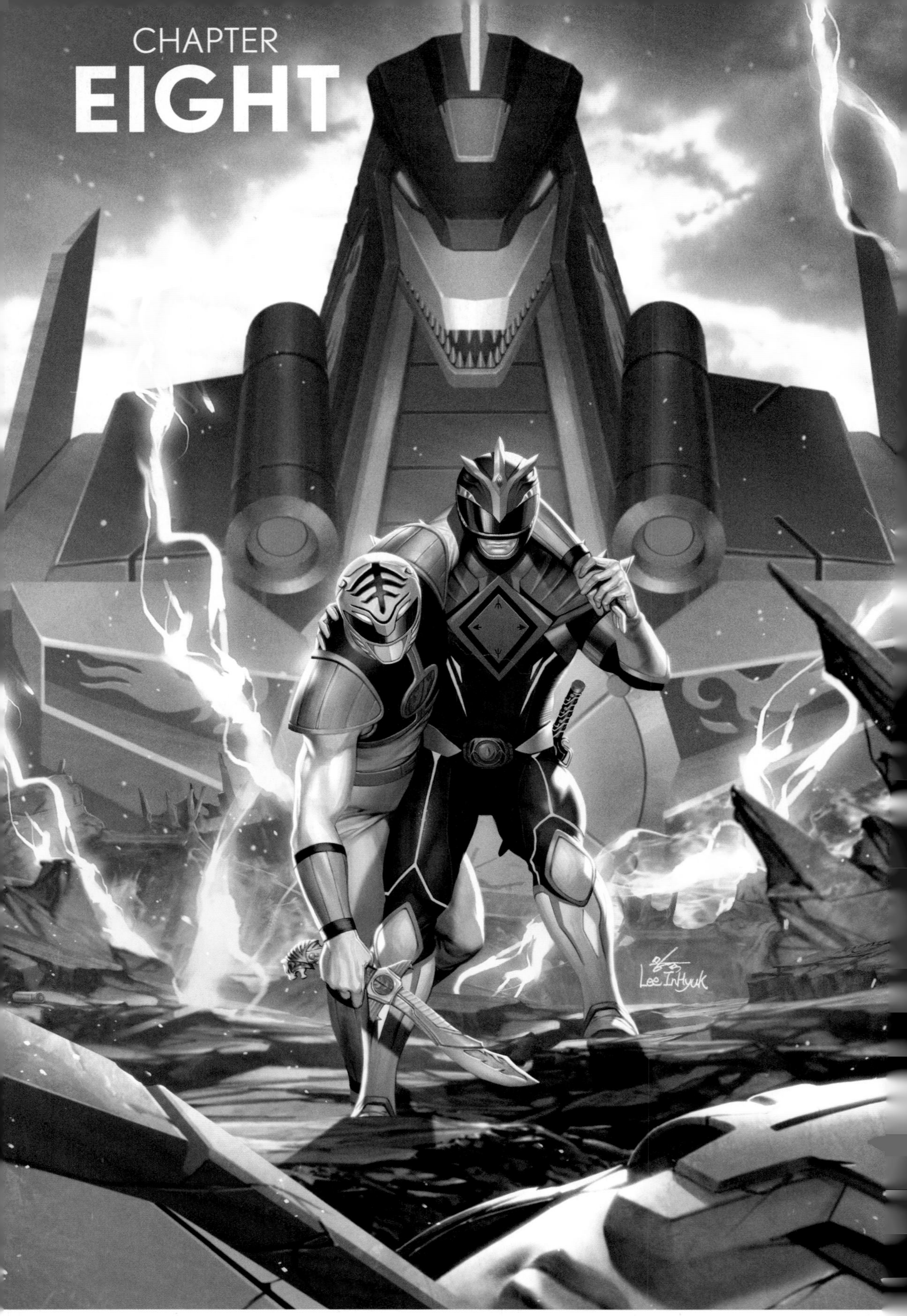
Lee InHyuk

INHYUK LEE ISSUE EIGHT COVER

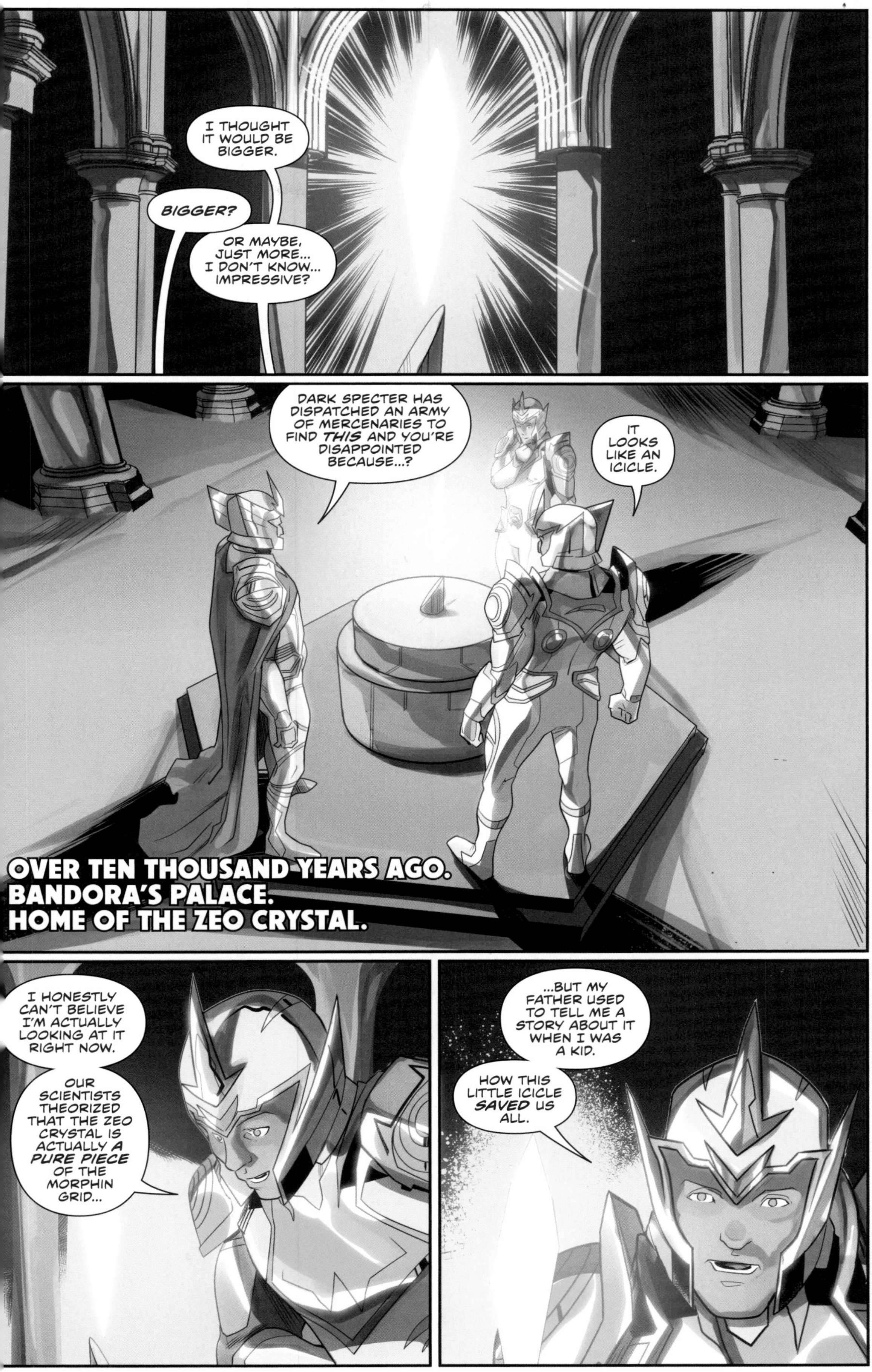
I THOUGHT IT WOULD BE BIGGER.
BIGGER?
OR MAYBE, JUST MORE... I DON'T KNOW... IMPRESSIVE?
DARK SPECTER HAS DISPATCHED AN ARMY OF MERCENARIES TO FIND THIS AND YOU'RE DISAPPOINTED BECAUSE...?
IT LOOKS LIKE AN ICICLE.
OVER TEN THOUSAND YEARS AGO.
BANDORA'S PALACE.
HOME OF THE ZEO CRYSTAL.
I HONESTLY CAN'T BELIEVE I'M ACTUALLY LOOKING AT IT RIGHT NOW.
OUR SCIENTISTS THEORIZED THAT THE ZEO CRYSTAL IS ACTUALLY A PURE PIECE OF THE MORPHIN GRID...
...BUT MY FATHER USED TO TELL ME A STORY ABOUT IT WHEN I WAS A KID.
HOW THIS LITTLE ICICLE SAVED US ALL.

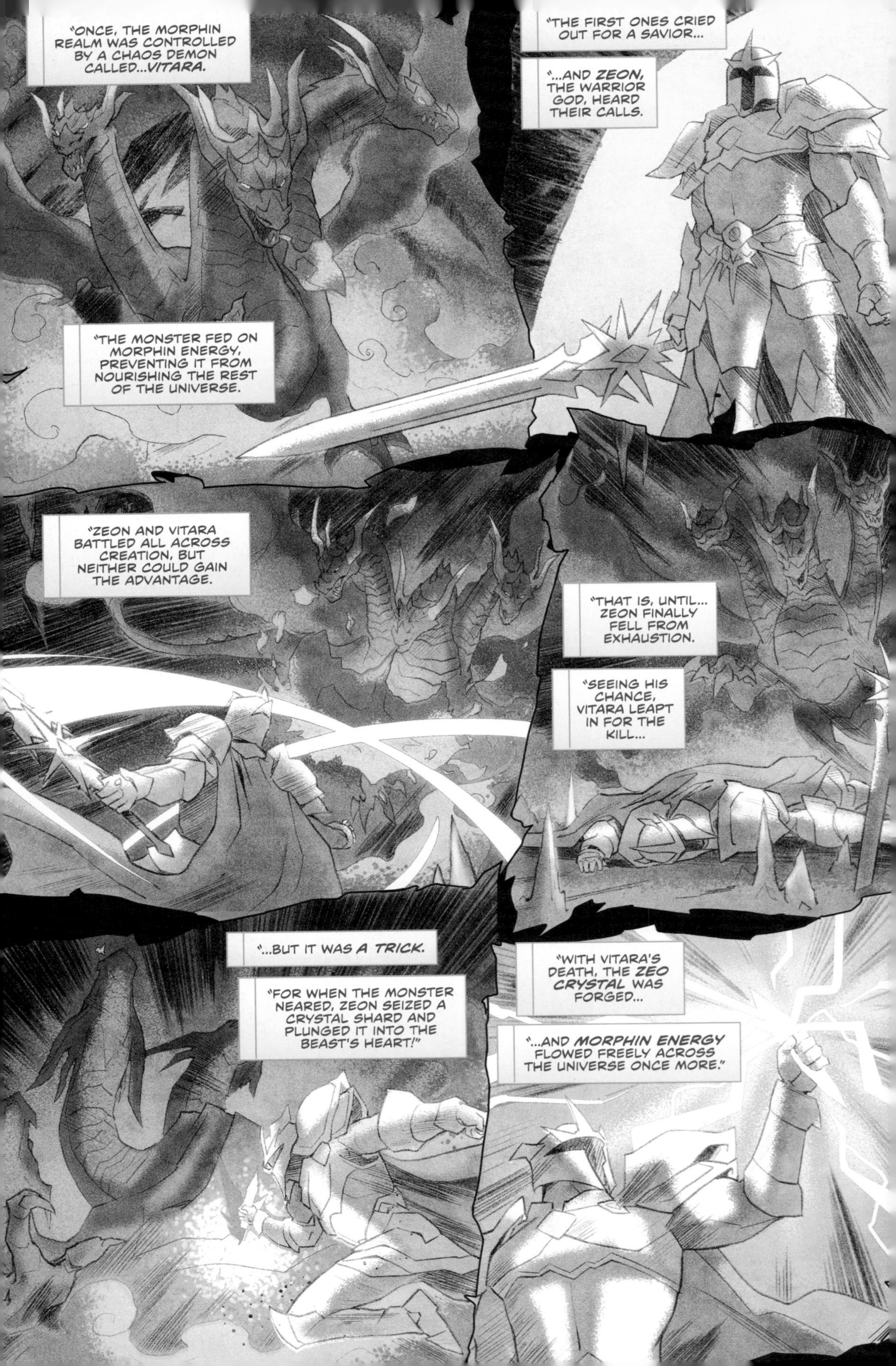
"ONCE, THE MORPHIN REALM WAS CONTROLLED BY A CHAOS DEMON CALLED...VITARA.
"THE MONSTER FED ON MORPHIN ENERGY, PREVENTING IT FROM NOURISHING THE REST OF THE UNIVERSE.
"THE FIRST ONES CRIED OUT FOR A SAVIOR...
"...AND ZEON, THE WARRIOR GOD, HEARD THEIR CALLS.
"ZEON AND VITARA BATTLED ALL ACROSS CREATION, BUT NEITHER COULD GAIN THE ADVANTAGE.
"THAT IS, UNTIL... ZEON FINALLY FELL FROM EXHAUSTION.
"SEEING HIS CHANCE, VITARA LEAPT IN FOR THE KILL...
"...BUT IT WAS A TRICK.
"FOR WHEN THE MONSTER NEARED, ZEON SEIZED A CRYSTAL SHARD AND PLUNGED IT INTO THE BEAST'S HEART!"
"WITH VITARA'S DEATH, THE ZEO CRYSTAL WAS FORGED...
"...AND MORPHIN ENERGY FLOWED FREELY ACROSS THE UNIVERSE ONCE MORE."

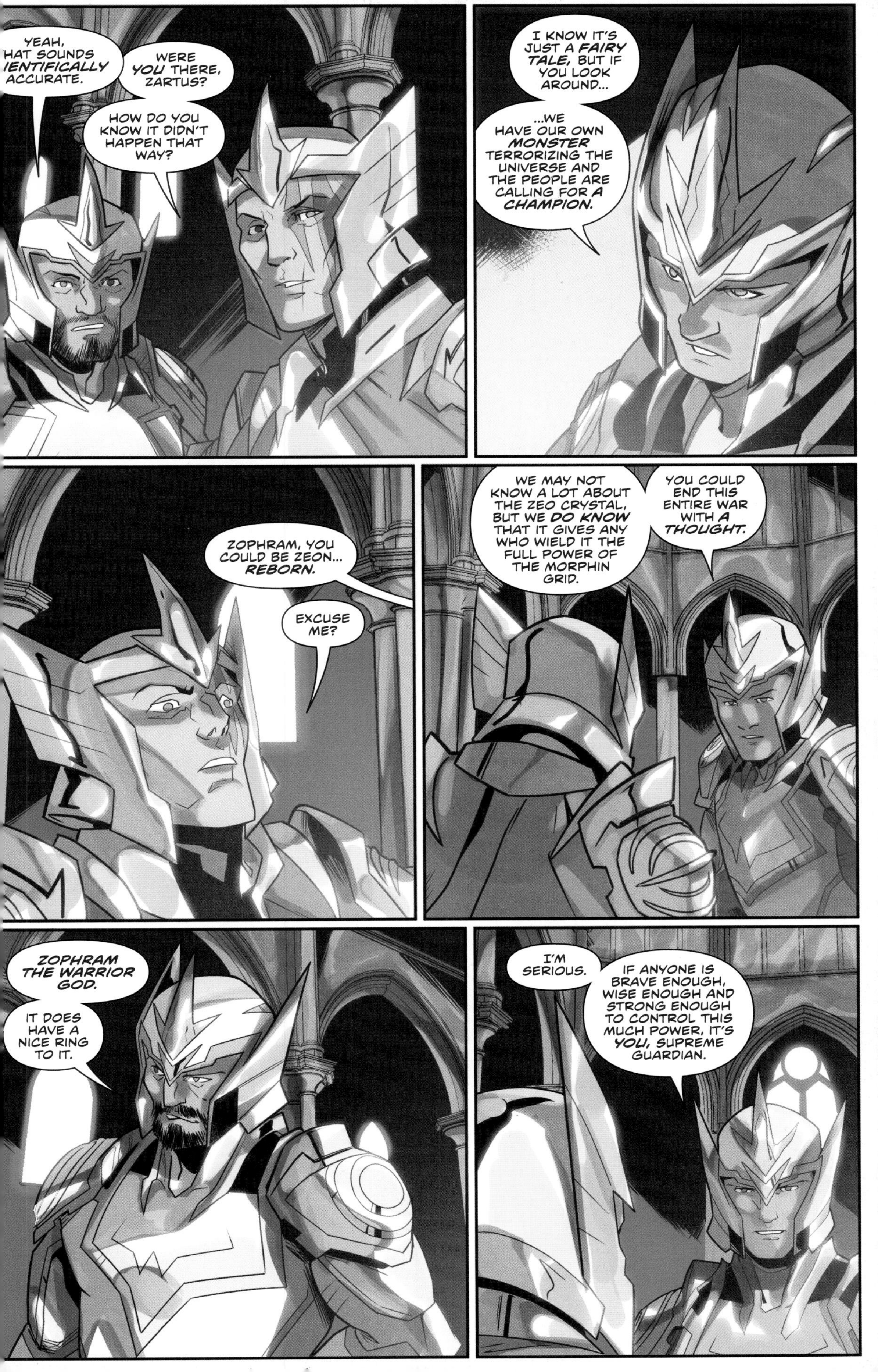
YEAH, HAT SOUNDS IENTIFICALLY ACCURATE.
WERE YOU THERE, ZARTUS?
HOW DO YOU KNOW IT DIDN'T HAPPEN THAT WAY?
I KNOW IT'S JUST A FAIRY TALE, BUT IF YOU LOOK AROUND...
...WE HAVE OUR OWN MONSTER TERRORIZING THE UNIVERSE AND THE PEOPLE ARE CALLING FOR A CHAMPION.
ZOPHRAM, YOU COULD BE ZEON... REBORN.
EXCUSE ME?
WE MAY NOT KNOW A LOT ABOUT THE ZEO CRYSTAL, BUT WE DO KNOW THAT IT GIVES ANY WHO WIELD IT THE FULL POWER OF THE MORPHIN GRID.
YOU COULD END THIS ENTIRE WAR WITH A THOUGHT.
ZOPHRAM THE WARRIOR GOD.
IT DOES HAVE A NICE RING TO IT.
I'M SERIOUS.
IF ANYONE IS BRAVE ENOUGH, WISE ENOUGH AND STRONG ENOUGH TO CONTROL THIS MUCH POWER, IT'S YOU, SUPREME GUARDIAN.

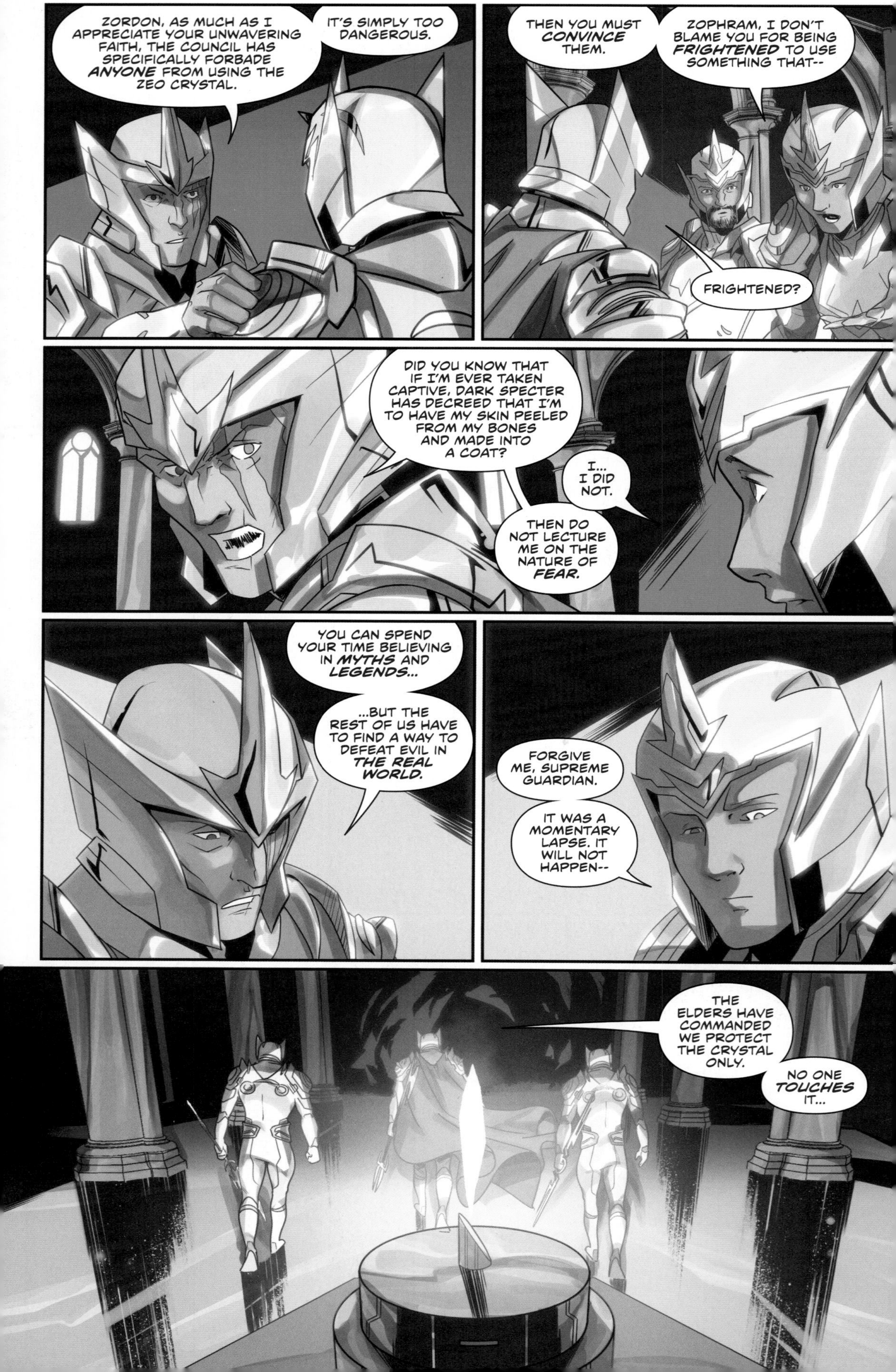
ZORDON, AS MUCH AS I APPRECIATE YOUR UNWAVERING FAITH, THE COUNCIL HAS SPECIFICALLY FORBADE ANYONE FROM USING THE ZEO CRYSTAL.
IT'S SIMPLY TOO DANGEROUS.
THEN YOU MUST CONVINCE THEM.
ZOPHRAM, I DON'T BLAME YOU FOR BEING FRIGHTENED TO USE SOMETHING THAT--
FRIGHTENED?
DID YOU KNOW THAT IF I'M EVER TAKEN CAPTIVE, DARK SPECTER HAS DECREED THAT I'M TO HAVE MY SKIN PEELED FROM MY BONES AND MADE INTO A COAT?
I... I DID NOT.
THEN DO NOT LECTURE ME ON THE NATURE OF FEAR.
YOU CAN SPEND YOUR TIME BELIEVING IN MYTHS AND LEGENDS...
...BUT THE REST OF US HAVE TO FIND A WAY TO DEFEAT EVIL IN THE REAL WORLD.
FORGIVE ME, SUPREME GUARDIAN.
IT WAS A MOMENTARY LAPSE. IT WILL NOT HAPPEN--
THE ELDERS HAVE COMMANDED WE PROTECT THE CRYSTAL ONLY.
NO ONE TOUCHES IT...

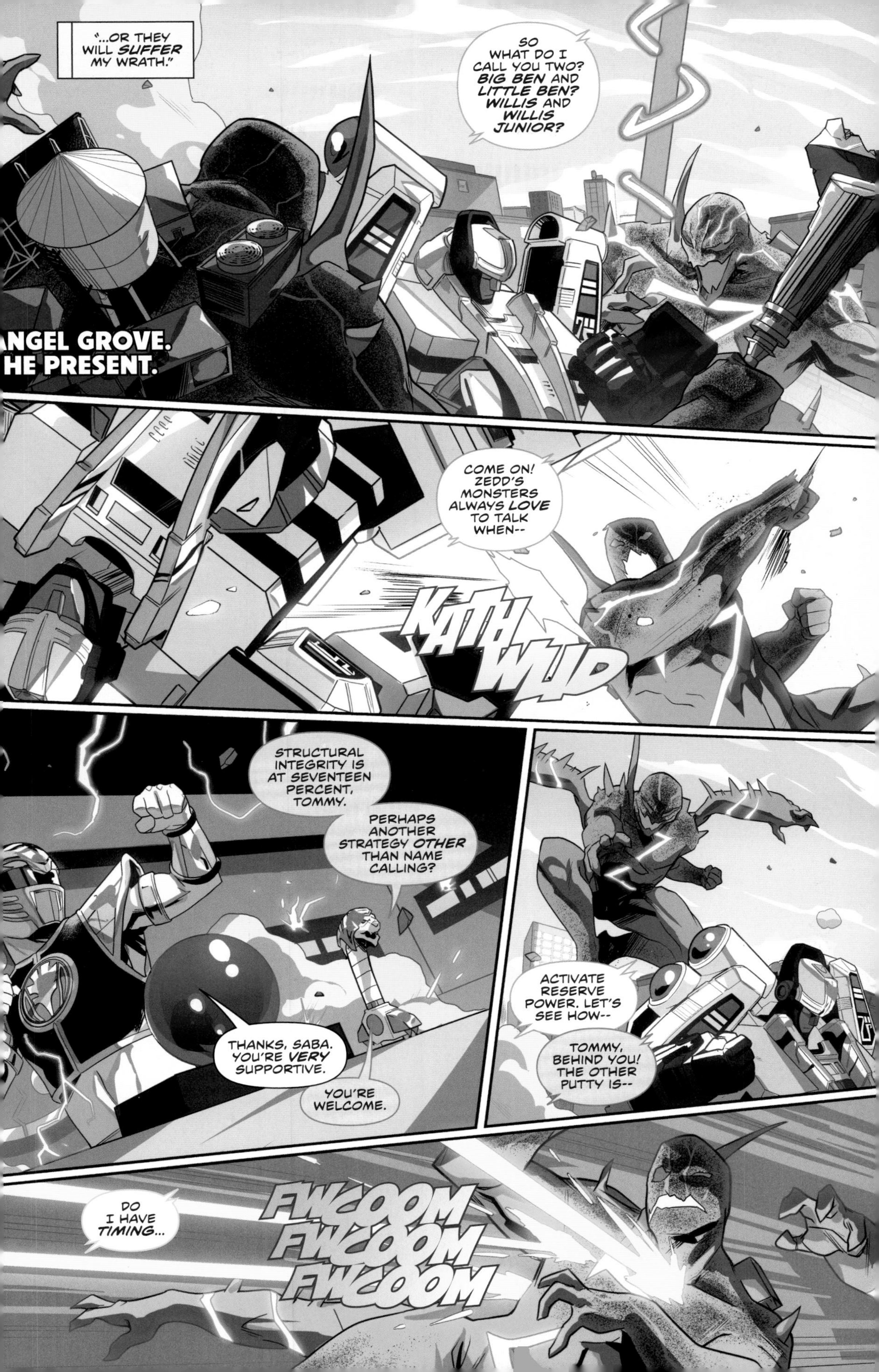
"...OR THEY WILL SUFFER MY WRATH."
SO WHAT DO I CALL YOU TWO? BIG BEN AND LITTLE BEN? WILLIS AND WILLIS JUNIOR?
NGEL GROVE.
HE PRESENT.
COME ON! ZEDD'S MONSTERS ALWAYS LOVE TO TALK WHEN--
KATHWUD
STRUCTURAL INTEGRITY IS AT SEVENTEEN PERCENT, TOMMY.
PERHAPS ANOTHER STRATEGY OTHER THAN NAME CALLING?
THANKS, SABA. YOU'RE VERY SUPPORTIVE.
YOU'RE WELCOME.
ACTIVATE RESERVE POWER. LET'S SEE HOW--
TOMMY, BEHIND YOU! THE OTHER PUTTY IS--
DO I HAVE TIMING...
FWCOOM
FWCOOM
FWCOOM

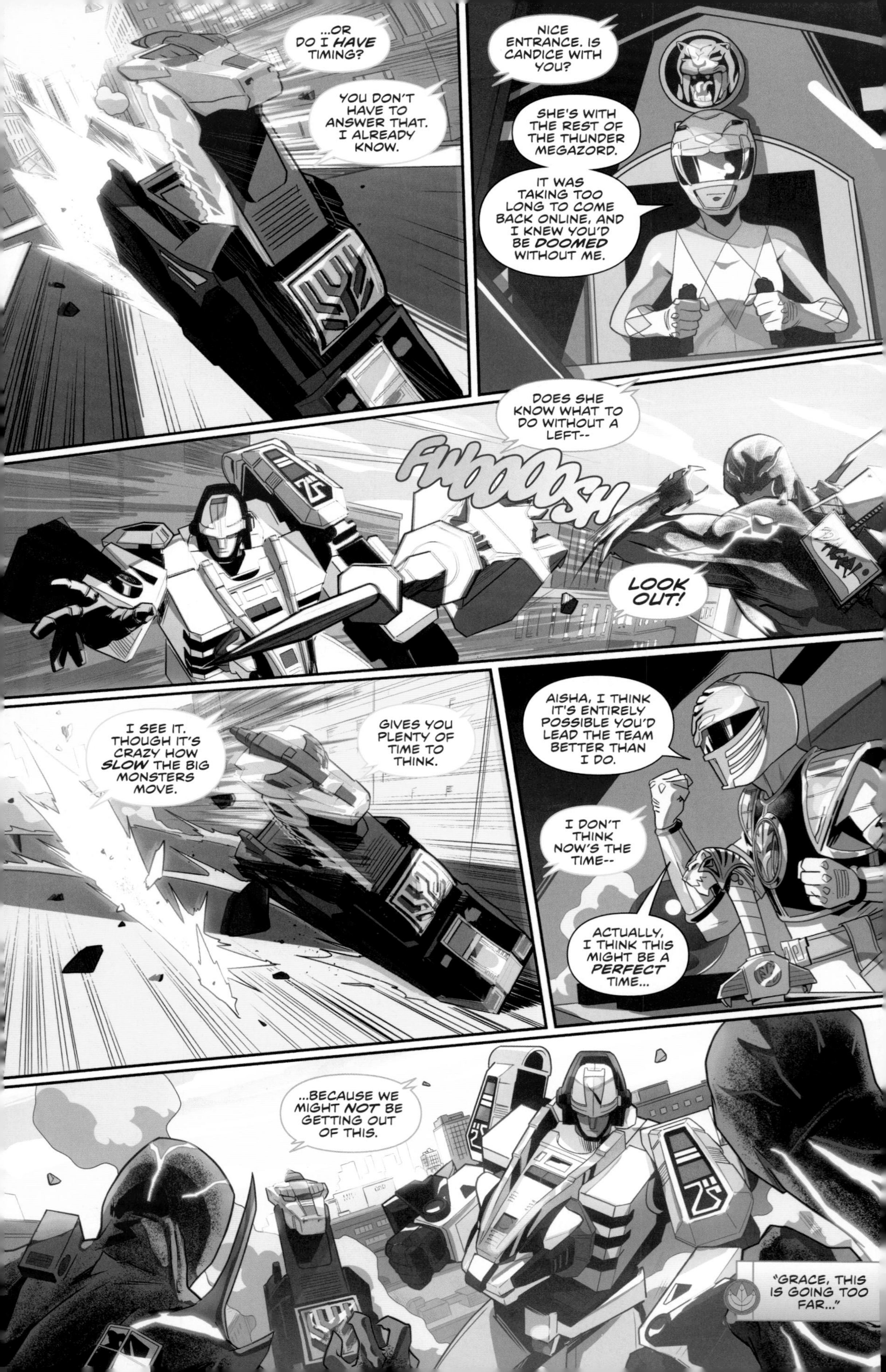
...OR DO I HAVE TIMING?
YOU DON'T HAVE TO ANSWER THAT. I ALREADY KNOW.
NICE ENTRANCE. IS CANDICE WITH YOU?
SHE'S WITH THE REST OF THE THUNDER MEGAZORD.
IT WAS TAKING TOO LONG TO COME BACK ONLINE, AND I KNEW YOU'D BE DOOMED WITHOUT ME.
DOES SHE KNOW WHAT TO DO WITHOUT A LEFT--
FWOOOOSH
LOOK OUT!
I SEE IT. THOUGH IT'S CRAZY HOW SLOW THE BIG MONSTERS MOVE.
GIVES YOU PLENTY OF TIME TO THINK.
AISHA, I THINK IT'S ENTIRELY POSSIBLE YOU'D LEAD THE TEAM BETTER THAN I DO.
I DON'T THINK NOW'S THE TIME--
ACTUALLY, I THINK THIS MIGHT BE A PERFECT TIME...
...BECAUSE WE MIGHT NOT BE GETTING OUT OF THIS.
"GRACE, THIS IS GOING TOO FAR..."

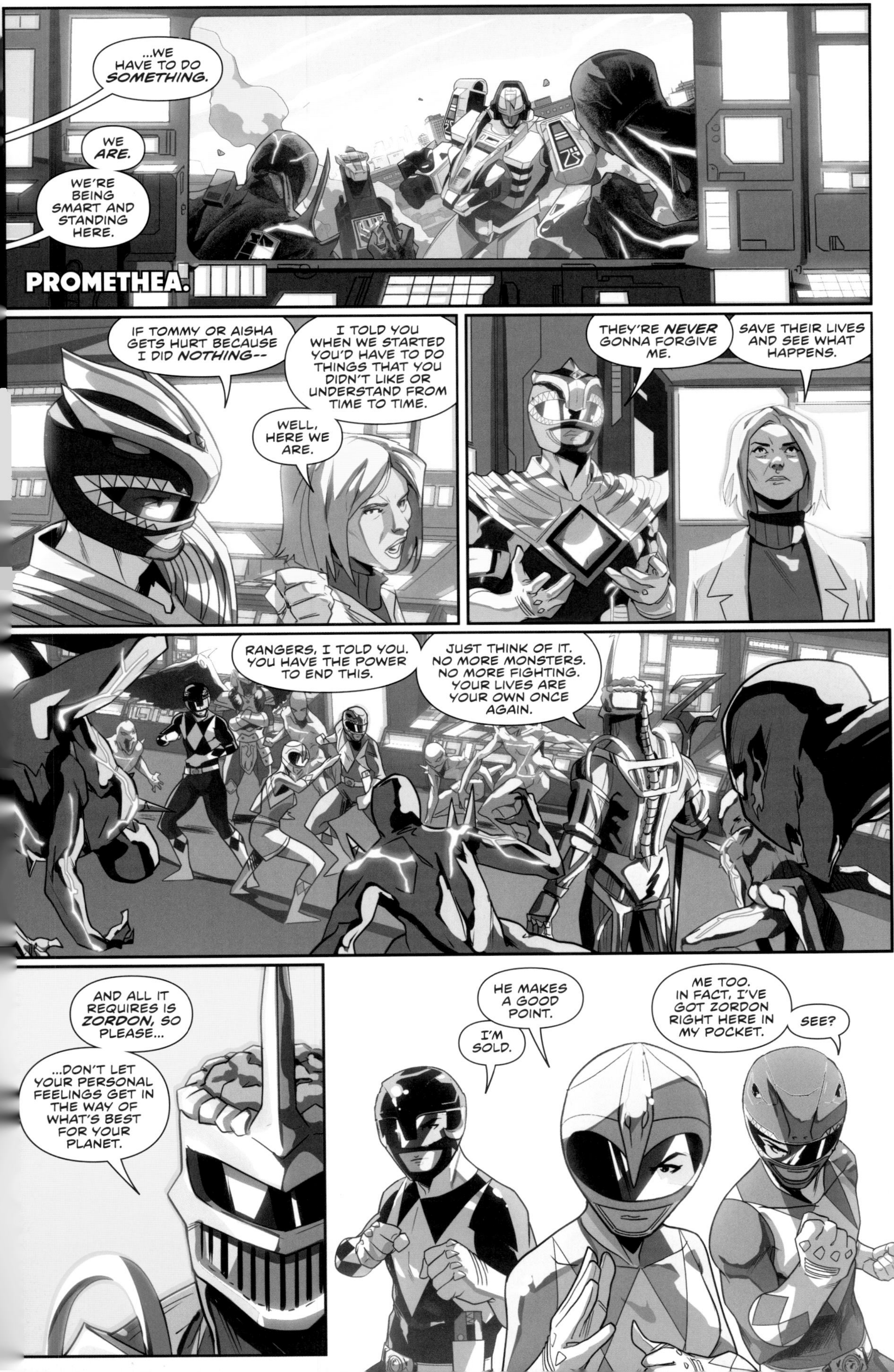
...WE HAVE TO DO *SOMETHING.*
WE *ARE.*
WE'RE BEING SMART AND STANDING HERE.
PROMETHEA.
IF TOMMY OR AISHA GETS HURT BECAUSE I DID *NOTHING*--
I TOLD YOU WHEN WE STARTED YOU'D HAVE TO DO THINGS THAT YOU DIDN'T LIKE OR UNDERSTAND FROM TIME TO TIME.
WELL, HERE WE ARE.
THEY'RE *NEVER* GONNA FORGIVE ME.
SAVE THEIR LIVES AND SEE WHAT HAPPENS.
RANGERS, I TOLD YOU. YOU HAVE THE POWER TO END THIS.
JUST THINK OF IT. NO MORE MONSTERS. NO MORE FIGHTING. YOUR LIVES ARE YOUR OWN ONCE AGAIN.
AND ALL IT REQUIRES IS *ZORDON,* SO PLEASE...
...DON'T LET YOUR PERSONAL FEELINGS GET IN THE WAY OF WHAT'S BEST FOR YOUR PLANET.
I'M SOLD.
HE MAKES A GOOD POINT.
ME TOO. IN FACT, I'VE GOT ZORDON RIGHT HERE IN MY POCKET.
SEE?

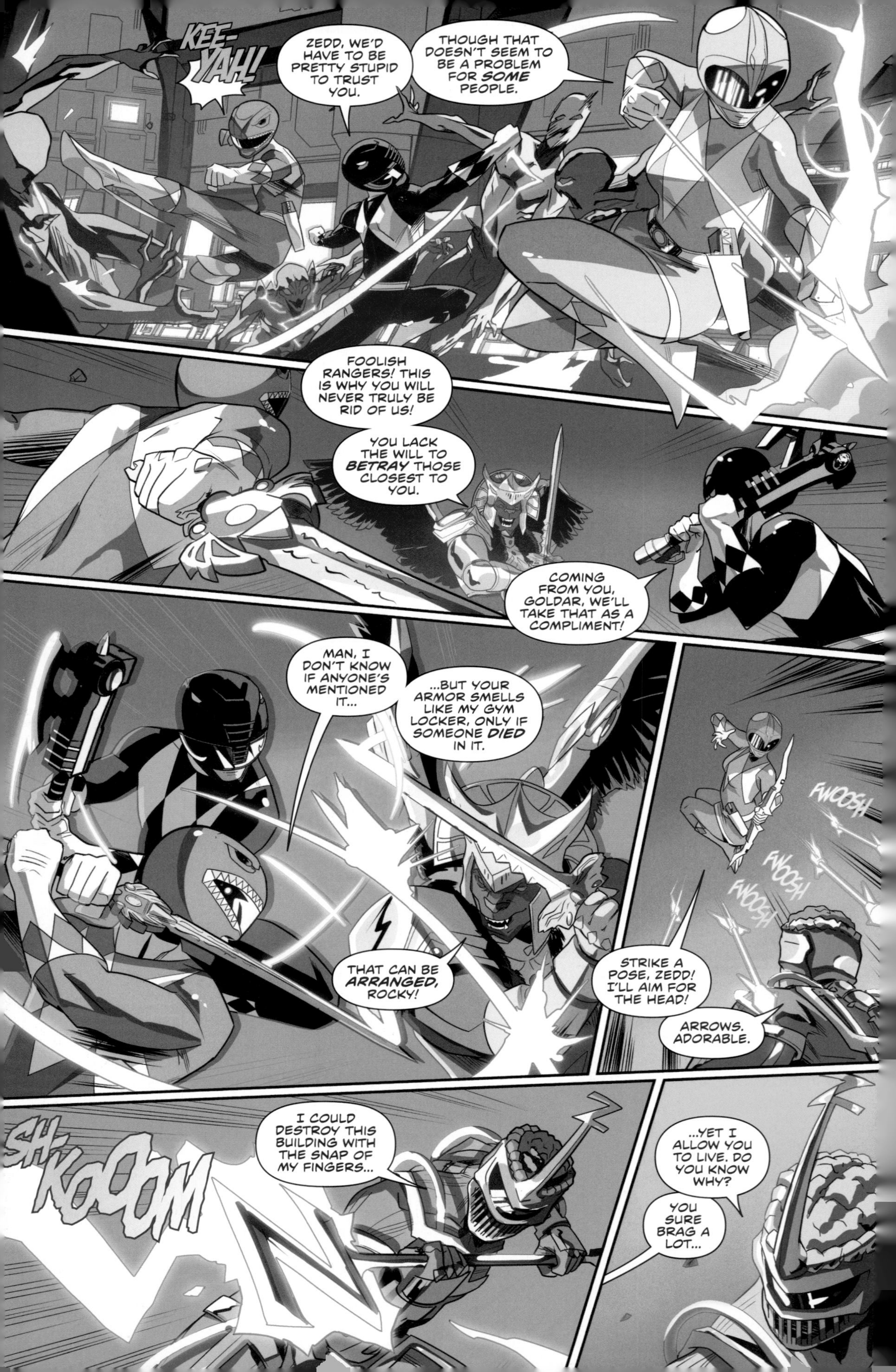
KEE-YAH!
ZEDD, WE'D HAVE TO BE PRETTY STUPID TO TRUST YOU.
THOUGH THAT DOESN'T SEEM TO BE A PROBLEM FOR SOME PEOPLE.
FOOLISH RANGERS! THIS IS WHY YOU WILL NEVER TRULY BE RID OF US!
YOU LACK THE WILL TO BETRAY THOSE CLOSEST TO YOU.
COMING FROM YOU, GOLDAR, WE'LL TAKE THAT AS A COMPLIMENT!
MAN, I DON'T KNOW IF ANYONE'S MENTIONED IT...
...BUT YOUR ARMOR SMELLS LIKE MY GYM LOCKER, ONLY IF SOMEONE DIED IN IT.
THAT CAN BE ARRANGED, ROCKY!
FWOOSH
FWOOSH
FWOOSH
STRIKE A POSE, ZEDD! I'LL AIM FOR THE HEAD!
ARROWS. ADORABLE.
SH-KOOOM
I COULD DESTROY THIS BUILDING WITH THE SNAP OF MY FINGERS...
...YET I ALLOW YOU TO LIVE. DO YOU KNOW WHY?
YOU SURE BRAG A LOT...

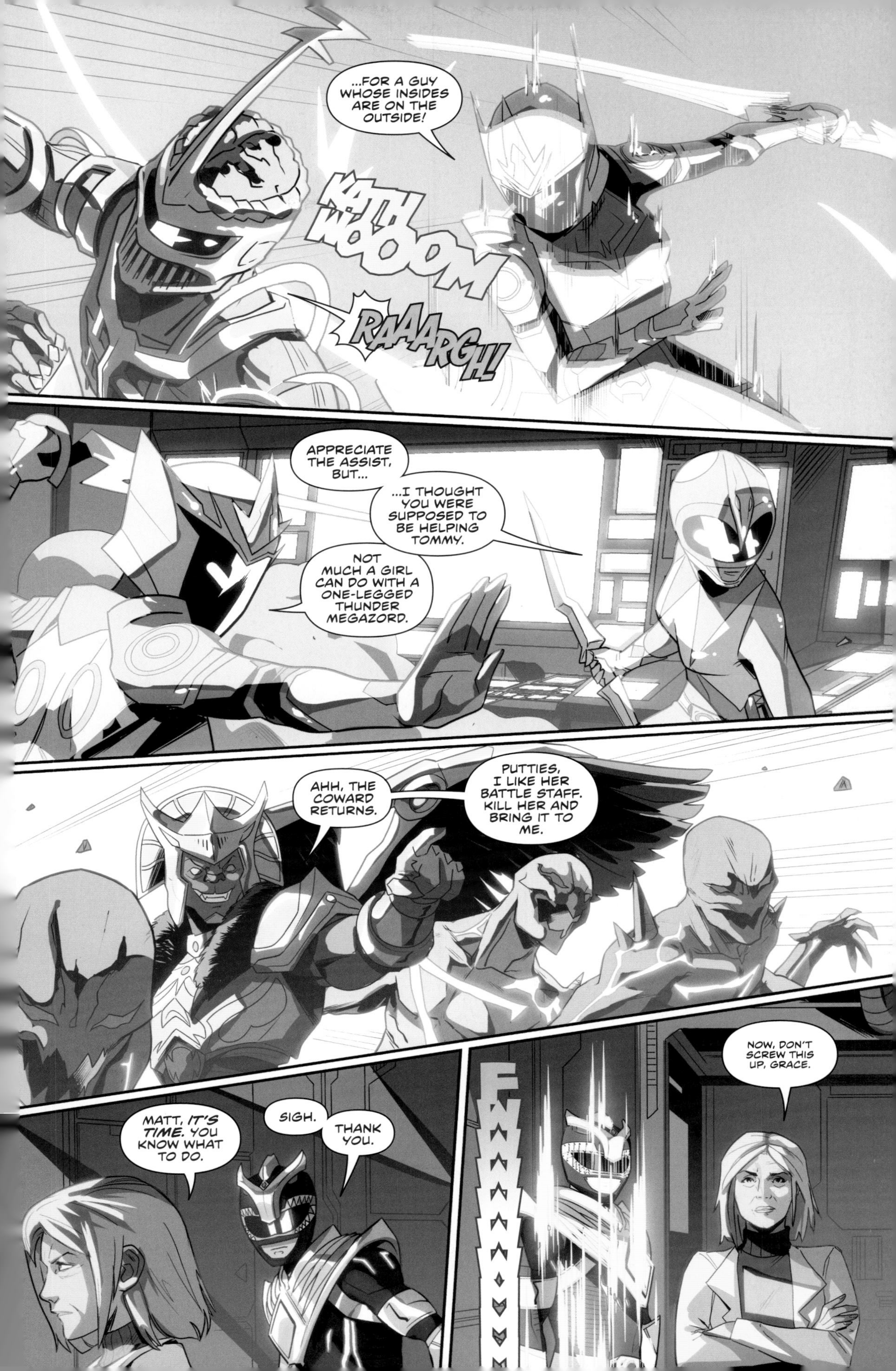
...FOR A GUY WHOSE INSIDES ARE ON THE OUTSIDE!
KATHWOOOM
RAAARGH!
APPRECIATE THE ASSIST, BUT...
...I THOUGHT YOU WERE SUPPOSED TO BE HELPING TOMMY.
NOT MUCH A GIRL CAN DO WITH A ONE-LEGGED THUNDER MEGAZORD.
AHH, THE COWARD RETURNS.
PUTTIES, I LIKE HER BATTLE STAFF. KILL HER AND BRING IT TO ME.
MATT, *IT'S TIME.* YOU KNOW WHAT TO DO.
SIGH.
THANK YOU.
NOW, DON'T SCREW THIS UP, GRACE.

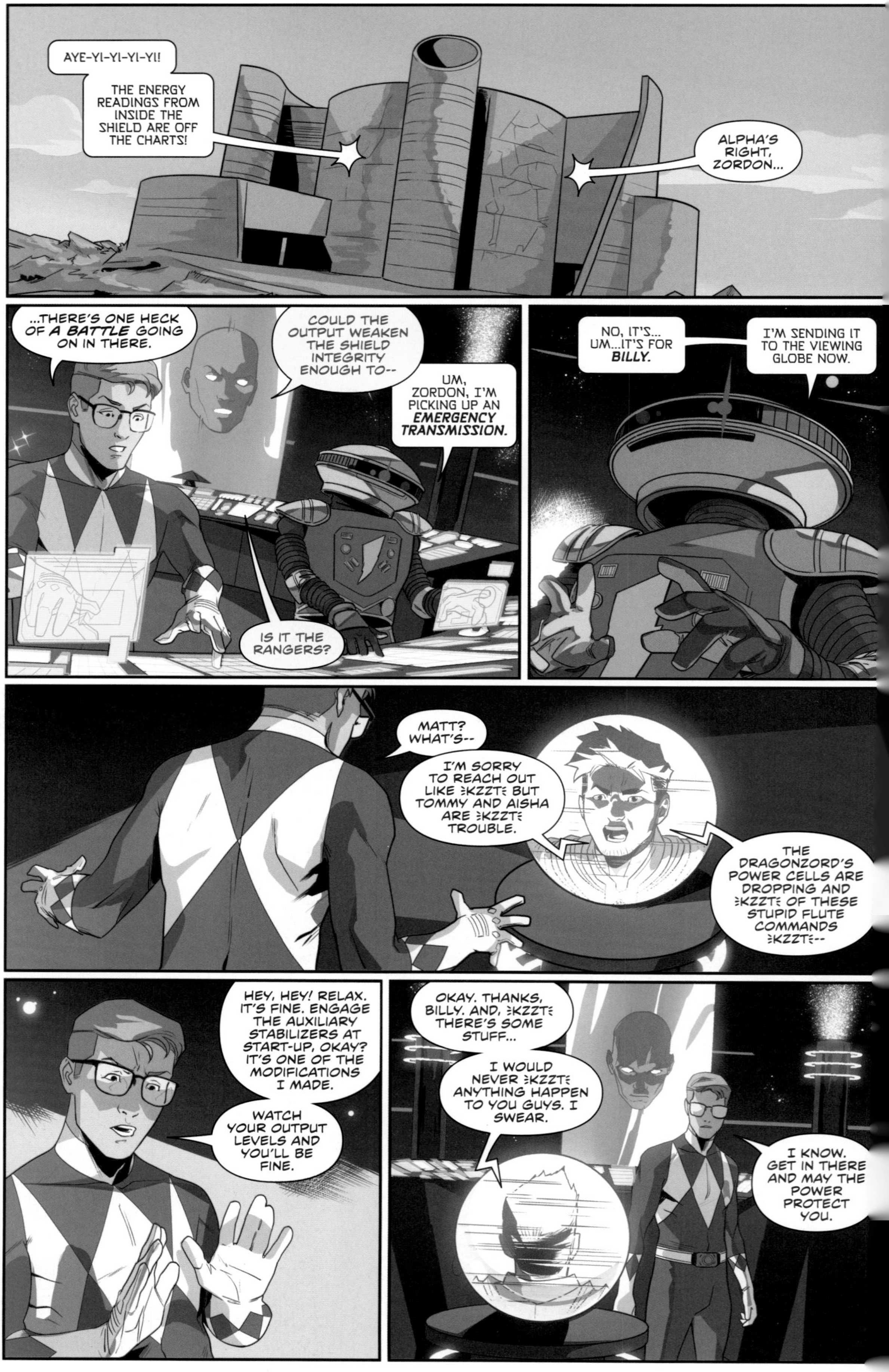
AYE-YI-YI-YI-YI!
THE ENERGY READINGS FROM INSIDE THE SHIELD ARE OFF THE CHARTS!
ALPHA'S RIGHT, ZORDON...
...THERE'S ONE HECK OF A BATTLE GOING ON IN THERE.
COULD THE OUTPUT WEAKEN THE SHIELD INTEGRITY ENOUGH TO--
UM, ZORDON, I'M PICKING UP AN EMERGENCY TRANSMISSION.
IS IT THE RANGERS?
NO, IT'S... UM...IT'S FOR BILLY.
I'M SENDING IT TO THE VIEWING GLOBE NOW.
MATT? WHAT'S--
I'M SORRY TO REACH OUT LIKE ≷KZZT≶ BUT TOMMY AND AISHA ARE ≷KZZT≶ TROUBLE.
THE DRAGONZORD'S POWER CELLS ARE DROPPING AND ≷KZZT≶ OF THESE STUPID FLUTE COMMANDS ≷KZZT≶--
HEY, HEY! RELAX. IT'S FINE. ENGAGE THE AUXILIARY STABILIZERS AT START-UP, OKAY? IT'S ONE OF THE MODIFICATIONS I MADE.
WATCH YOUR OUTPUT LEVELS AND YOU'LL BE FINE.
OKAY. THANKS, BILLY. AND, ≷KZZT≶ THERE'S SOME STUFF...
I WOULD NEVER ≷KZZT≶ ANYTHING HAPPEN TO YOU GUYS. I SWEAR.
I KNOW. GET IN THERE AND MAY THE POWER PROTECT YOU.

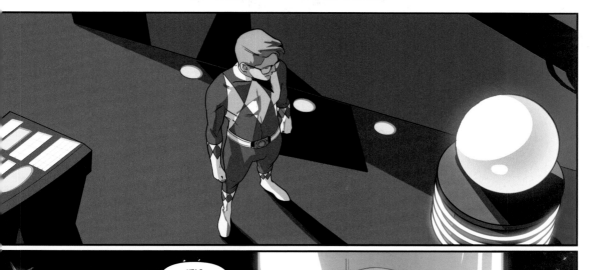

IT'S NOT WHAT IT--

YOU **STOLE** THE DRAGON POWER COIN. YOU HELPED BRING BACK THE GREEN RANGER, AND YOU'VE BEEN ASSISTING GRACE BEHIND MY BACK THIS **WHOLE TIME.**

WOULD YOU CARE TO EXPLAIN YOURSELF?

WHEN TOMMY LOST HIS POWERS, I GOT... I GOT REALLY SCARED.

I COULDN'T STOP THINKING ABOUT WHAT WOULD HAPPEN TO OUR PLANET IF WE ALL LOST THEM?

AND WHEN IT WAS CLEAR THAT YOU NOT ONLY **COULDN'T** FIX IT BUT THAT YOU WOULDN'T TRY EVERY POSSIBLE OPTION...

...I JUST, I HAD TO DO **SOMETHING.**

AND YOU DID. YOU GAVE AWAY ONE OF OUR MOST POWERFUL WEAPONS.

ZORDON, GRACE AND MATT CAN--

BILLY, YOU'VE PROVEN YOU CAN SOLVE ANY PROBLEM YOU PUT YOUR MIND TO. SO I HAVE **ONE** FOR YOU...

...AFTER MONTHS OF LIES, DECEPTION, AND BETRAYAL, HOW ARE THE RANGERS AND I **EVER** SUPPOSED TO TRUST YOU WITH ANYTHING EVER AGAIN?

BECAUSE IF YOU CAN SOLVE THAT...

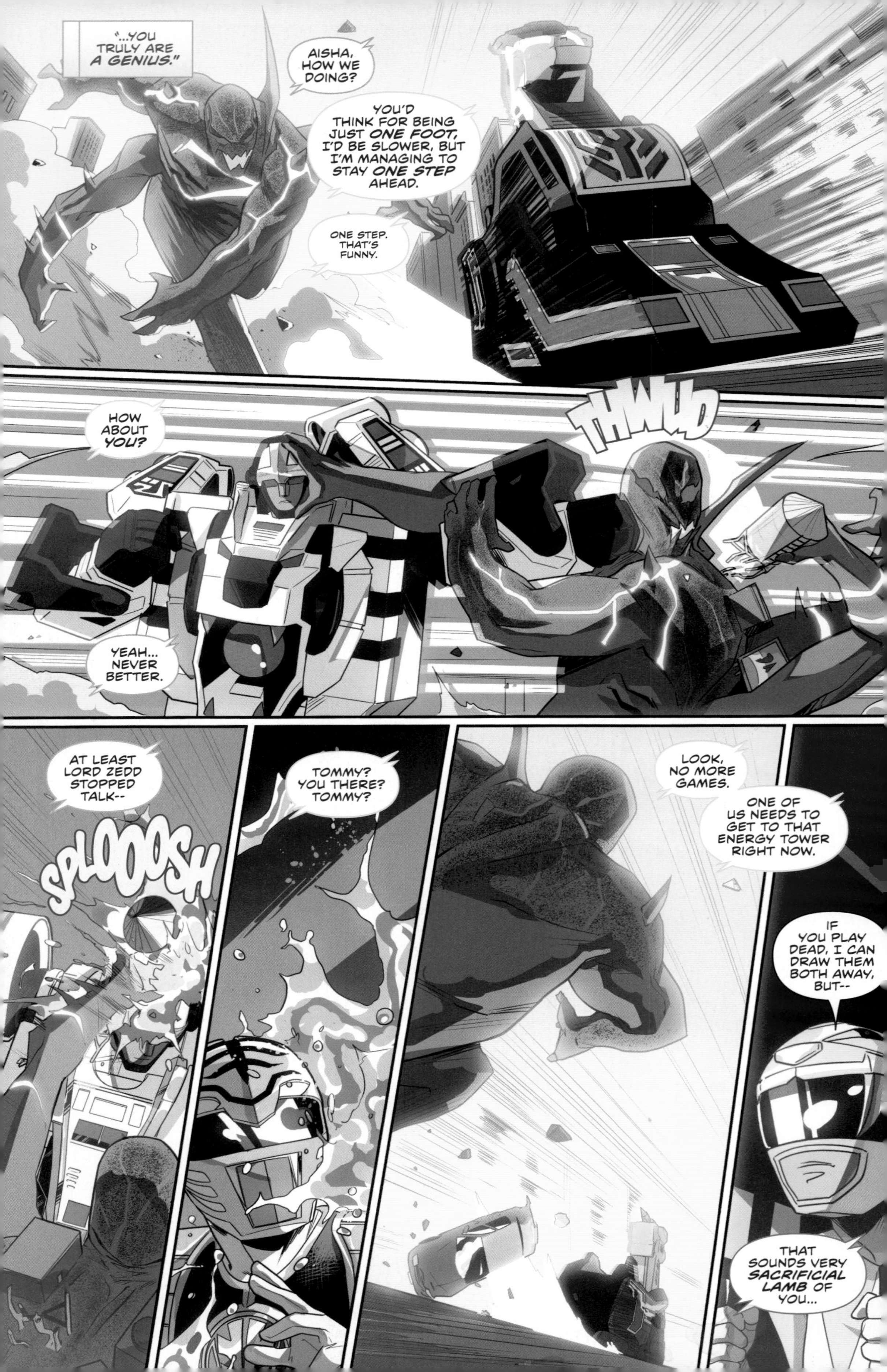
"...YOU TRULY ARE A GENIUS."
AISHA, HOW WE DOING?
YOU'D THINK FOR BEING JUST ONE FOOT, I'D BE SLOWER, BUT I'M MANAGING TO STAY ONE STEP AHEAD.
ONE STEP. THAT'S FUNNY.
HOW ABOUT YOU?
THWUD
YEAH... NEVER BETTER.
AT LEAST LORD ZEDD STOPPED TALK--
SPLOOOSH
TOMMY? YOU THERE? TOMMY?
LOOK, NO MORE GAMES.
ONE OF US NEEDS TO GET TO THAT ENERGY TOWER RIGHT NOW.
IF YOU PLAY DEAD, I CAN DRAW THEM BOTH AWAY, BUT--
THAT SOUNDS VERY SACRIFICIAL LAMB OF YOU...

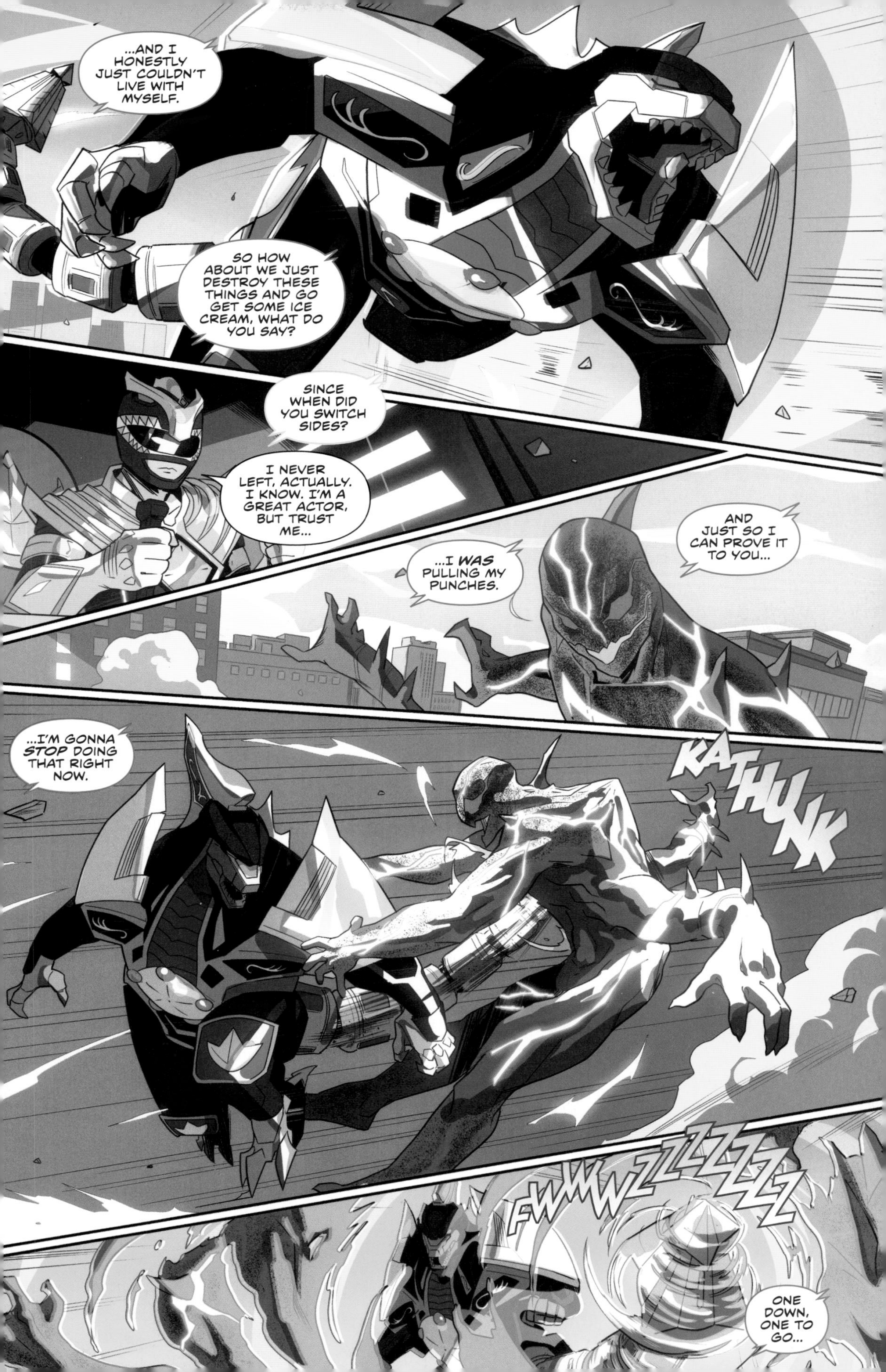
...AND I HONESTLY JUST COULDN'T LIVE WITH MYSELF.
SO HOW ABOUT WE JUST DESTROY THESE THINGS AND GO GET SOME ICE CREAM, WHAT DO YOU SAY?
SINCE WHEN DID YOU SWITCH SIDES?
I NEVER LEFT, ACTUALLY. I KNOW. I'M A GREAT ACTOR, BUT TRUST ME...
...I *WAS* PULLING MY PUNCHES.
AND JUST SO I CAN PROVE IT TO YOU...
...I'M GONNA *STOP* DOING THAT RIGHT NOW.
KATHUNK
FWWWZZZZZZZ
ONE DOWN, ONE TO GO...

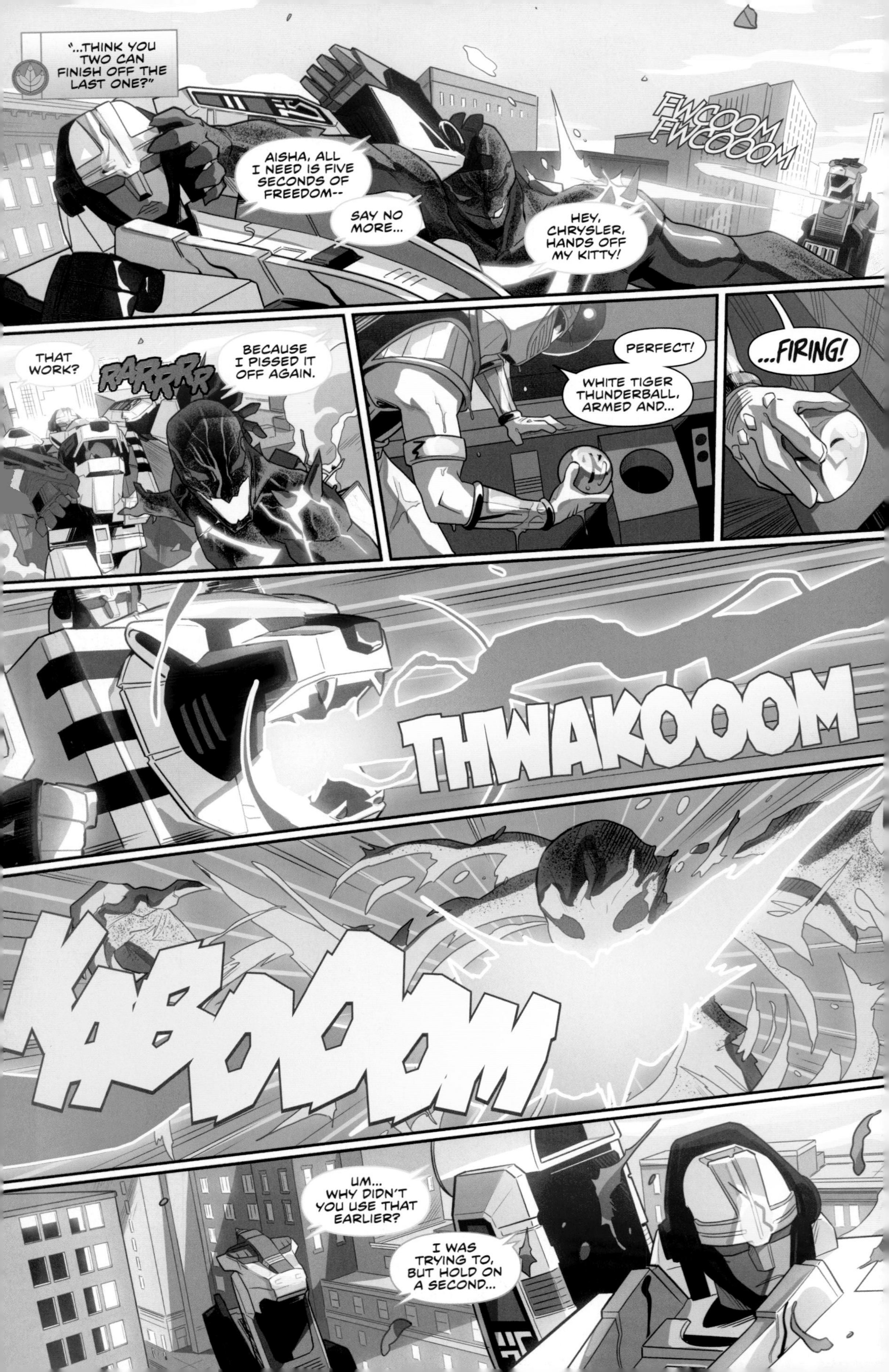
"...THINK YOU TWO CAN FINISH OFF THE LAST ONE?"
AISHA, ALL I NEED IS FIVE SECONDS OF FREEDOM--
SAY NO MORE...
HEY, CHRYSLER, HANDS OFF MY KITTY!
FWCOOM FWCOOOM
THAT WORK?
RARRRR
BECAUSE I PISSED IT OFF AGAIN.
PERFECT!
WHITE TIGER THUNDERBALL, ARMED AND...
...FIRING!
THWAKOOOM
KABOOOM
UM... WHY DIDN'T YOU USE THAT EARLIER?
I WAS TRYING TO, BUT HOLD ON A SECOND...

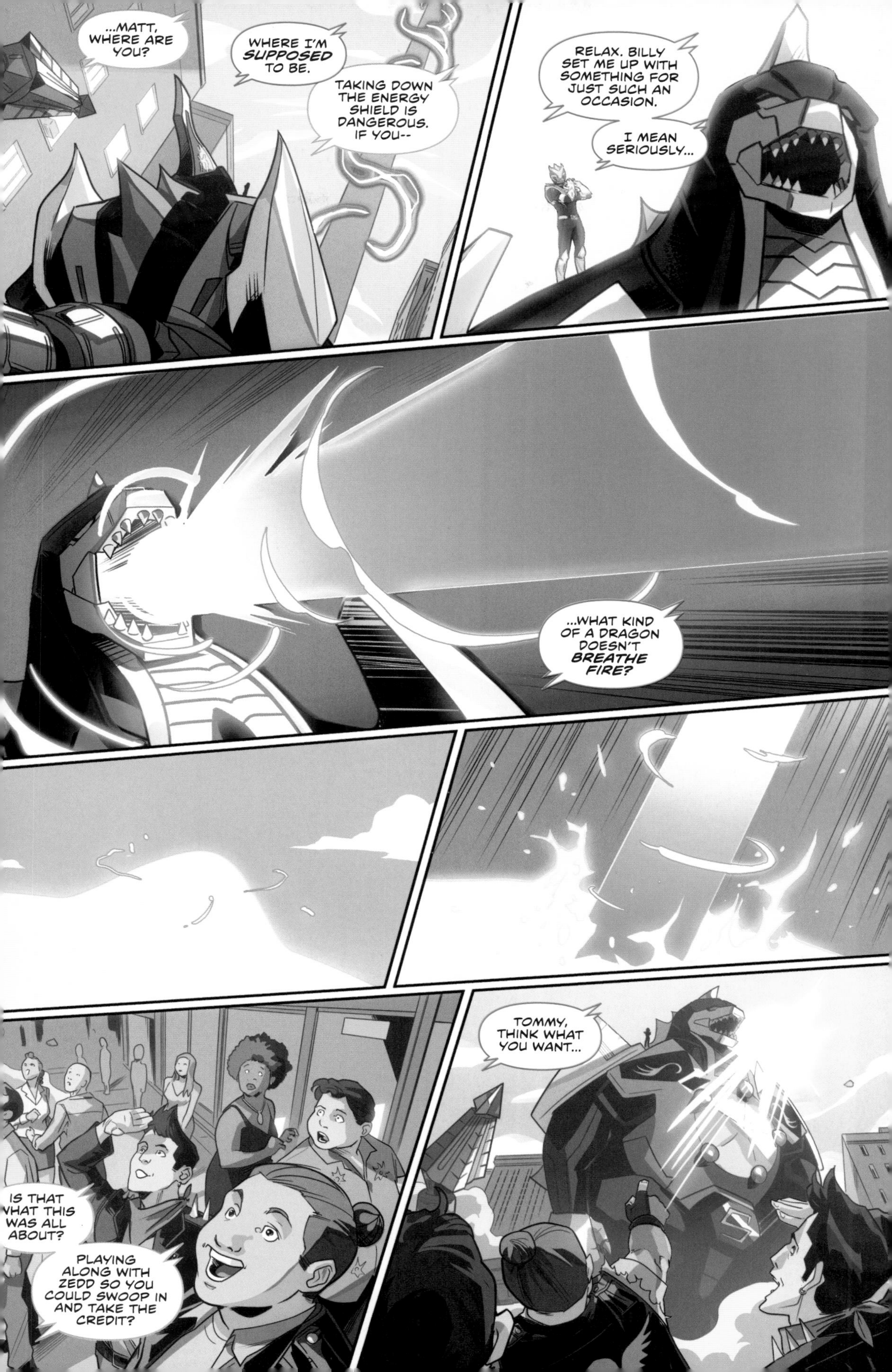
...MATT, WHERE ARE YOU?
WHERE I'M *SUPPOSED* TO BE.
TAKING DOWN THE ENERGY SHIELD IS DANGEROUS. IF YOU--
RELAX. BILLY SET ME UP WITH SOMETHING FOR JUST SUCH AN OCCASION.
I MEAN SERIOUSLY...
...WHAT KIND OF A DRAGON DOESN'T *BREATHE FIRE?*
TOMMY, THINK WHAT YOU WANT...
IS THAT WHAT THIS WAS ALL ABOUT?
PLAYING ALONG WITH ZEDD SO YOU COULD SWOOP IN AND TAKE THE CREDIT?

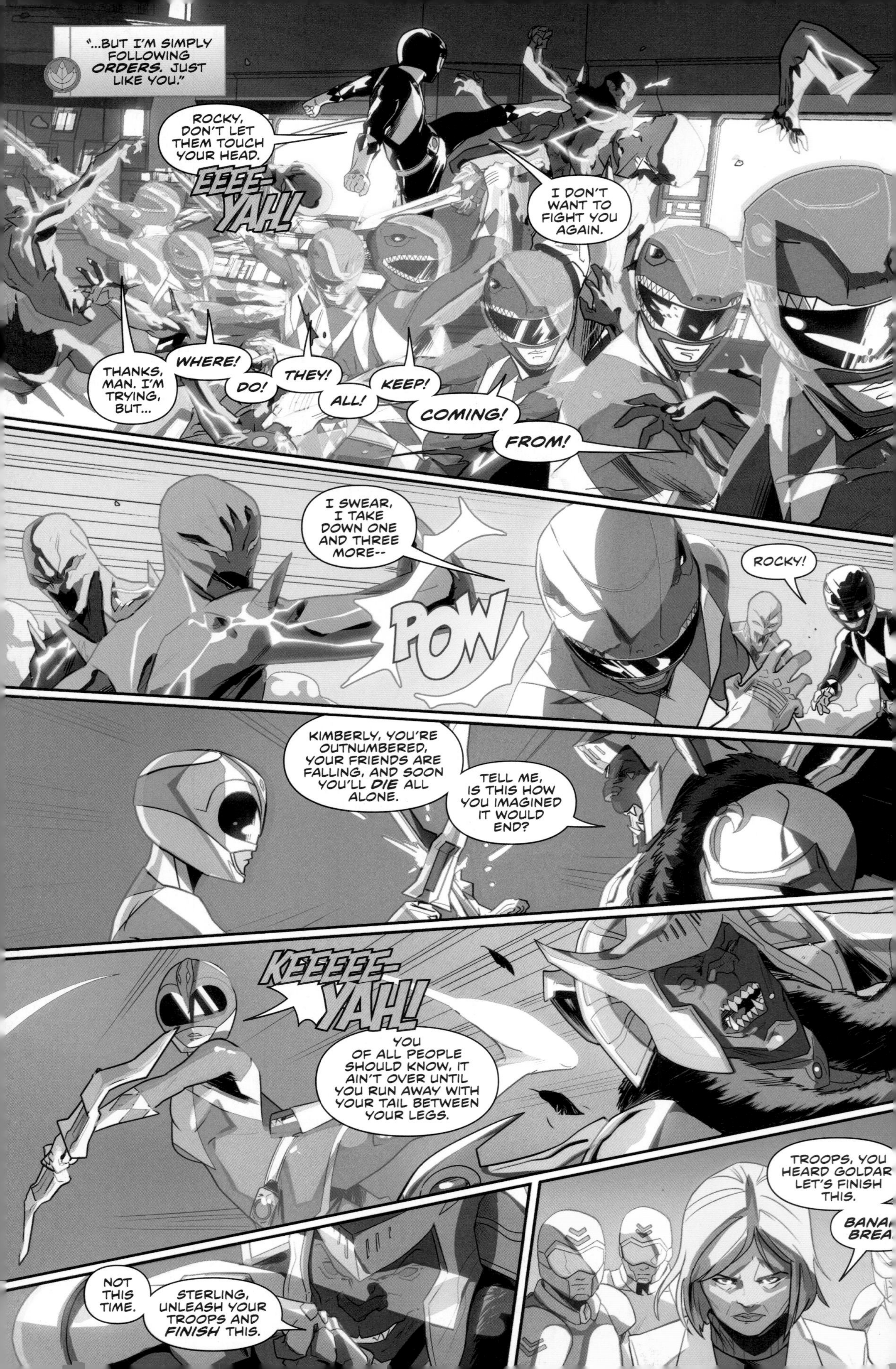
"...BUT I'M SIMPLY FOLLOWING ORDERS. JUST LIKE YOU."
ROCKY, DON'T LET THEM TOUCH YOUR HEAD.
EEEE-YAH!
I DON'T WANT TO FIGHT YOU AGAIN.
THANKS, MAN. I'M TRYING, BUT...
WHERE!
DO!
THEY!
ALL!
KEEP!
COMING!
FROM!
I SWEAR, I TAKE DOWN ONE AND THREE MORE--
POW
ROCKY!
KIMBERLY, YOU'RE OUTNUMBERED, YOUR FRIENDS ARE FALLING, AND SOON YOU'LL DIE ALL ALONE.
TELL ME, IS THIS HOW YOU IMAGINED IT WOULD END?
KEEEEE-YAH!
YOU OF ALL PEOPLE SHOULD KNOW, IT AIN'T OVER UNTIL YOU RUN AWAY WITH YOUR TAIL BETWEEN YOUR LEGS.
NOT THIS TIME.
STERLING, UNLEASH YOUR TROOPS AND FINISH THIS.
TROOPS, YOU HEARD GOLDAR. LET'S FINISH THIS.

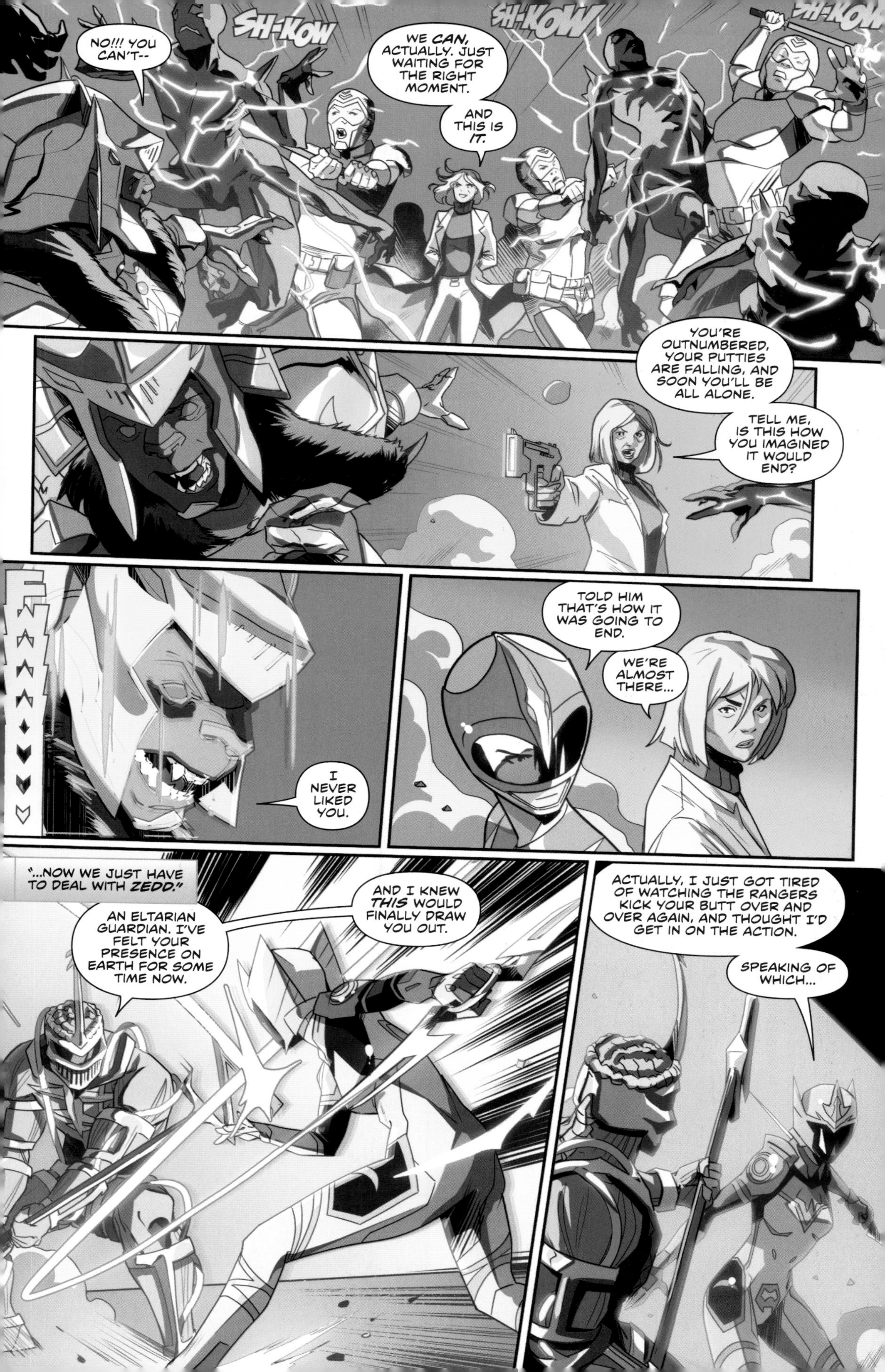
SH-KOW
SH-KOW
SH-KOW
NO!!! YOU CAN'T--
WE CAN, ACTUALLY. JUST WAITING FOR THE RIGHT MOMENT.
AND THIS IS IT.
YOU'RE OUTNUMBERED, YOUR PUTTIES ARE FALLING, AND SOON YOU'LL BE ALL ALONE.
TELL ME, IS THIS HOW YOU IMAGINED IT WOULD END?
FWAAAAAA
I NEVER LIKED YOU.
TOLD HIM THAT'S HOW IT WAS GOING TO END.
WE'RE ALMOST THERE...
"...NOW WE JUST HAVE TO DEAL WITH ZEDD."
AN ELTARIAN GUARDIAN. I'VE FELT YOUR PRESENCE ON EARTH FOR SOME TIME NOW.
AND I KNEW THIS WOULD FINALLY DRAW YOU OUT.
ACTUALLY, I JUST GOT TIRED OF WATCHING THE RANGERS KICK YOUR BUTT OVER AND OVER AGAIN, AND THOUGHT I'D GET IN ON THE ACTION.
SPEAKING OF WHICH...

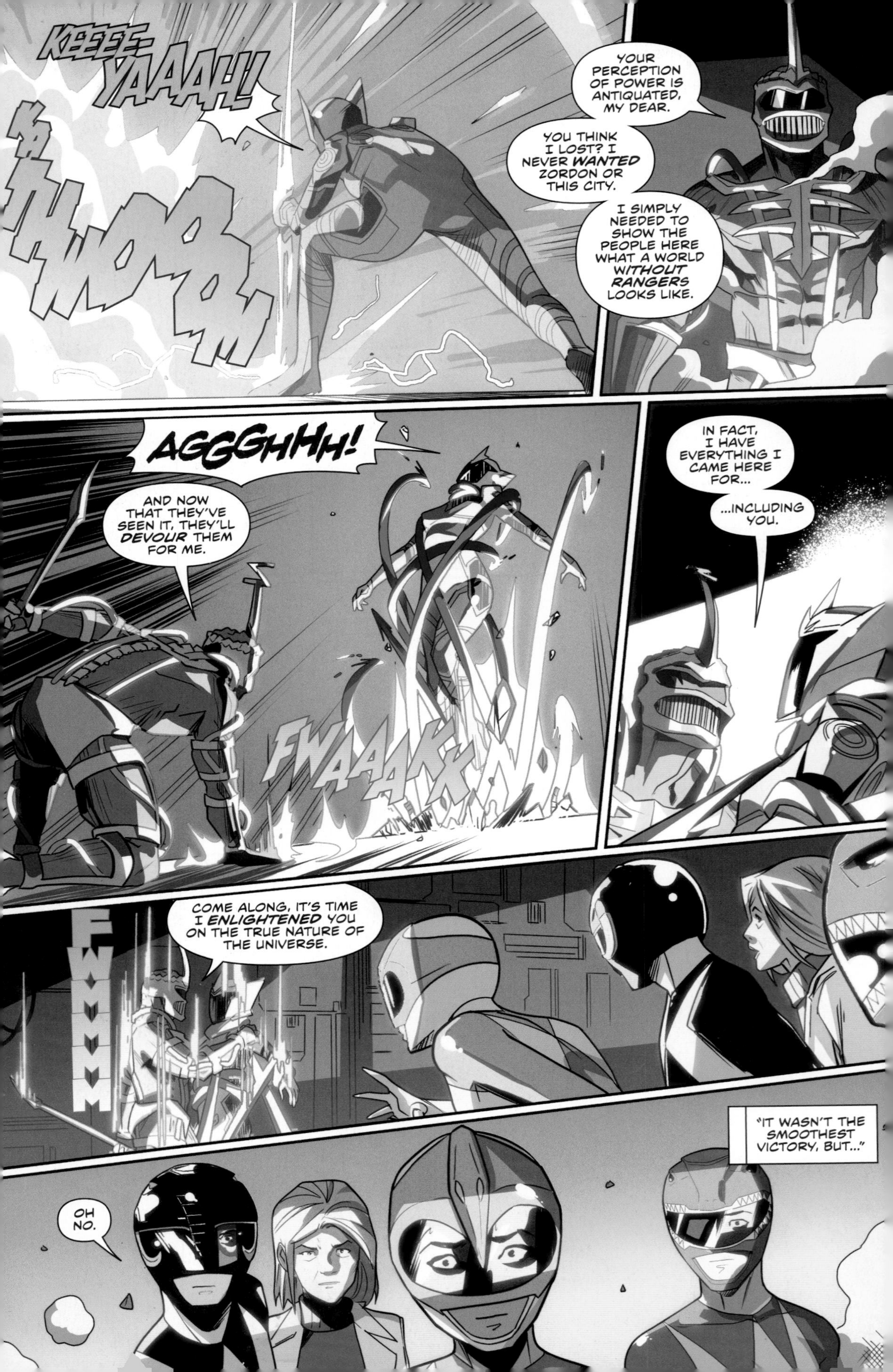
KEEEE-YAAAH!!
THWOOM
YOUR PERCEPTION OF POWER IS ANTIQUATED, MY DEAR.
YOU THINK I LOST? I NEVER WANTED ZORDON OR THIS CITY.
I SIMPLY NEEDED TO SHOW THE PEOPLE HERE WHAT A WORLD WITHOUT RANGERS LOOKS LIKE.
AGGGHHH!
AND NOW THAT THEY'VE SEEN IT, THEY'LL DEVOUR THEM FOR ME.
FWAAAKKK
IN FACT, I HAVE EVERYTHING I CAME HERE FOR...
...INCLUDING YOU.
FWMMMM
COME ALONG, IT'S TIME I ENLIGHTENED YOU ON THE TRUE NATURE OF THE UNIVERSE.
"IT WASN'T THE SMOOTHEST VICTORY, BUT..."
OH NO.

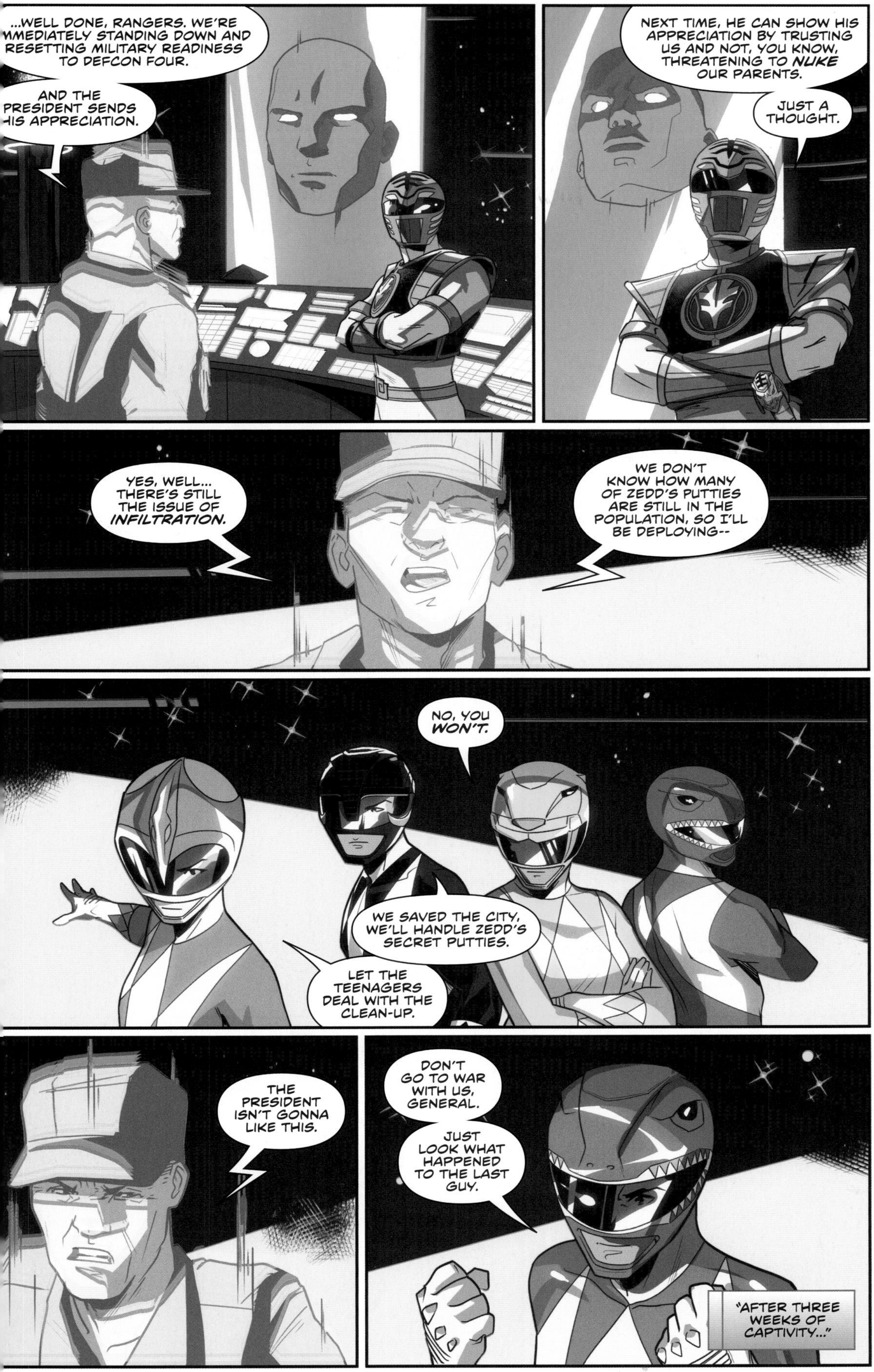
...WELL DONE, RANGERS. WE'RE IMMEDIATELY STANDING DOWN AND RESETTING MILITARY READINESS TO DEFCON FOUR.
AND THE PRESIDENT SENDS HIS APPRECIATION.
NEXT TIME, HE CAN SHOW HIS APPRECIATION BY TRUSTING US AND NOT, YOU KNOW, THREATENING TO NUKE OUR PARENTS.
JUST A THOUGHT.
YES, WELL... THERE'S STILL THE ISSUE OF INFILTRATION.
WE DON'T KNOW HOW MANY OF ZEDD'S PUTTIES ARE STILL IN THE POPULATION, SO I'LL BE DEPLOYING--
NO, YOU WON'T.
WE SAVED THE CITY, WE'LL HANDLE ZEDD'S SECRET PUTTIES.
LET THE TEENAGERS DEAL WITH THE CLEAN-UP.
THE PRESIDENT ISN'T GONNA LIKE THIS.
DON'T GO TO WAR WITH US, GENERAL.
JUST LOOK WHAT HAPPENED TO THE LAST GUY.
"AFTER THREE WEEKS OF CAPTIVITY..."

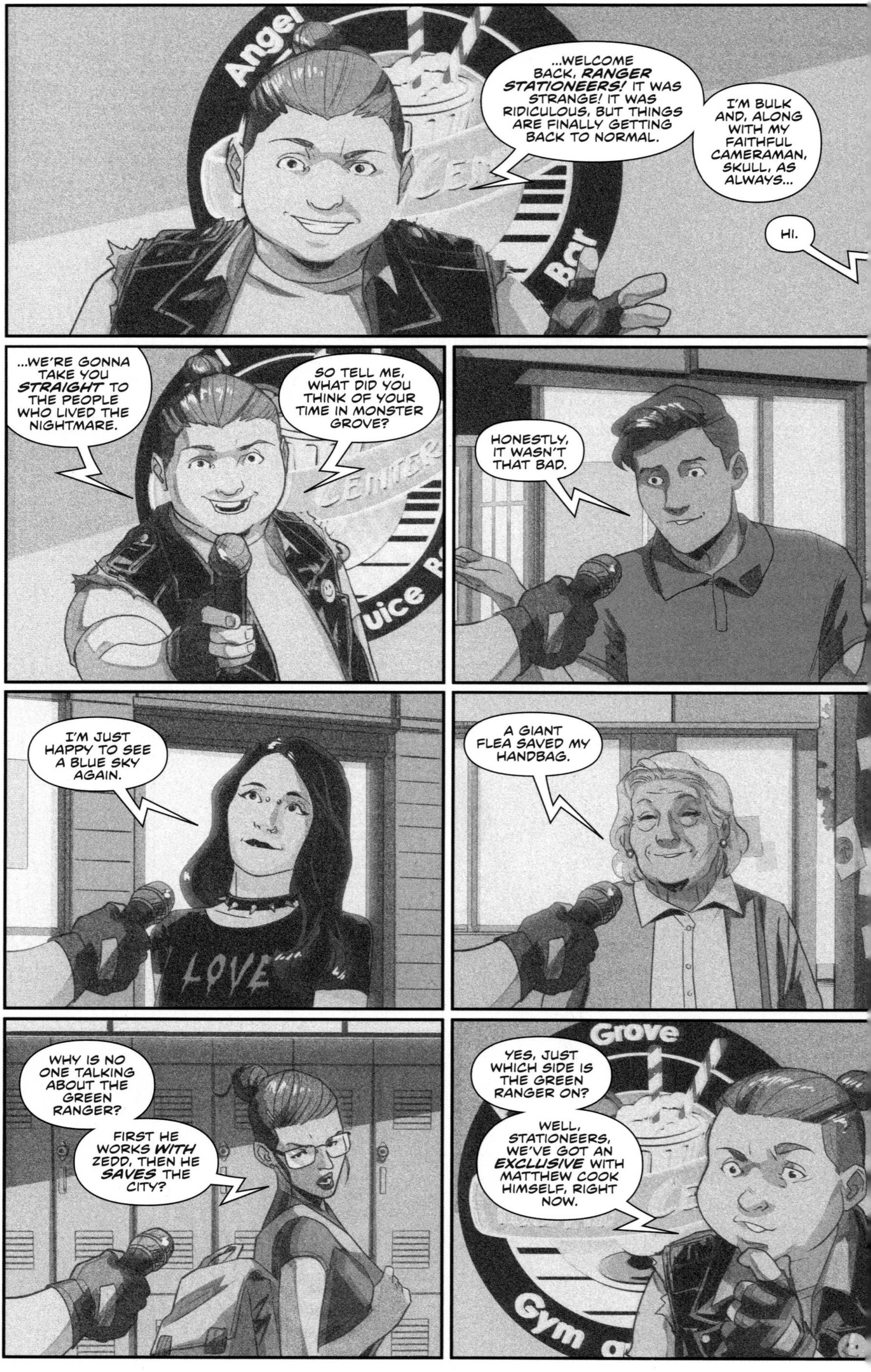
...WELCOME BACK, RANGER STATIONEERS! IT WAS STRANGE! IT WAS RIDICULOUS, BUT THINGS ARE FINALLY GETTING BACK TO NORMAL.
I'M BULK AND, ALONG WITH MY FAITHFUL CAMERAMAN, SKULL, AS ALWAYS...
HI.
...WE'RE GONNA TAKE YOU STRAIGHT TO THE PEOPLE WHO LIVED THE NIGHTMARE.
SO TELL ME, WHAT DID YOU THINK OF YOUR TIME IN MONSTER GROVE?
HONESTLY, IT WASN'T THAT BAD.
I'M JUST HAPPY TO SEE A BLUE SKY AGAIN.
A GIANT FLEA SAVED MY HANDBAG.
WHY IS NO ONE TALKING ABOUT THE GREEN RANGER?
FIRST HE WORKS WITH ZEDD, THEN HE SAVES THE CITY?
YES, JUST WHICH SIDE IS THE GREEN RANGER ON?
WELL, STATIONEERS, WE'VE GOT AN EXCLUSIVE WITH MATTHEW COOK HIMSELF, RIGHT NOW.

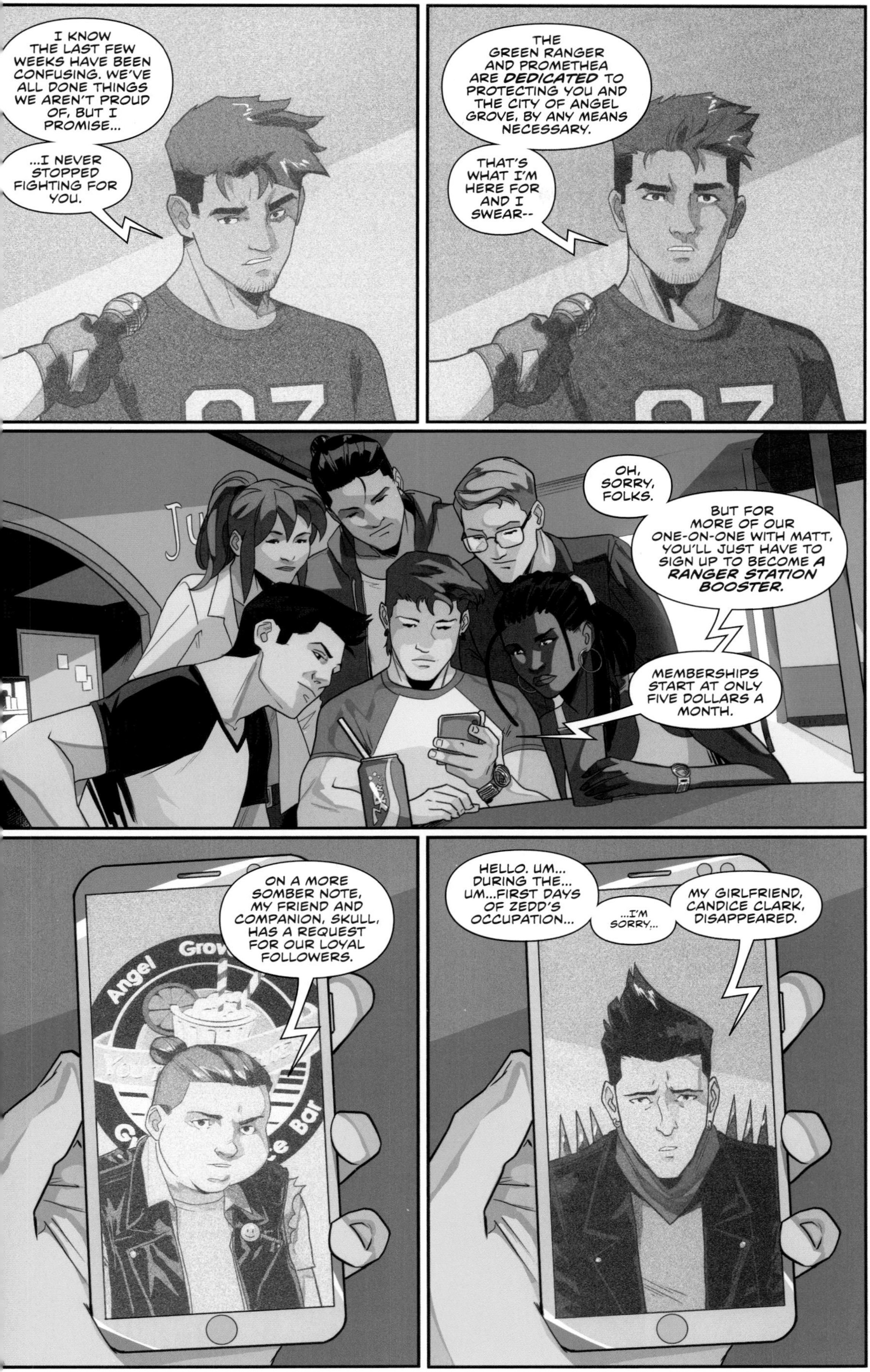
I KNOW THE LAST FEW WEEKS HAVE BEEN CONFUSING. WE'VE ALL DONE THINGS WE AREN'T PROUD OF, BUT I PROMISE...
...I NEVER STOPPED FIGHTING FOR YOU.
THE GREEN RANGER AND PROMETHEA ARE *DEDICATED* TO PROTECTING YOU AND THE CITY OF ANGEL GROVE, BY ANY MEANS NECESSARY.
THAT'S WHAT I'M HERE FOR AND I SWEAR--
OH, SORRY, FOLKS.
BUT FOR MORE OF OUR ONE-ON-ONE WITH MATT, YOU'LL JUST HAVE TO SIGN UP TO BECOME ***A RANGER STATION BOOSTER.***
MEMBERSHIPS START AT ONLY FIVE DOLLARS A MONTH.
ON A MORE SOMBER NOTE, MY FRIEND AND COMPANION, SKULL, HAS A REQUEST FOR OUR LOYAL FOLLOWERS.
HELLO. UM... DURING THE... UM...FIRST DAYS OF ZEDD'S OCCUPATION...
...I'M SORRY...
MY GIRLFRIEND, CANDICE CLARK, DISAPPEARED.

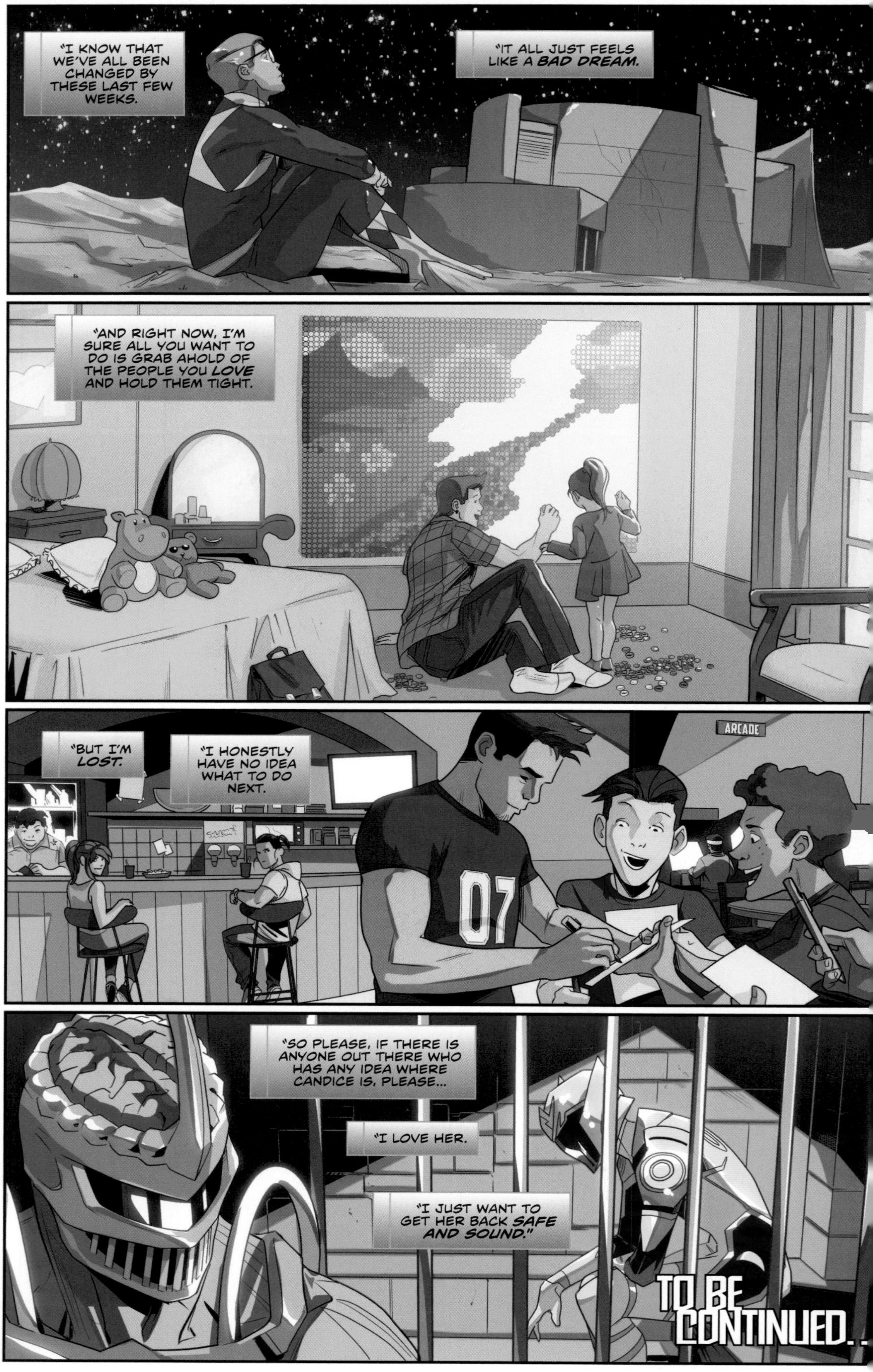
"I KNOW THAT WE'VE ALL BEEN CHANGED BY THESE LAST FEW WEEKS.
"IT ALL JUST FEELS LIKE A BAD DREAM.
"AND RIGHT NOW, I'M SURE ALL YOU WANT TO DO IS GRAB AHOLD OF THE PEOPLE YOU LOVE AND HOLD THEM TIGHT.
"BUT I'M LOST.
"I HONESTLY HAVE NO IDEA WHAT TO DO NEXT.
ARCADE
07
"SO PLEASE, IF THERE IS ANYONE OUT THERE WHO HAS ANY IDEA WHERE CANDICE IS, PLEASE...
"I LOVE HER.
"I JUST WANT TO GET HER BACK SAFE AND SOUND."
TO BE CONTINUED...

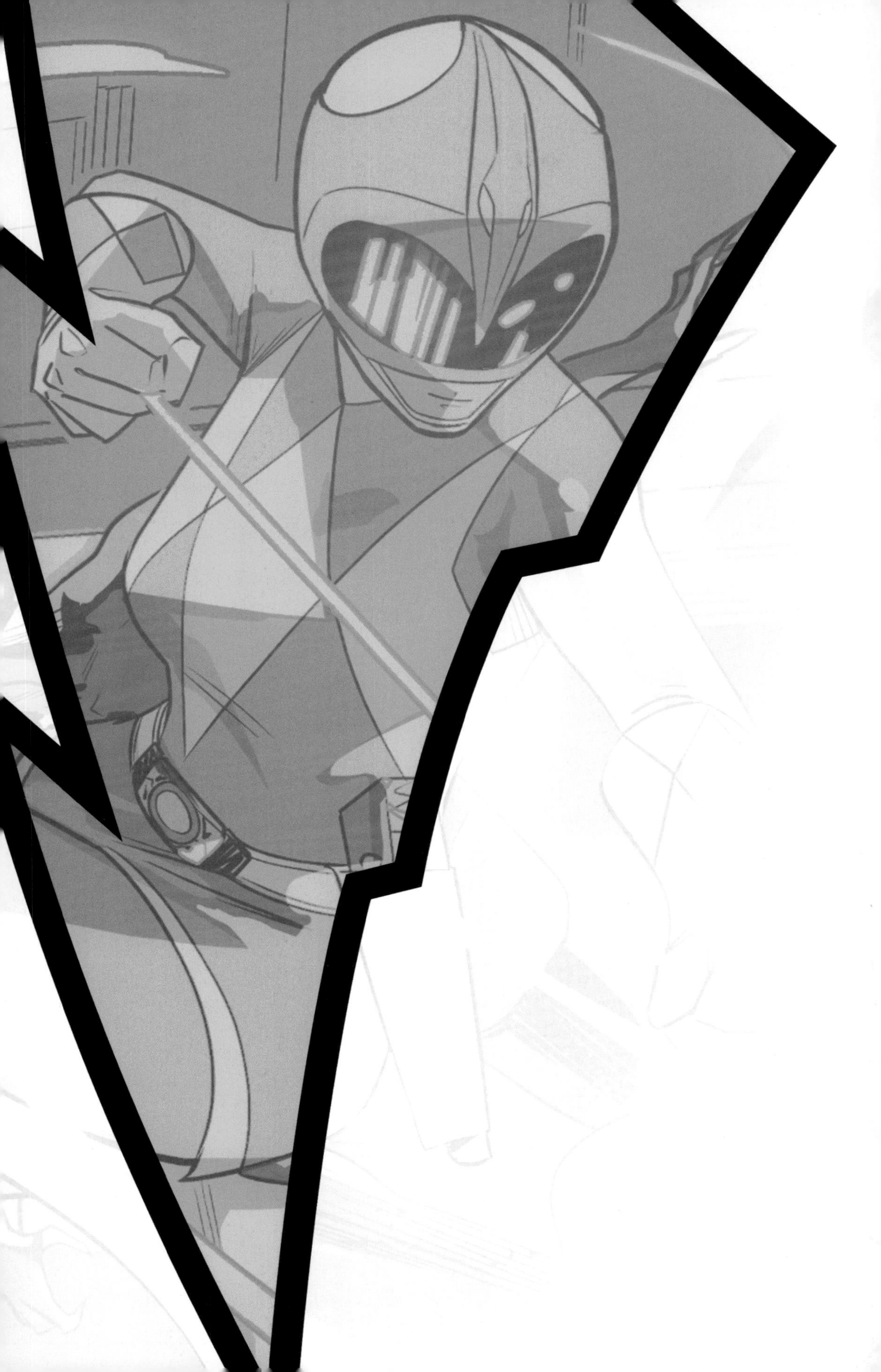

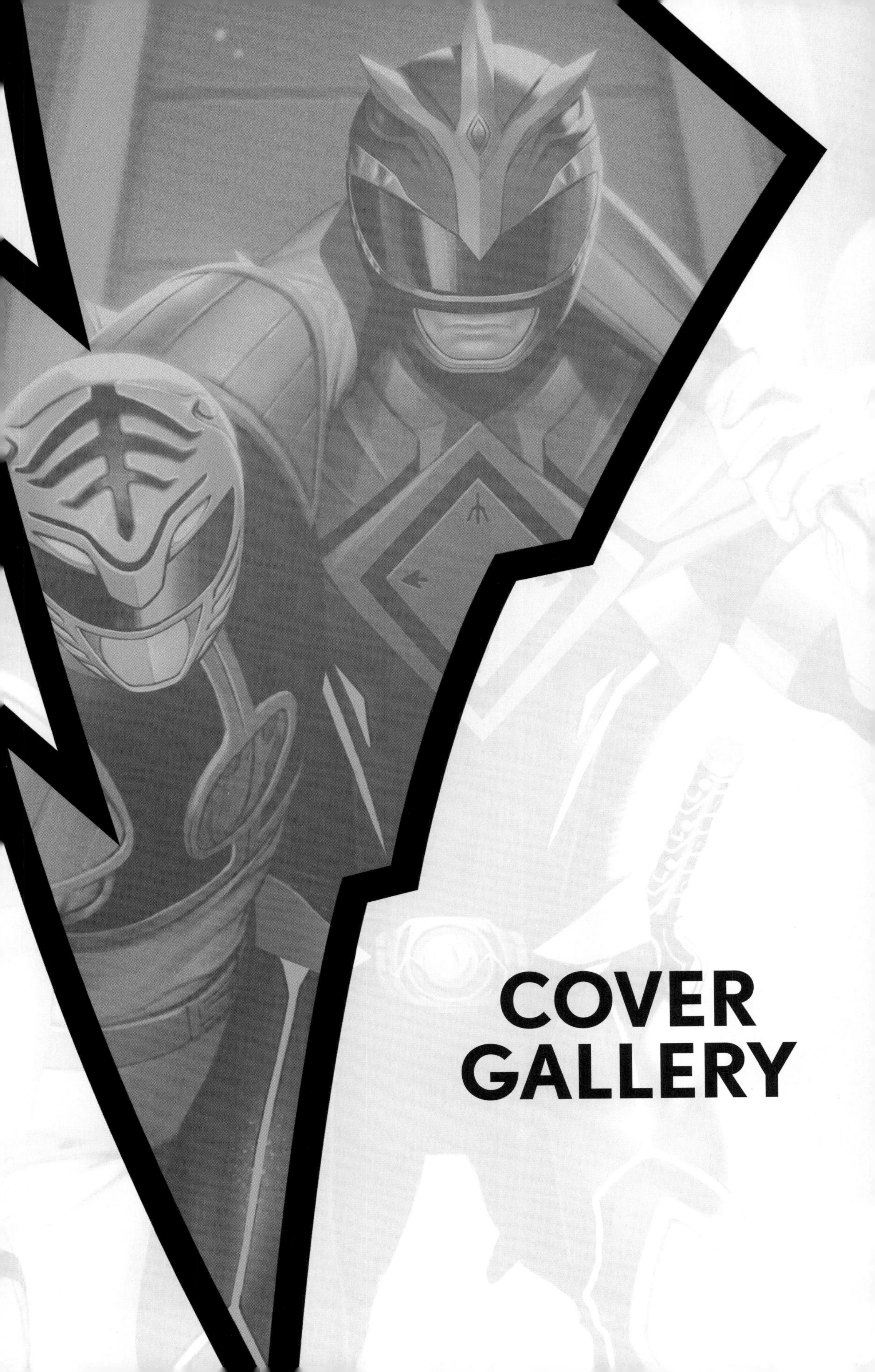

COVER GALLERY

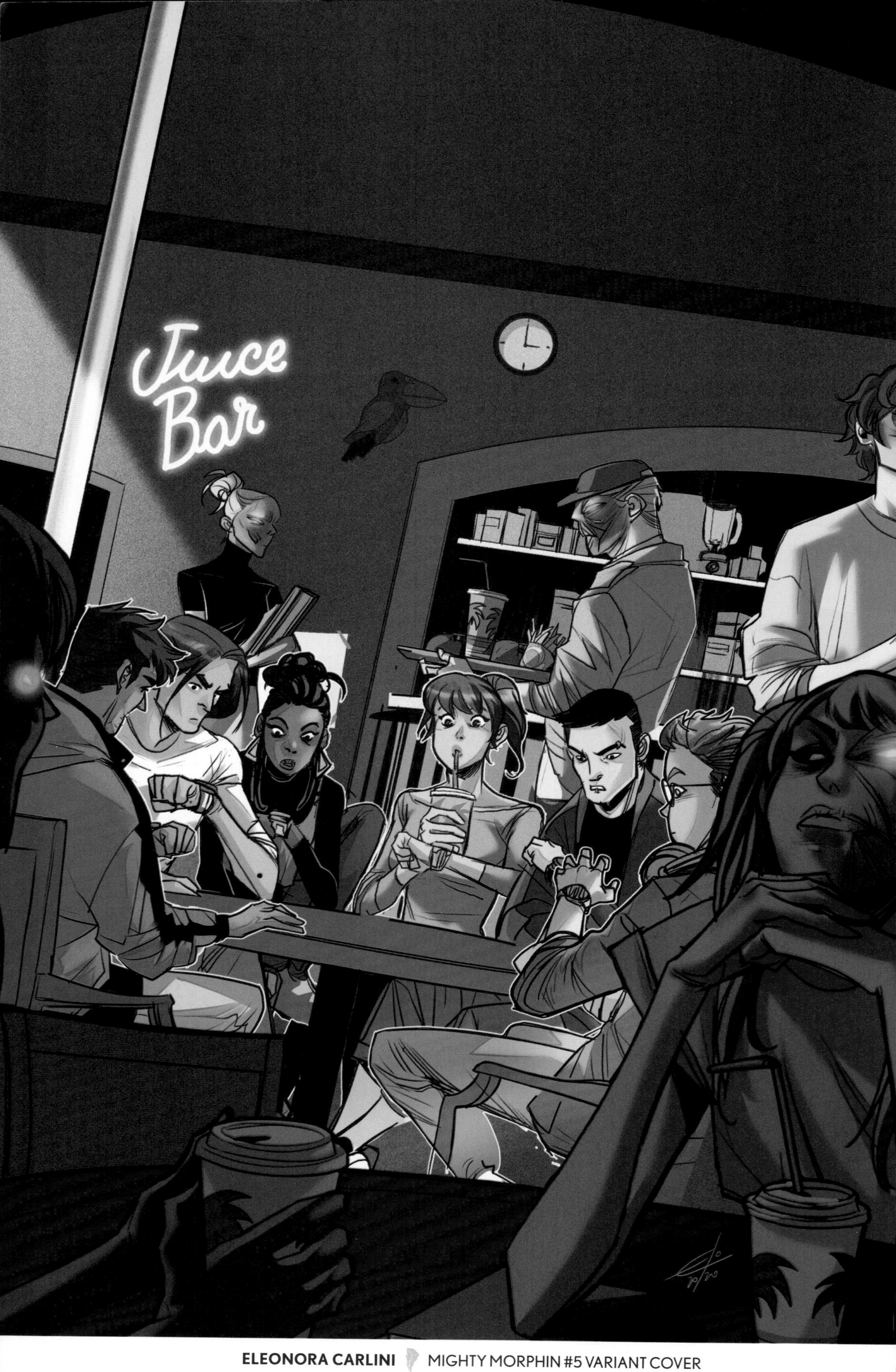
Juice Bar

ELEONORA CARLINI MIGHTY MORPHIN #5 VARIANT COVER

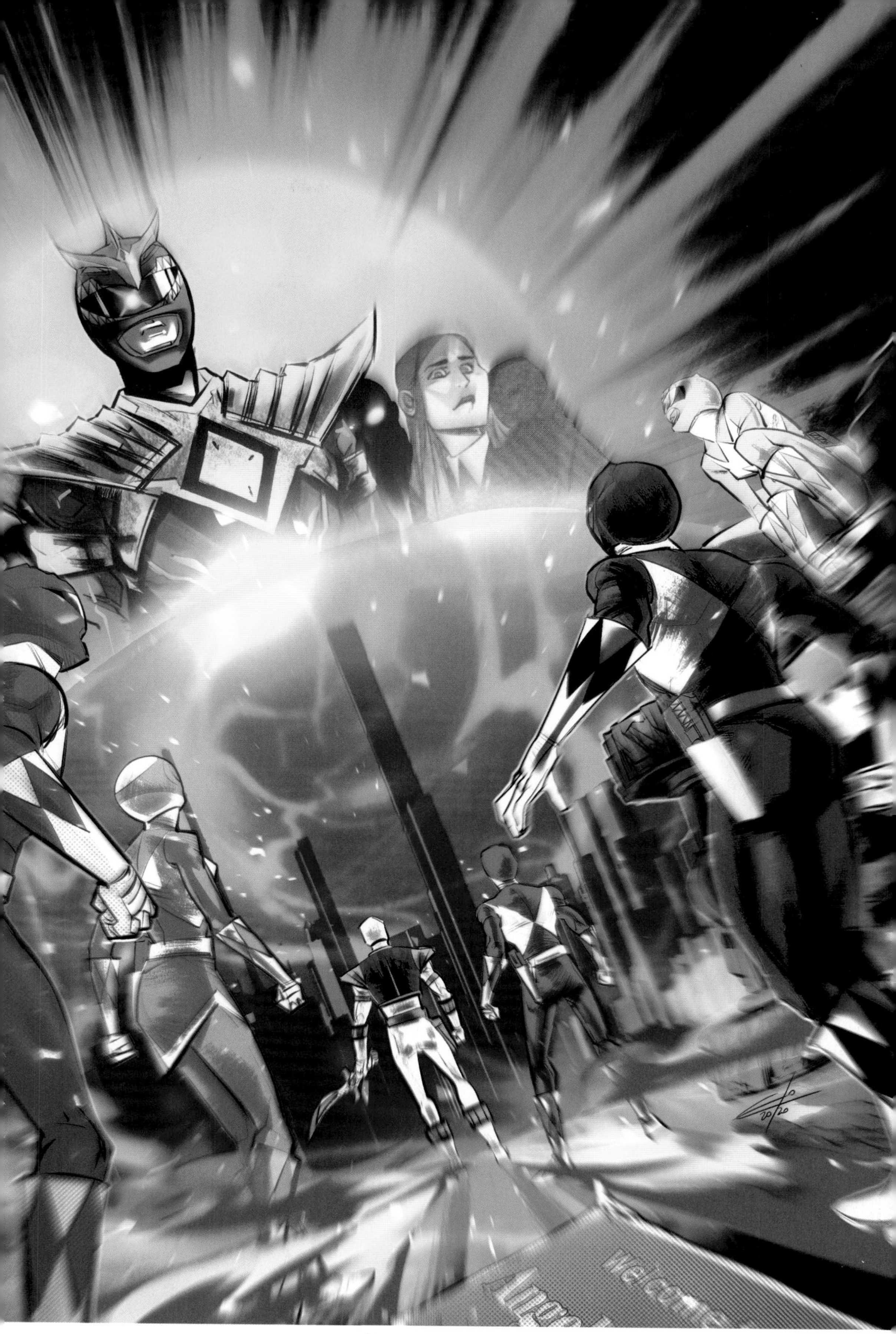

ELEONORA CARLINI MIGHTY MORPHIN #6 VARIANT COVER

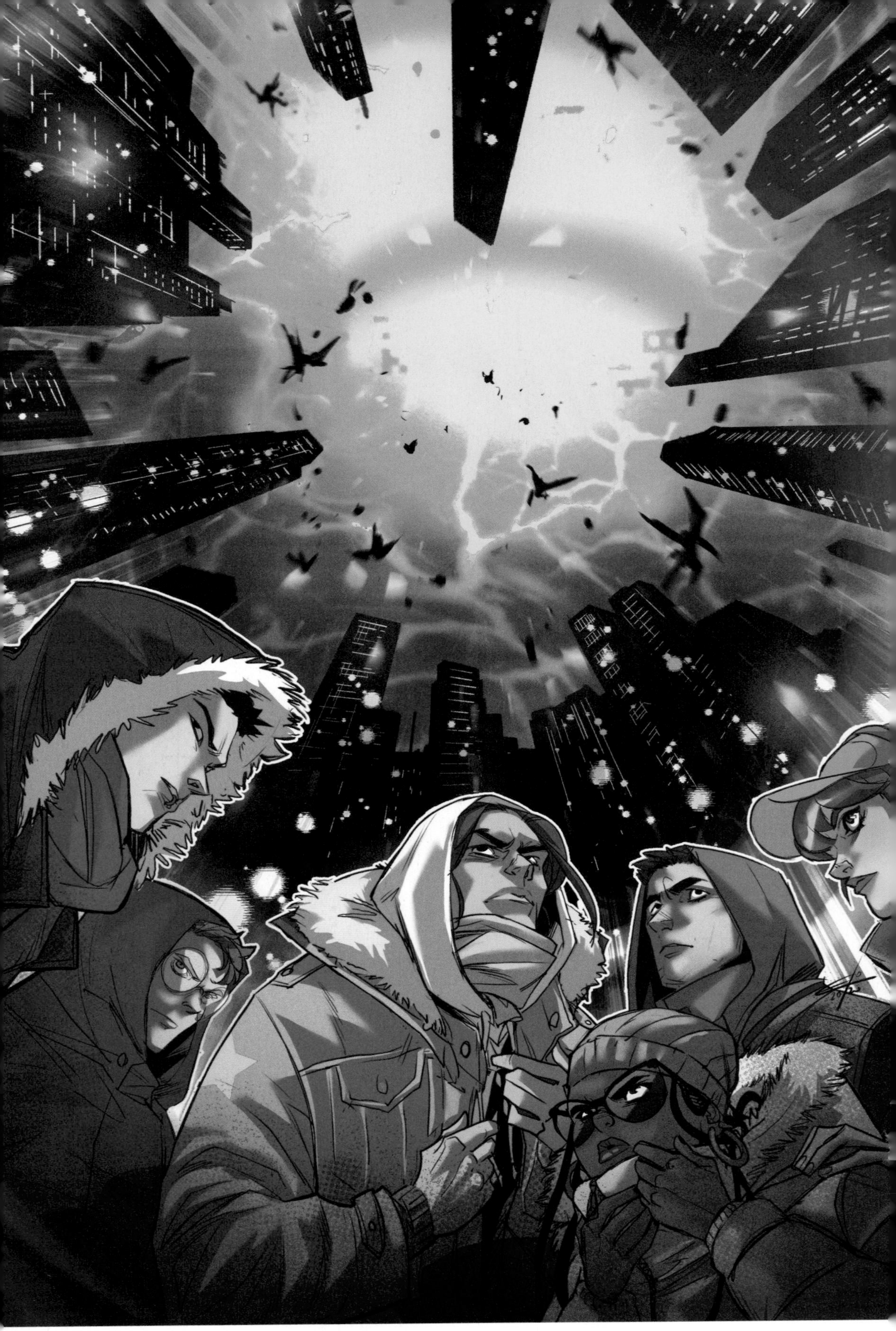

ELEONORA CARLINI MIGHTY MORPHIN #7 VARIANT COVER

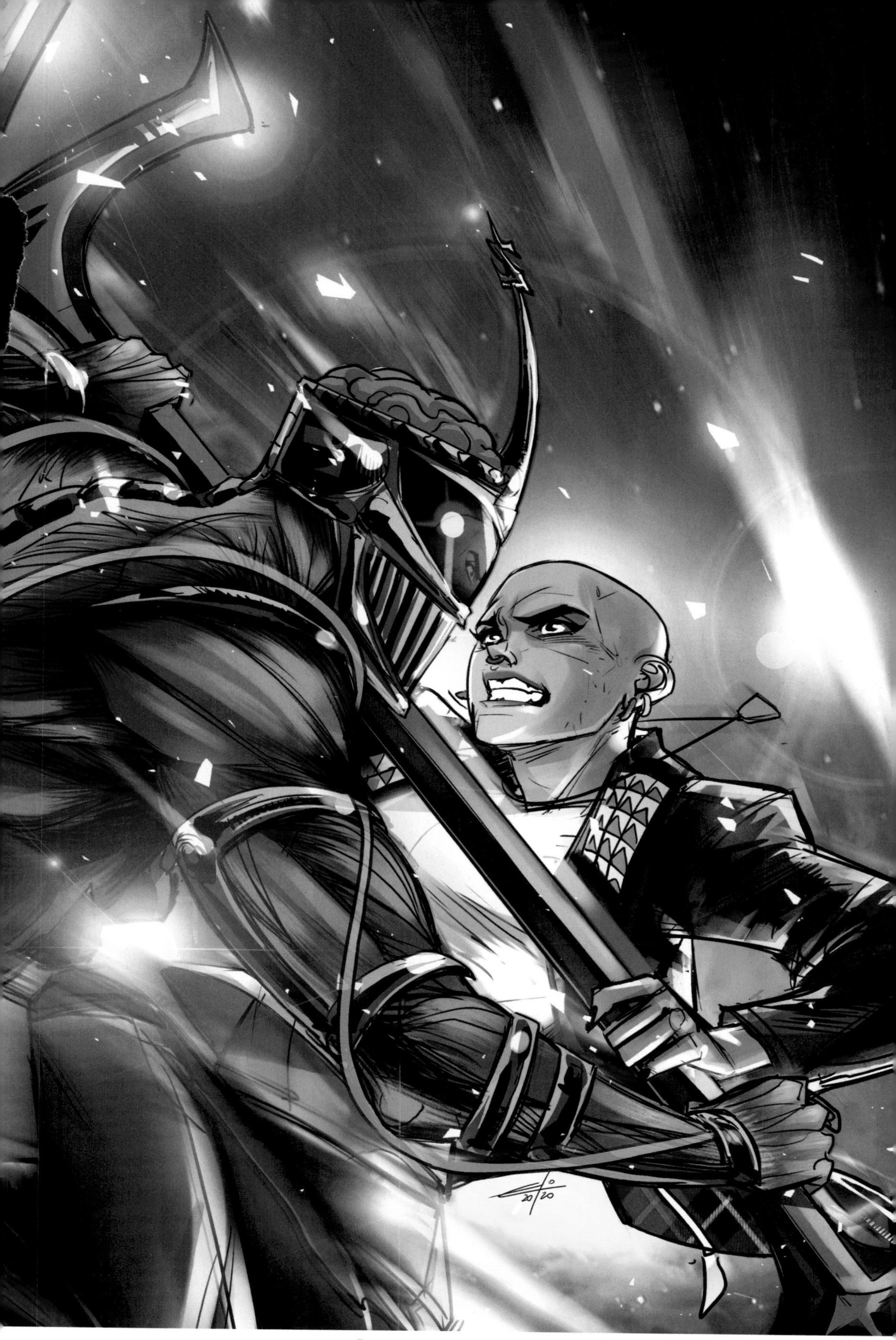

ELEONORA CARLINI MIGHTY MORPHIN #8 VARIANT COVER

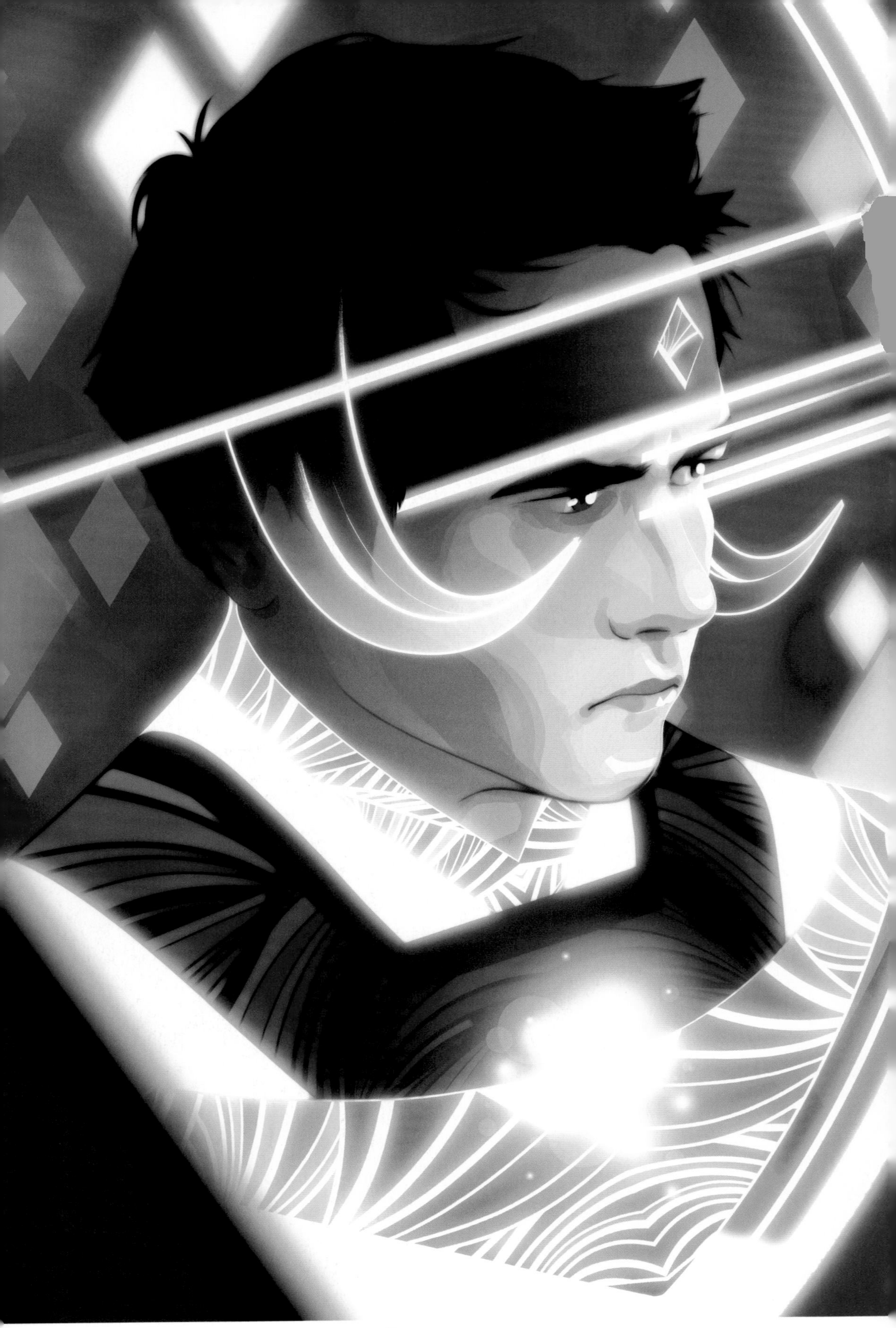

GOÑI MONTES MIGHTY MORPHIN #5 VARIANT COVER

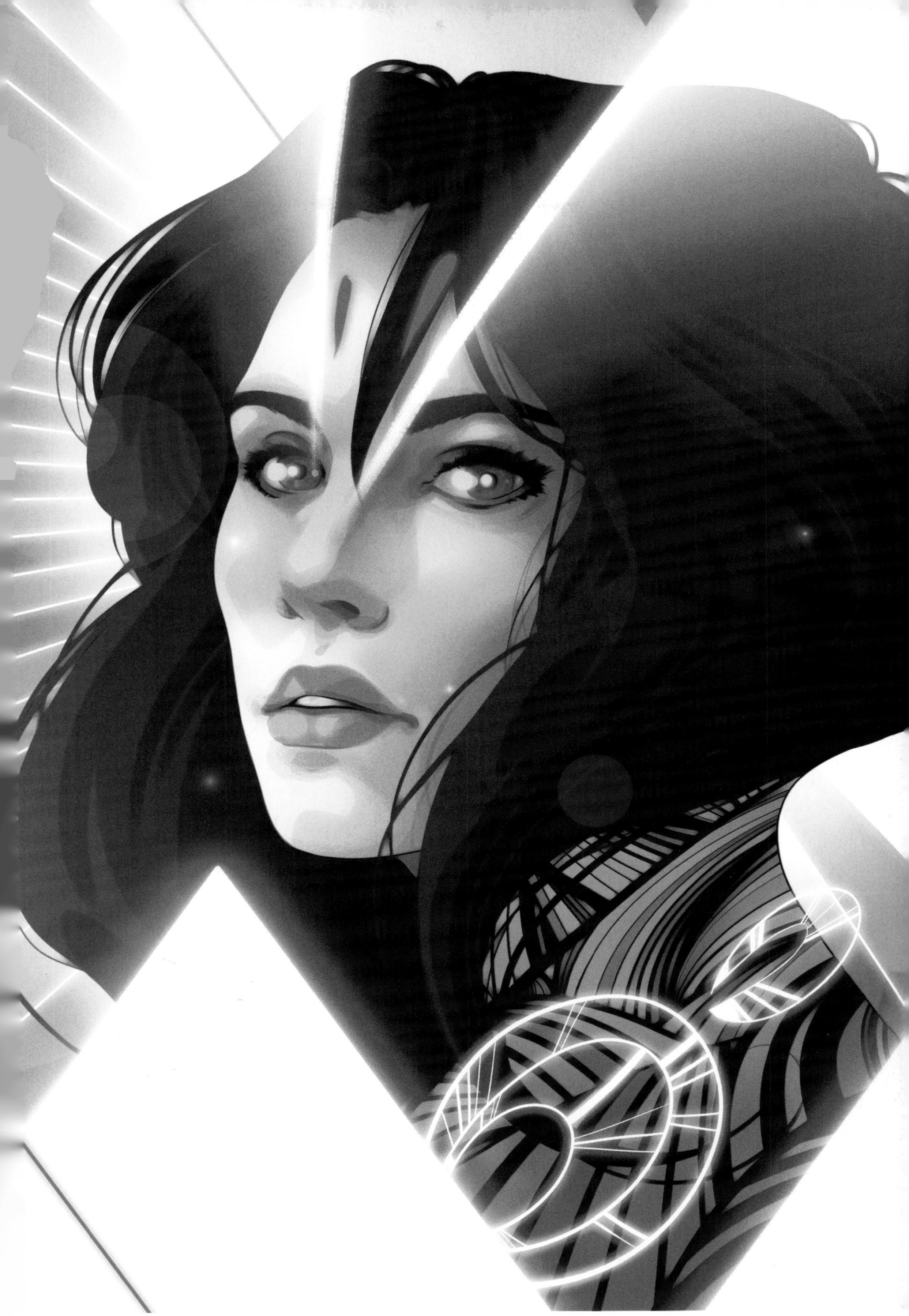

GOÑI MONTES MIGHTY MORPHIN #7 VARIANT COVER

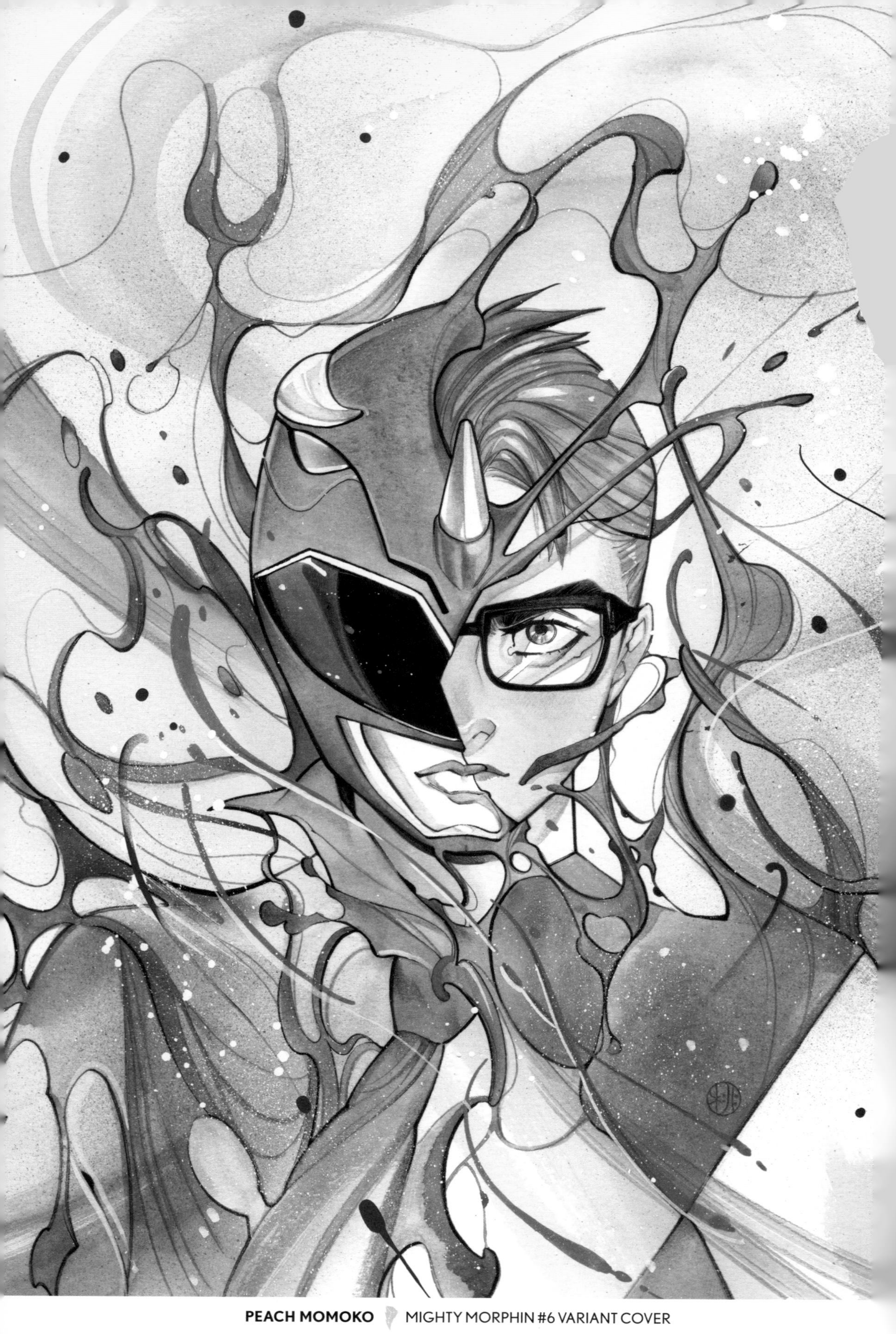

PEACH MOMOKO MIGHTY MORPHIN #6 VARIANT COVER

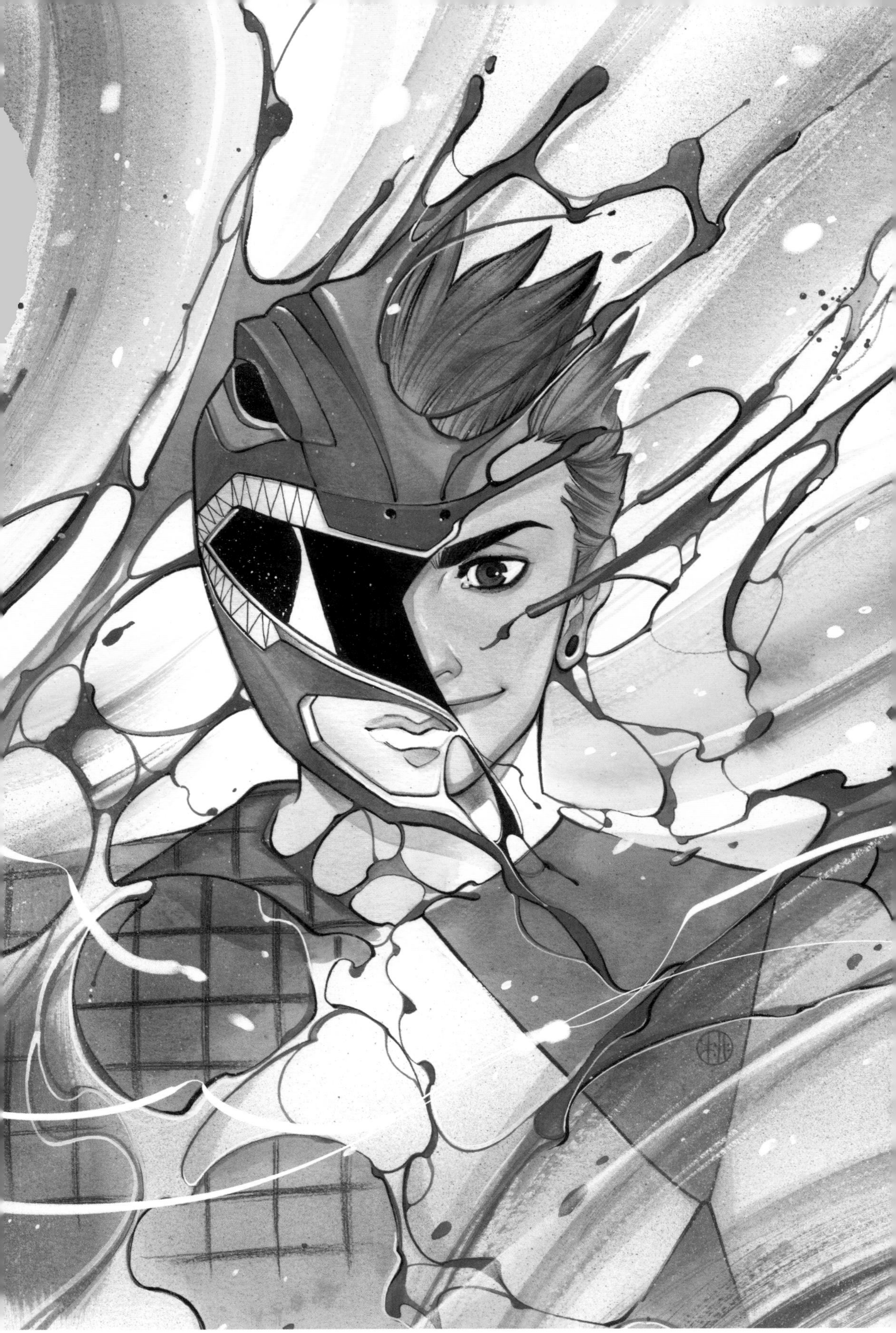

PEACH MOMOKO MIGHTY MORPHIN #8 VARIANT COVER

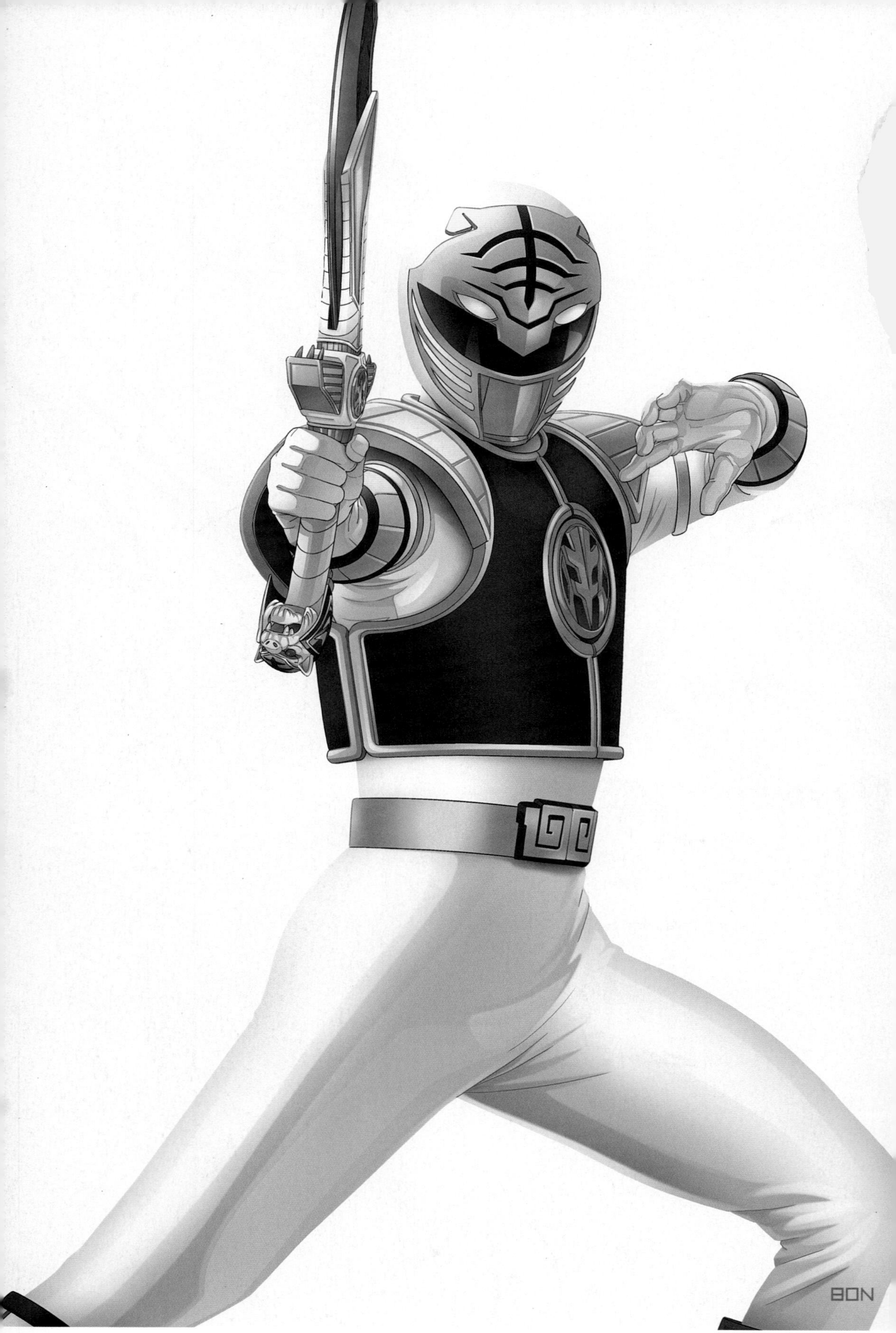
BON

BON BERNARDO MIGHTY MORPHIN #8 VARIANT COVER

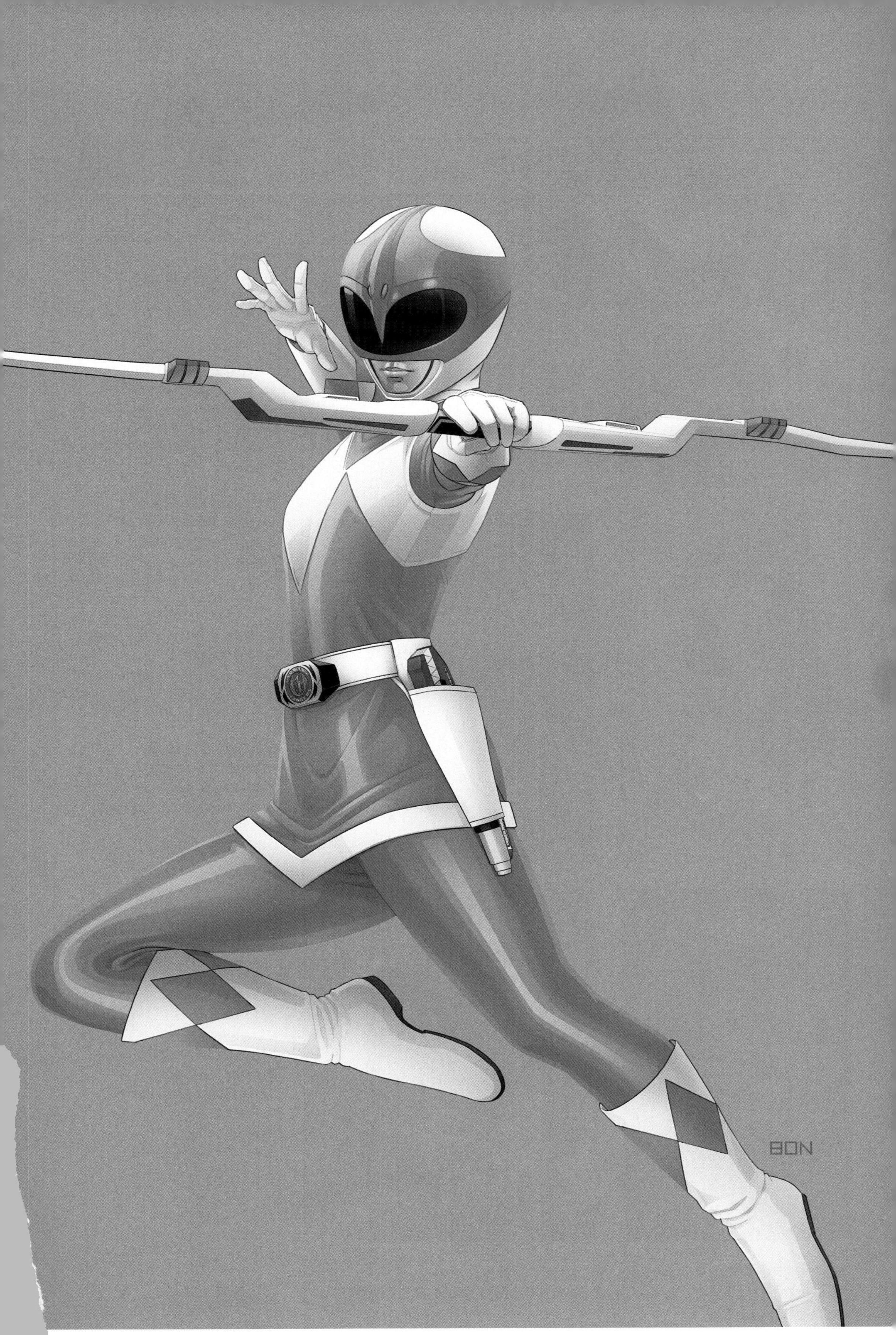
BON

BON BERNARDO MIGHTY MORPHIN #8 VARIANT COVER

DISCOVER
MORE POWER RANGERS!

HIGGINS • PRASETYA • HERMS
ORLANDO • HOWELL • LAWSON
MIGHTY MORPHIN POWER RANGERS
VOLUME ONE
INTRODUCTION BY POWER RANGERS' EXECUTIVE PRODUCER JUDD "CHIP" LYNN

HIGGINS • PRASETYA
SILAS • HERMS
VALENZA • ORLANDO
HOWELL • LAWSON
MIGHTY MORPHIN POWER RANGERS
VOLUME TWO

FLETCHER
THOMPSON
HOWARD
DI NICUOLO
STERN
MIGHTY MORPHIN POWER RANGERS
PINK
INTRODUCTION BY AMY JO JOHNSON KIMBERLY HART, THE ORIGINAL PINK RANGER

SABAN'S
POWER RANGERS
AFTERSHOCK
RYAN PARROTT LUCAS WERNECK JOANA LAFUENTE

MIGHTY MORPHIN POWER RANGERS
POSTER BOOK
FEATURING 20 REMOVABLE POSTERS

PARROTT • MORA • ANGULO
SABAN'S
GO GO POWER RANGERS
VOLUME ONE

BOOM! STUDIOS

AVAILABLE AT YOUR LOCAL COMICS SHOP AND BOOKSTORE

Find a comic shop near you at www.comicshoplocator.com

WWW.**BOOM-STUDIOS**.COM

Mighty Morphin Power Rangers
Kyle Higgins, Hendry Prasetya, Matt Herms
Volume 1
ISBN: 978-1-60886-893-3 | $19.99
Volume 2
ISBN: 978-1-60886-942-8 | $16.99
Volume 3
ISBN: 978-1-60886-977-0 | $16.99
Volume 4
ISBN: 978-1-68415-031-1 | $16.99

Mighty Morphin Power Rangers: Pink
Kelly Thompson, Brenden Fletcher, Tini Howard, Daniele Di Nicuolo
ISBN: 978-1-60886-952-7 | $19.99

Saban's Go Go Power Rangers
Ryan Parrott, Dan Mora
Volume 1
ISBN: 978-1-68415-193-6 | $16.99

Saban's Power Rangers: Aftershock
Ryan Parrott, Lucas Werneck
ISBN: 978-1-60886-937-4 | $14.99

Mighty Morphin Power Rangers Poster Book
Goñi Montes, Jamal Campbell, Joe Quinones
ISBN: 978-1-60886-966-4 | $19.99

Mighty Morphin Power Rangers Adult Coloring Book
Goñi Montes, Jamal Campbell, Hendry Prasetya
ISBN: 978-1-60886-955-8 | $16.99

Mighty Morphin Power Rangers Year One: Deluxe HC
Kyle Higgins, Hendry Prasetya, Steve Orlando
ISBN: 978-1-68415-012-0 | $75.00

Licensed by: Hasbro